CRE▲TIVE
HOMEOWNER®

TOP-SELLING
FAMILY LIVING
HOME PLANS

SCHAUMBURG TOWNSHIP DISTRICT LIBRARY
130 SOUTH ROSELLE ROAD
SCHAUMBURG, ILLINOIS 60193

CREATIVE HOMEOWNER®, Upper Saddle River, New Jersey

COPYRIGHT © 2004

CREATIVE
HOMEOWNER®

A Division of Federal Marketing Corp.
Upper Saddle River, NJ

3 1257 01633 0648

All floor plans and elevations copyright by the individual designers and may not be reproduced by any means without permission. All text and other illustrative material ©2004 Creative Homeowner and may not be reproduced, either in part or in its entirety, in any form, by any means, without written permission from the publisher, with the exception of brief excerpts for purposes of radio, television, or published review. All rights, including the right of translation, are reserved. Although all possible measures have been taken to ensure the accuracy of the material presented, the publisher is not liable in case of misinterpretation or typographical error.

Creative Homeowner® is a registered trademark of Federal Marketing Corporation.

VP/Business Development: Brian H. Toolan
VP/Editorial Director: Timothy O. Bakke
Production Manager: Kimberly H. Vivas

Home Plans Publishing Consultant: James D. McNair III
Editorial Assistant: Jennifer Doolittle

Design and Layout: Arrowhead Direct (David Kroha, Cindy DiPierdomenico, Judith Kroha)

Cover Design: David Geer

Current Printing (last digit)
10 9 8 7 6 5 4 3 2 1

Top-Selling Family-Living Home Plans
Library of Congress Control Number: 2003113427
ISBN: 1-58011-187-4

CREATIVE HOMEOWNER®
A Division of Federal Marketing Corp.
24 Park Way
Upper Saddle River, NJ 07458
www.creativehomeowner.com

Printed in China

Note: The homes as shown in the photographs and renderings in this book may differ from the actual blueprints. When studying the house of your choice, please check the floor plans carefully.

PHOTO CREDITS

Front cover: *top* plan 121061, page 237; *bottom row left to right* plan 141026, page 22; plan 141021, page 225; plan 181151, page 134; plan 121082, page 244

Back cover: *top* plan 161029, page 248; *center* plan 121062, page 245; *bottom right* plan 161029, page 248; *bottom center* plan 211076, page 266; *bottom left* plan 181151, page 134

page 4: courtesy of Trus Joist MacMillan

page 5: Paul M. Schumm/CH

page 6: *top* Freeze Frame Studio/CH; *bottom* courtesy of Trus Joist MacMillan

page 7: Kim, Jin Hong Photo Studio

page 8: *top right* plan 321057, page 76; *bottom right* plan 321060, page 76; *bottom left* Motif Designs/CH

pages 68–69: courtesy of Kraftmaid Cabinetry, Inc.

page 70: *both* courtesy of Wellborn Cabinets

page 71: courtesy of Kraftmaid Cabinetry, Inc.

page 72: courtesy of Wellborn Cabinets

page 73: *top left* courtesy of Merillat Industries; *top right* courtesy of Wellborn Cabinets; *bottom left* courtesy of Merillat Industries

page 110: *top* plan 321051, page 199; *bottom left* George Ross/CH

page 130: courtesy of Central Fireplaces

page 131: *top* illustrations by Robert LaPointe; *bottom* courtesy of Heatilator, Inc.

pages 132–133: courtesy of Aladdin Steel Products

page 200: *bottom right* George Ross/CH; *bottom left* plan 321041, page 127

page 236: *top* George Ross/CH

pages 250–251: *both* courtesy of Kraftmaid Cabinetry, Inc.

page 252: courtesy of Sylvania

pages 253–252: *both* Kraftmaid Cabinetry, Inc.

page 255: courtesy of Ikea

page 288: *center right* George Ross/CH

page 312: *bottom left* George Ross/CH

page 319: *top* courtesy of Weber; *bottom right* courtesy of Frontgate; *bottom left* courtesy of Broilmaster

page 320: courtesy of Sub-Zero

page 321: courtesy of Malibu Lighting/Intermatic

pages 322–323: *top left* courtesy of Malibu Lighting/Intermatic; *center* Marvin Slobin/courtesy of California Redwood Assoc.; *bottom* courtesy of Southern Forest Products Assoc.

Contents

Getting Started

Maybe you can't wait to bang the first nail. Or you may be just as happy leaving town until the windows are cleaned. The extent of your involvement with the construction phase is up to you. Your time, interests, and abilities can help you decide how to get the project from lines on paper to reality. But building a house requires more than putting pieces together. Whoever is in charge of the process must competently manage people as well as supplies, materials, and construction. He or she will have to

- Make a project schedule to plan the orderly progress of the work. This can be a bar chart that shows the time period of activity by each trade.
- Establish a budget for each category of work, such as foundation, framing, and finish carpentry.
- Arrange for a source of construction financing.
- Get a building permit and post it conspicuously at the construction site.
- Line up supply sources and order materials.
- Find subcontractors and negotiate their contracts.
- Coordinate the work so that it progresses smoothly with the fewest conflicts.
- Notify inspectors at the appropriate milestones.
- Make payments to suppliers and subcontractors.

You as the Builder

You'll have to take care of every logistical detail yourself if you decide to act as your own bulder or general contractor. But along with the responsibilities of managing the project, you gain the flexibility to do as much of your own work as you want and subcontract out the rest. Before taking this path, however, be sure you have the time and capabilities. Do you also have the

time and ability to schedule the work, hire and coordinate subs, order materials, and keep ahead of the accounting required to manage the project successfully? If you do, you stand to save the amount that a general contractor would charge to take on these responsibilities, normally 15 to 30 percent of the construction cost. If you take this responsibility on but mismanage the project, the potential savings will erode and may even cost you more than if you had hired a builder in the first place. A subcontractor might charge extra for hav-

Acting as the builder, above, requires the ability to hire and manage subcontractors.

Building a home, opposite, includes the need to schedule building inspections at the appropriate milestones.

ing to return to the site to complete work that was originally scheduled for an earlier date. Or perhaps because you didn't order the windows at the beginning, you now have to pay for a recent cost increase. (If you had hired a builder in the first place he or she would absorb the increase.)

Hiring a Builder to Handle Construction

A builder or general contractor will manage every aspect of the construction process. Your role after signing the construction contract will be to make regular progress payments and ensure that the work for which you are paying has been completed. You will also consult with the builder and agree to any changes that may have to be made along the way.

Leads for finding builders might come from friends or neighbors who have had contractors build, remodel, or add to their homes. Real-estate agents and bankers may have some names handy but are more likely familiar with the builder's ability to complete projects on time and budget than the quality of the work itself.

The next step is to narrow your list of candidates to three or four who you think can do a quality job and work harmoniously with you. Phone each builder to see whether he or she is interested in being considered for your project. If so, invite the builder to an interview at your home. The meeting will serve two purposes. You'll be able to ask the candidate about his or her experience, and you'll be able to see whether or not your personalities are compatible. Go over the plans with the builder to make certain that he or she understands the scope of the project. Ask if they have constructed similar houses. Get references, and check the builder's standing with the Better Business Bureau. Develop a short list of builders, say three, and ask them to submit bids for the project.

Contracts

Lump-Sum Contracts

A lump-sum, or fixed-fee, contract lets you know from the beginning just what the project will cost, barring any changes made because of your requests or unforeseen conditions. This form works well for projects that promise few surprises and are well defined from the outset by a complete set of contract documents. You can enter into a fixed-price contract by negotiating with a single builder on your short list or by obtaining bids from three or four builders. If you go the latter route, give each bidder a set of documents and allow at least two weeks for them to submit their bids. When you get the bids, decide who you want and call the others to thank them for their efforts. You don't have to accept the lowest bid, but it probably makes sense to do so since you have already honed the list to builders you trust. Inform this builder of your intentions to finalize a contract.

Cost-Plus-Fee Contracts

Under a cost-plus-fee contract, you agree to pay the builder for the costs of labor and materials, as verified by receipts, plus a fee that represents the builder's overhead and profit. This arrangement is sometimes referred to as "time and materials." The fee can range between 15 and 30 percent of the incurred costs. Because you ultimately pick up the tab—whatever the costs—the contractor is never at risk, as he is with a lump-sum contract. You won't know the final total cost of a cost-plus-fee contract until the project is built and paid for. If you can live with that uncertainty, there are offsetting advantages. First, this form allows you to accommodate unknown conditions much more easily than does a lump-sum contract. And rather than being tied down by the project documents, you will be free to make changes at any point along the way. This can be a trap, though. Watching the project take shape will spark the desire to add something or do something differently. Each change costs more, and the accumulation can easily exceed your budget. Because of the uncertainty of the final tab and the built-in advantage to the contractor, you should think twice before entering into this form of contract.

Contract Content

The conditions of your agreement should be spelled out thoroughly in writing and signed by both parties, whatever contractual arrangement you make with your builder. Your contract should include provisions for the following:

- The names and addresses of the owner and builder.
- A description of the work to be included ("As described in the plans and specifications dated . . .").
- The date that the work will be completed if time is of the essence.
- The contract price for lump-sum contracts and the builder's allowed profit and overhead costs for changes.
- The builder's fee for cost-plus-fee contracts and the method of accounting and requesting payment.
- The criteria for progress payments (monthly, by project milestones) and the conditions of final payment.
- A list of each drawing and specification section that is to be included as part of the contract.
- Requirements for guarantees. (One year is the standard period for which contractors guarantee the entire project, but you may require specific guarantees on

When submitting bids, all of the builders should base their estimates on the same specifications. Once the work begins, communicate with your builder to keep the work proceeding smoothly.

Inspect your newly built home, if possible, before the builder closes it up and finishes it.

certain parts of the project, such as a 20-year guarantee on the roofing.)

- Provisions for insurance.
- A description of how changes in the work orders will be handled.

The builder may have a standard contract that you can tailor to the specifics of your project. These contain complete specific conditions with blanks that you can fill in to fit your project and a set of "general conditions" that cover a host of issues from insurance to termination provisions. It's always a good idea to have an attorney review the draft of your completed contract before signing it.

Working with Your Builder

The construction phase officially begins when you have a signed copy of the contract and copies of any insurance required from the builder. It's not unheard of for a builder to request an initial payment of 10 to 20 percent of the total cost to cover mobilization costs, those costs associated with obtaining permits and getting set up to begin the actual construction. If you agree to this, keep a careful eye on the progress of the work to ensure that the total paid out at any one time doesn't get too far out of sync with the actual work completed.

What about changes? From here on, it's up to you and your builder to proceed in good faith and to keep the channels of communication open. Even so, changes of one sort or another beset every project, and they usually add to its cost.

Light at the End of the Tunnel.

The builder's request for a final inspection marks the end of the construction phase— almost. At the final inspection meeting, you and the builder will inspect the work, noting any defects or incomplete items on a "punch list." When the builder tidies up the punch list items, you should reinspect. Sometimes, builders go on to another job and take forever to clean up the last few details, so only after all items on the list have been completed satisfactorily should you release the final payment, which often accounts for the builder's profit.

Some Final Words

Having a positive attitude is important when undertaking a project as large as building a home. A positive attitude can help you ride out the rigors and stress of the construction process.

Stay Flexible. Expect problems, because they certainly will occur. Weather can upset the schedule you have established for subcontractors. A supplier may get behind on deliveries, which also affects the schedule. An unexpected pipe may surprise you during excavation. Just as certain, every problem that comes along has a solution if you are open to it.

Be Patient. The extra days it may take to resolve a construction problem will be forgotten once the project is completed.

Express Yourself. If what you see isn't exactly what you thought you were getting, don't be afraid to look into changing it. Or you may spot an unforeseen opportunity for an improvement. Changes usually cost more money, though, so don't make frivolous decisions.

Finally, watching your home go up is exciting, so stay upbeat. Get away from your project from time to time. Dine out. Take time to relax. A positive attitude will make for smoother relations with your builder. An optimistic outlook will yield better-quality work if you are doing your own construction. And though the project might seem endless while it is under way, keep in mind that all the planning and construction will fade to a faint memory at some time in the future, and you will be getting a lifetime of pleasure from a home that is just right for you.

Start-Up Homes

There is nothing like the excitement of building your first house, and the rewards are many. Financially, you are making a wise investment in your future. Plus, you're saving money right now: the cost per square foot of remodeled space in a typical fixer-upper is often higher than that of new construction. But it is in the personal sense that you stand to gain the most. Having a place of your own will enhance your lifestyle and provide the opportunity to create a home that is perfect for you *now*.

Although starter homes are compact (1,500 sq. ft. or less), today's designs live larger than the ones that were built a generation ago. Features that were once regarded as luxury options, such as master baths and two-car garages, are now standard to many basic plans. So you're getting a lot more for your money than you might expect.

Personal space, below, is just one of the rewards of home ownership.

A compact design, top right, may be all that you need to start.

A two-car garage, bottom right, is a standard feature of some plans.

In addition, architects have been re-thinking ways to configure space and designing open floor plans that are better suited to today's casual style of living. An airy great room or a combined living and dining room have replaced small separate rooms, leaving space in the plan for an extra bedroom or a

home office. Vaulted ceilings and open interiors "feel" larger, too. Thanks to energy-efficient glass, dramatic windows and large glass doors visually extend the house beyond the walls and ease the flow between indoors and outdoors, increasing the amount of actual living space, as well.

Plan #121084

Dimensions: 40' W x 42' D
Levels: 2
Square Footage: 1,728
Main Level Sq. Ft.: 845
Upper Level Sq. Ft.: 883
Bedrooms: 4
Bathrooms: 2½
Foundation: Basement
Materials List Available: Yes
Price Category: C

Photo provided by designer/architect.

If you're looking for a home where the whole family will be comfortable, you'll love this design.

Features:

- **Great Room:** The heart of the home, this great room has a fireplace with a raised hearth, a sloped ceiling, and transom-topped windows.

- **Dining Room:** A cased opening lets you flow from the great room into this formal dining room. A built-in display hutch is the highlight here.

- **Kitchen:** What could be nicer than this wraparound kitchen with peninsula snack bar? The sunny, attached breakfast area has a pantry and built-in desk.

- **Master Suite:** A double vanity, whirlpool tub, shower, and walk-in closet exude luxury in this upper floor master suite.

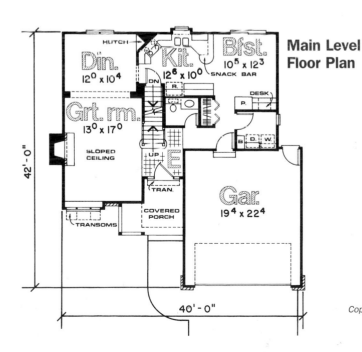

Main Level Floor Plan

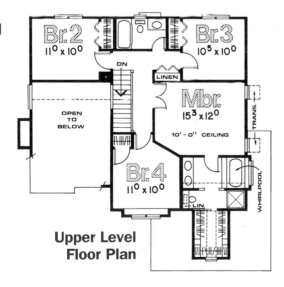

Upper Level Floor Plan

Copyright by designer/architect.

Illustration provided by designer/architect.

Plan #291009

Dimensions: 74'8" W x 41'4" D

Levels: 2

Square Footage: 1,655

Main Level Sq. Ft.: 1,277

Upper Level Sq. Ft.: 378

Bedrooms: 3

Bathrooms: 2

Foundation: Basement

Materials List Available: No

Price Category: C

If your family loves a northern European look, they'll appreciate the curved eaves and arched window that give this lovely home its character.

Features:

• Entryway: The front door welcomes both friends and family into a lovely open design on the first floor of this home.

• Living Room: The enormous arched window floods this room with natural light in the daytime. At night, draw drapes across it to create a warm, intimate feeling.

• Dining Room: Windows are the highlight of this room, too, but here, the angled bay window area opens to the rear deck.

• Kitchen: The family cook will be delighted with this well-planned kitchen, which is a snap to organize.

• Master Suite: Located on the first floor, this suite includes a private bath for total convenience.

Main Level Floor Plan

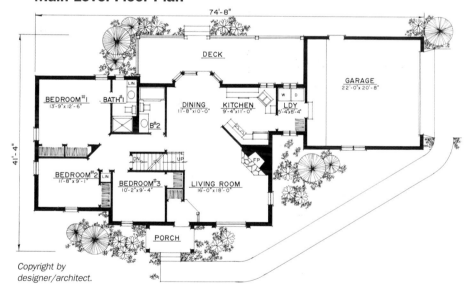

Copyright by designer/architect.

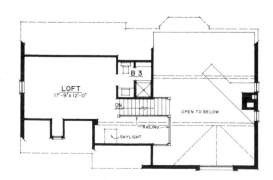

Upper Level Floor Plan

Plan #341004

Dimensions: 56'10" W x 28'6" D

Levels: 1

Square Footage: 1,101

Bedrooms: 3

Bathrooms: 2

Foundation: Crawl space, slab, or basement

Materials List Available: Yes

Price Category: B

Images provided by designer/architect.

You'll love the romantic feeling that the gables and front porch give to this well designed home, with its family-oriented layout.

Features:

- **Living Room:** The open design between this spacious room and the kitchen/dining area makes this home as ideal for family activities as it is for entertaining.

- **Outdoor Living Space:** French doors open to the back deck, where you're sure to host alfresco dinners or easy summer brunches.

- **Kitchen:** Designed for the cook's convenience, this kitchen features ample work area as well as excellent storage space in the nearby pantry.

- **Laundry Area:** Located behind closed doors to shut out the noise, this laundry closet is conveniently placed.

- **Master Suite:** With triple windows, a wide closet, and a private bath, this is a luxurious suite.

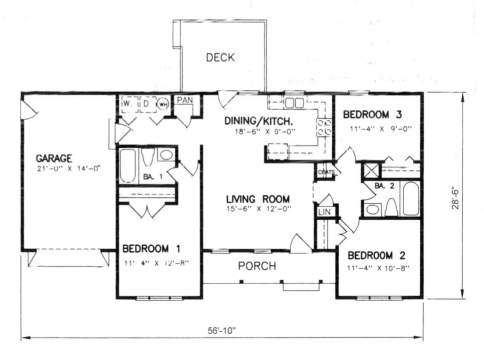

Copyright by designer/architect.

Plan #131007

Dimensions: 59'10" W x 47'8" D
Levels: 1
Square Footage: 1,595
Bedrooms: 3
Bathrooms: 2
Foundation: Crawl space, slab, basement, or walkout
Materials List Available: Yes
Price Category: D

Imagine living in this home, with its traditional country comfort and individual brand of charm.

Features:

• Exterior elements: The mixture of a front porch with a cameo front door, decorative posts, bay windows, and dormers will delight you.

• Great Room: A tray ceiling gives distinction to this large room, and a wet bar eases entertaining.

• Screened Porch: At dusk and dawn, this porch is sure to be your favorite outdoor spot.

• Kitchen: Eat any meal in this large kitchen for a touch of homey charm.

• Dining Room: Perfect for hosting a formal dinner, this bayed dining room can increase your enjoyment of simple family meals.

• Master Bedroom: For the sake of privacy, this room is somewhat secluded. Decorate to emphasize the elegant tray ceiling.

Images provided by designer/architect.

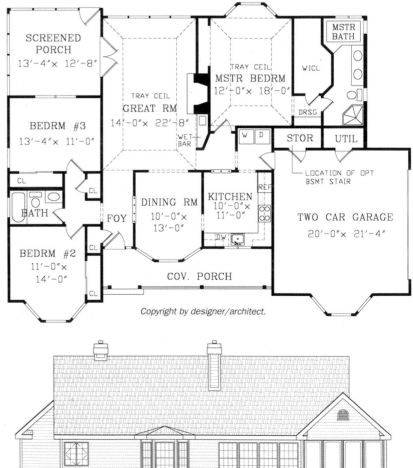

Copyright by designer/architect.

Rear Elevation

Alternate Front View

Foyer / Dining Room

Great Room

Add the Extras

Simple or plain, it's the little conveniences and miscellaneous touches that push the dining experience to perfection. Here are some extra things to think about.

- You can never have too many serving trays when you entertain outside. For carrying food or drinks from the kitchen or the grill, trays are indispensable.

- A serving cart on wheels makes a perfect movable outdoor bar and provides an additional serving surface. Look for one at yard sales or buy one new.

- Chances are you won't have a sideboard, but a few small tables to hold excess items are great substitutes for one. They're also easier to position in the different places where you need them.

- For cooler weather or even a summer's evening with a bit of nip in the air, nothing beats an outdoor fireplace for comfort. You could build one into the house, but various types of stand-alone units are sold in home centers. To add a Southwest ambiance, consider a chiminea, a clay fireplace. Try burning some piñon pine, and you'll feel as if you're in Santa Fe. Be sure to follow manufacturers' instructions when using these fireplaces. You might also have to store them during the winter.

- Pots of fragrant plants —lavender, scented geraniums, flowering tobacco, or jasmine—provide a sensual aroma. Flowers such as roses climbing up an arbor or trellis are beautiful, evoke a romantic feeling, and lend a delicate scent to the atmosphere as well.

Nothing adds romance and intrigue to an evening soiree as candlelight does. Include just a few candles for an intimate dinner. Use more for a larger gathering, placing one or more on each table. Scatter luminaries around the yard. As the beautiful evening dusk begins, light candles, a few at a time, so your eyes can adjust to the dimming light. Not only do the candles illuminate the night in a magical way but they can also keep bugs at bay.

Plan #341003

Dimensions: 60' W x 30' D

Levels: 1

Square Footage: 1,200

Bedrooms: 3

Bathrooms: 2

Foundation: Crawl space, slab, or basement

Materials List Available: Yes

Price Category: B

Images provided by designer/architect.

If you're looking for the ideal plan for a first home or an empty-nester, this romantic cottage will meet your needs with style.

Features:

• Outdoor Living Space: Use the porch at the front of the house and the deck at the back as extra living area in fine weather.

• Living Room: Open to both the dining area and the kitchen, this room also looks out to the deck and backyard.

• Kitchen: This well-planned area combines a step-saving layout with conveniently placed counter and storage space.

• Laundry Closet: Open the door to this centrally located closet to find a full washer and dryer.

• Bedrooms: Choose between the bedrooms with spacious walk-in closets for your room, and depending on need, use the others for children's rooms, a guest room, or an office.

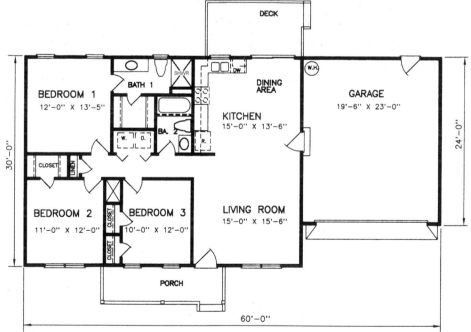

Copyright by designer/architect.

Images provided by designer/architect.

Plan #251005

Dimensions: 50' W x 44'2" D
Levels: 1
Square Footage: 1,631
Bedrooms: 3
Bathrooms: 2
Foundation: Basement
Materials List Available: Yes
Price Category: C

This elegant home features hip roof lines that will add appeal in any neighborhood.

Features:

- Ceiling Height: 9 ft.
- Front Porch: The porch stretches across the entire front of the home, offering plenty of space to sit and enjoy evening breezes.
- Family Room: This family room features a handsome fireplace and has plenty of room for all kinds of family activities.
- Dining Room: This dining room has plenty of room for dinner parties. After dinner, guests can step through French doors onto the rear deck.
- Kitchen: This kitchen is a pleasure in which to work. It features an angled snack bar with plenty of room for informal family meals.
- Master Bedroom: You'll enjoy retiring at day's end to this master bedroom, with its large walk-in closet.
- Master Bath: This master bath features a double vanity, a deluxe tub, and a walk-in shower.

SMARTtip

Victorian Style

Victorian, today, is a very romantic look. To underscore this, add the scent of lavender or some other dried flower to the room or use potpourri, which you can keep in a bowl on the vanity. Hang a fragrant pomander on a hook, display lavender soaps on a wall shelf, or tuck sachets between towels on a shelf. For an authentic touch, display a Victorian favorite, the spider plant.

Copyright by designer/architect.

Main Level Floor Plan

DR 11-6x9-0
Nook
KITCHEN 12-2x9-0
dw
F R
up
rail
dn
GARAGE 13-6x20-6
LIVINGROOM 11-6x17-8
BRM
D W
Foyer
Lav
Porch

Main Level Floor Plan

Illustration provided by designer/architect.

Plan #281007

Dimensions: 37' W x 31' D

Levels: 2

Square Footage: 1,206

Main Level Sq. Ft.: 670

Upper Level Sq. Ft.: 536

Bedrooms: 3

Bathrooms: 1 full, 2 half

Foundation: Full basement

Materials List Available: Yes

Price Category: B

Upper Level Floor Plan

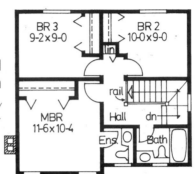

BR 3 9-2x9-0
BR 2 10-0x9-0
lin
rail
MBR 11-6x10-4
Hall
dn
Ens
Bath

Copyright by designer/architect.

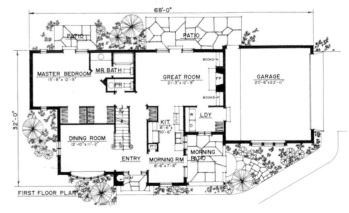

Main Level Floor Plan

68'-0"

PATIO
PATIO
MASTER BEDROOM 15'-8"x12'-9"
MR.BATH
GREAT ROOM 21'-3"x12'-9"
GARAGE 20'-6"x22'-0"
BOOKS
PR
BOOKS
32'-0"
KIT. 8'-6"
W D
LDY
DINING ROOM 12'-10"x11'-2"
MORNING PATIO
ENTRY
MORNING RM 8'-6"x7'-8"
SEAT
FIRST FLOOR PLAN

Copyright by designer/architect.

Plan #291011

Dimensions: 68'6" W x 33' D

Levels: 2

Square Footage: 1,898

Main Level Sq. Ft.: 1,182

Upper Level Sq. Ft.: 716

Bedrooms: 4

Bathrooms: 2½

Foundation: Basement

Materials List Available: No

Price Category: D

Illustrations provided by designer/architect.

Upper Level Floor Plan

BATH#2
BEDROOM#4 11'-6"x10'-2"
BEDROOM#2 13'-4"x14'-4"
BEDROOM#3 11'-0"x14'-11"

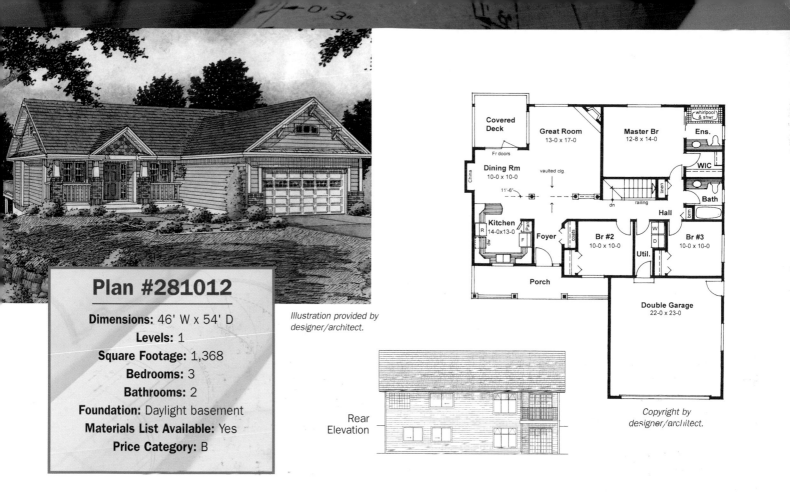

Plan #281012

Dimensions: 46' W x 54' D

Levels: 1

Square Footage: 1,368

Bedrooms: 3

Bathrooms: 2

Foundation: Daylight basement

Materials List Available: Yes

Price Category: B

Illustration provided by designer/architect.

Rear Elevation

Copyright by designer/architect.

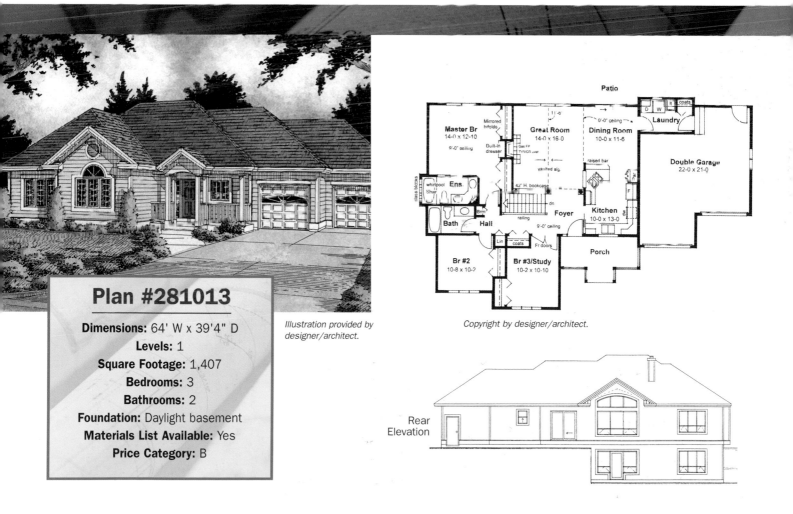

Plan #281013

Dimensions: 64' W x 39'4" D

Levels: 1

Square Footage: 1,407

Bedrooms: 3

Bathrooms: 2

Foundation: Daylight basement

Materials List Available: Yes

Price Category: B

Illustration provided by designer/architect.

Copyright by designer/architect.

Rear Elevation

Plan #221004

Dimensions: 67'8" W x 43' D

Levels: 1

Square Footage: 1,763

Bedrooms: 3

Bathrooms: 2

Foundation: Basement

Materials List Available: No

Price Category: C

Illustration provided by designer/architect.

Rear Elevation

You'll love the spacious feeling provided by the open design of this traditional ranch.

Features:

- Ceiling Height: 8 ft.

- Dining Room: This formal room is perfect for entertaining groups both large and small, and the open design makes it easy to serve.

- Living Room: The vaulted ceiling here and in the dining room adds to the elegance of these rooms. Use window treatments that emphasize these ceilings for a truly sumptuous look.

- Kitchen: Designed for practicality and efficiency, this kitchen will thrill all the cooks in the family. An attached dining nook makes a natural gathering place for friends and family.

- Master Suite: The private bath in this suite features a double vanity and whirlpool tub. You'll find a walk-in closet in the bedroom.

- Garage: You'll love the extra storage space in this two-car garage.

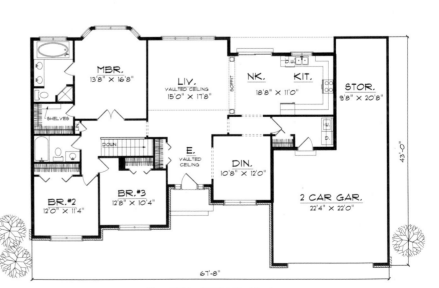

Copyright by designer/architect.

Plan #321001

Dimensions: 83' W x 42' D

Levels: 1

Square Footage: 1,721

Bedrooms: 3

Bathrooms: 2

Foundation: Basement, crawl space, or slab

Materials List Available: Yes

Price Category: C

You'll love the atrium that creates a warm, naturally lit space inside this gracious home, as well as the roof dormers that give it wonderful curb appeal from the outside.

Features:

- **Great Room:** Bathed in light from the atrium window wall, this room, with its vaulted ceiling, will be the hub of your family life.

- **Dining Room:** This room also has a vaulted ceiling and is lit by the atrium, but you can draw drapes at night to create a cozy, warm feeling.

- **Kitchen:** Designed for functionality, this step-saving kitchen is easy to organize and makes cooking a pleasure.

- **Breakfast Room:** For convenience, this room is located between the kitchen and the rear covered porch.

- **Master Suite:** Retire with pleasure to this lovely retreat, with its luxurious bath.

Illustration provided by designer/architect.

Rear View

Copyright by designer/architect.

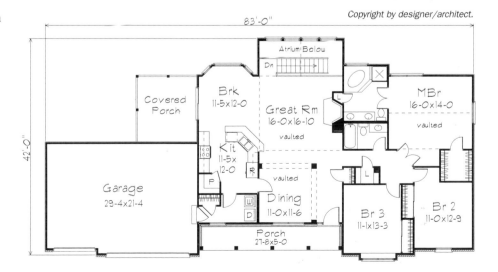

Plan #131002

Dimensions: 70'1" W x 60'7" D
Levels: 1
Square Footage: 1,709
Bedrooms: 3
Bathrooms: 2½
Foundation: Basement, crawl space, or slab
Materials List Available: Yes
Price Category: D

Images provided by designer/architect.

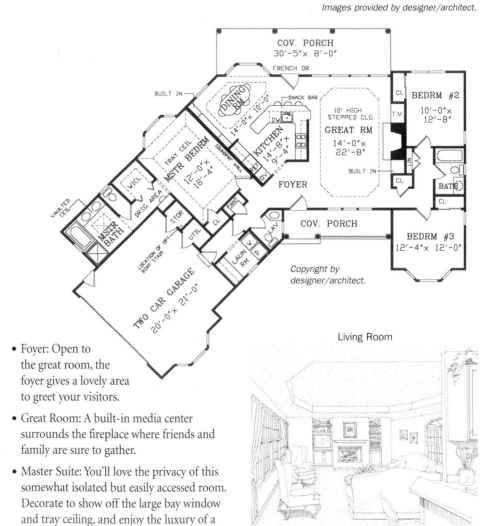

Rear View

Living Room

Copyright by designer/architect.

You'll love the way this angled ranch brings out the best in a corner lot or on a slope.

Features:

Ceiling Height: 8 ft.

- **Front Porch:** Hang baskets of plants from the roof of this porch, which is just the right size for a couple of rockers and a side table.

- **Dining Room:** Well-placed windows flood this room with sunlight during the day and a built-in cabinet gives ample storage space for all your china, linens, and collectables.

- **Foyer:** Open to the great room, the foyer gives a lovely area to greet your visitors.

- **Great Room:** A built-in media center surrounds the fireplace where friends and family are sure to gather.

- **Master Suite:** You'll love the privacy of this somewhat isolated but easily accessed room. Decorate to show off the large bay window and tray ceiling, and enjoy the luxury of a compartmented bathroom.

Plan #211002

Dimensions: 68' W x 62' D
Levels: 1
Square Footage: 1,792
Bedrooms: 3
Bathrooms: 2
Foundation: Crawl space
Materials List Available: Yes
Price Category: C

Images provided by designer/architect.

Arched windows on the front of this home give it a European style that you're sure to love.

SMARTtip

Water Features

Water features create the ambiance of a soothing oasis on a deck. A water-filled urn becomes a mirror that reflects the sky—making a small deck look larger. Fish flashing in an ornamental pool add color and act as a focal point for a deck with no view.

A water fountain introduces a pleasant rhythmical sound that helps drown out the background noises of traffic and nearby neighbors.

Features.

- **Living Room:** The 12-ft. ceiling in this large, open room enhances its spacious feeling. A fireplace adds warmth on chilly days and cool evenings.

- **Dining Room:** Decorate to accentuate the 12-ft. ceiling and formal feeling of this room.

- **Kitchen:** Designed for comfort and efficiency, this room also has a 12-ft. ceiling. The cozy breakfast bar is a natural gathering spot for friends and family.

- **Master Suite:** A split design guarantees privacy here. A sloped cathedral ceiling adds elegance, and a walk-in closet makes it practical. The bath has two vanities, a tub, and a walk-in shower.

- **Garage:** Park two cars here, and use the balance of this 520 sq. ft. area as a handy storage area.

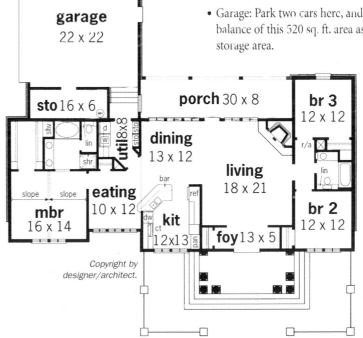

Copyright by designer/architect.

Plan #141026

Dimensions: 48' W x 48' D

Levels: 2

Square Footage: 1,993

Main Level Sq. Ft.: 1,038

Upper Level Sq. Ft.: 955

Bedrooms: 3

Bathrooms: 2½

Foundation: Basement

Materials List Available: Yes

Price Category: D

Images provided by designer/architect.

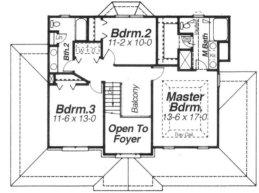

Main Level Floor Plan

Sundeck 17-6 x 13-6

Brkfst. 8-8 x 15-6

Kit. 11-10 x 10-0

Family 14-10 x 13-6

Dining 11-6 x 13-6

Lav.

Living 13-6 x 13-6

Open Foyer 7-8 x 9-8

© 1995, Jannis Vann & Associates, Inc.

48-0

48-0

Upper Level Floor Plan

Copyright by designer/architect.

Bdrm.2 11-2 x 10-0

Bth.2

Lin

W D

M.Bath

Bdrm.3 11-6 x 13-0

Balcony

Master Bdrm 13-6 x 17-0

Open To Foyer

Tray Ceil.

Plan #121055

Dimensions: 51' W x 52' D

Levels: 1

Square Footage: 1,622

Bedrooms: 3

Bathrooms: 2

Foundation: Basement

Materials List Available: Yes

Price Category: C

Images provided by designer/architect.

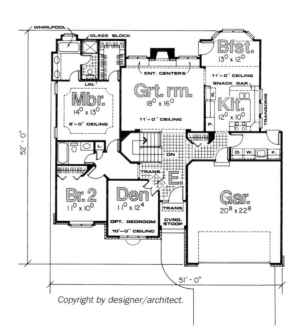

WHIRLPOOL

GLASS BLOCK

ENT. CENTERS

Bfst. 13⁰ x 12⁰

11'-0" CEILING

SNACK BAR

Mbr. 14⁰ x 13⁰

9'-0" CEILING

LIN.

Grt. rm. 18⁰ x 16⁰

11'-0" CEILING

Kit. 12⁰ x 10⁰

P.

TRANSOMS

D. W. F.

DN

Br. 2 11⁰ x 10⁰

Den 11⁰ x 12⁴

TRANS.

OPT. BEDROOM

10'-0" CEILING

Gar. 20⁸ x 22⁸

CVRD. STOOP

52' - 0"

51' - 0"

Copyright by designer/architect.

OPTIONAL Br.3 11⁰ x 10⁰

10'-0" CEILING

Optional Third Bedroom Floor Plan

Main Level Floor Plan

Fam. rm. 18⁰ x 14⁰
Bfst. 10⁰ x 14⁰
Kit. 9⁰ x 11⁰
Par. 11⁰ x 12⁰
Din. 11⁰ x 12²
Gar. 20⁰ x 24⁰
COVERED PORCH

40'-0"
50'-0"

Plan #121087

Dimensions: 50' W x 40' D
Levels: 2
Square Footage: 2,103
Main Level Sq. Ft.: 1,082
Upper Level Sq. Ft.: 1,021
Bedrooms: 4
Bathrooms: 2½
Foundation: Basement
Materials List Available: Yes
Price Category: D

Images provided by designer/architect.

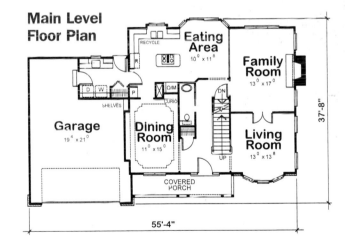

Br. 3 11⁰ x 10⁸
Br. 4 10³ x 10⁸
Mbr. 13⁰ x 15⁰ 9'-0" CEILING
SEAT
Br. 2 11⁰ x 11⁰
OPEN TO BELOW
GLASS BLOCK
WHIRLPOOL

Upper Level Floor Plan

Copyright by designer/architect.

Main Level Floor Plan

Eating Area 10⁰ x 11⁸
Family Room 13⁰ x 17⁰
Garage 19⁴ x 21⁰
Dining Room 11⁰ x 15⁰
Living Room 13⁰ x 13⁸
RECYCLE
SHELVES
CURIO
COVERED PORCH

37'-8"
55'-4"

Plan #121086

Dimensions: 55'4" W x 37'8" D
Levels: 2
Square Footage: 1,998
Main Level Sq. Ft.: 1,093
Upper Level Sq. Ft.: 905
Bedrooms: 3
Bathrooms: 2½
Foundation: Basement
Materials List Available: Yes
Price Category: D

Images provided by designer/architect.

Br. 2 10⁰ x 11⁰
10'-0" CEILING
Br. 3 11² x 15⁶
Mbr. 13⁰ x 17⁰ 10'-0" CEILING
OPEN TO BELOW

Upper Level Floor Plan

Copyright by designer/architect.

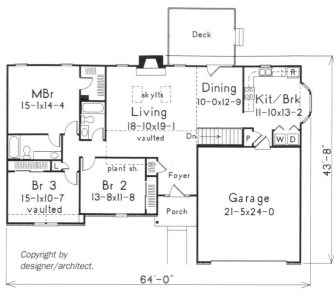

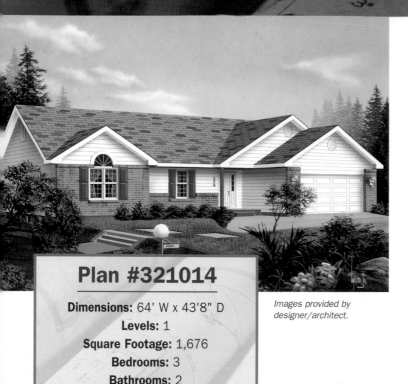

Plan #321014

Dimensions: 64' W x 43'8" D

Levels: 1

Square Footage: 1,676

Bedrooms: 3

Bathrooms: 2

Foundation: Basement

Materials List Available: Yes

Price Category: C

Images provided by designer/architect.

Copyright by designer/architect.

SMARTtip

Blending Architecture

An easy way to blend the new deck with the architecture of a house is with railings. Precut railings and caps come in many styles and sizes.

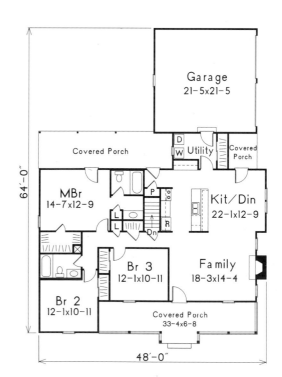

Plan #321015

Dimensions: 48' W x 64' D

Levels: 1

Square Footage: 1,501

Bedrooms: 3

Bathrooms: 2

Foundation: Basement

Materials List Available: Yes

Price Category: C

Images provided by designer/architect.

Copyright by designer/architect.

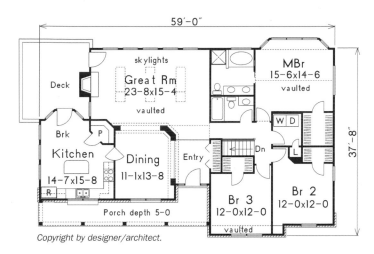

Copyright by designer/architect.

Plan #321010

Dimensions: 59' W x 37'8" D
Levels: 1
Square Footage: 1,787
Bedrooms: 3
Bathrooms: 2
Foundation: Basement
Materials List Available: Yes
Price Category: C

Images provided by designer/architect.

SMARTtip

Country Décor in Your Bathroom

Collections are often part of a country decor, even in the bathroom. All you need is three or more of anything that have size, shape, or color in common. You can mass them on walls, on shelves, on the windowsills, or even along the edge of the tub.

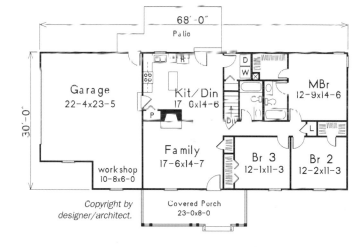

Copyright by designer/architect.

Plan #321013

Dimensions: 68' W x 30' D
Levels: 1
Square Footage: 1,360
Bedrooms: 3
Bathrooms: 2
Foundation: Basement
Materials List Available: Yes
Price Category: B

Images provided by designer/architect.

SMARTtip

Glass Doors and Fire Safety

Professionals recommend keeping glass doors open while a fire is burning. When the doors are left completely open, the burning flame has a more realistic appearance and the glass doesn't become soiled by swirling ashes. When the doors are closed, heat from a large hot fire can break the glass.

Plan #321003

Dimensions: 67'4" W x 48' D

Levels: 1

Square Footage: 1,791

Bedrooms: 4

Bathrooms: 2

Foundation: Basement

Materials List Available: Yes

Price Category: C

The traditional good looks of the exterior of this home are complemented by the stunning contemporary design of the interior.

Features:

- **Great Room:** With a vaulted ceiling to highlight its spacious dimensions, this room is certain to be the central gathering spot for friends and family.

- **Dining Room:** Also with a vaulted ceiling, this room has an octagonal shape for added interest. Windows here and in the great room look out to the covered patio.

- **Kitchen:** A center island gives a convenient work space in this well-designed kitchen, which features a pass-through to the dining room for easy serving, and large, walk-in pantry for storage.

- **Breakfast Room:** A bay window lets sunshine pour in to start your morning with a smile.

- **Master Bedroom:** A vaulted ceiling and a sitting area make you feel truly pampered in this room.

Images provided by designer/architect.

Great Rm 22-8x16-10 vaulted clg

MBr 15-8x13-9 vaulted clg

Covered Patio

Dining 12-0x12-0

Br 2 10-0x 9-0

Stor 8-0x 7-7

Laundry

48'-0"

Kit/ Brkfst 17-4x14-2

Foyer

Br 3 10-0x 10-0

Study Br 4 11-4x12-7 vaulted clg

Garage 19-4x21-0

Porch depth 5-10

67'-4"

Copyright by designer/architect.

SMARTtip

Bay & Bow Windows

Occasionally too little room exists between the window frame (if there is one) and the ceiling. In this situation you might be able to use ceiling-mounted hardware. Alternatively, a cornice across the top and a rod mounted inside the cornice will give you the dual benefit of visually lowering the top of the window and concealing the hardware.

Plan #341009

Dimensions: 44'5" W x 39'4" D

Levels: 1

Square Footage: 1,280

Bedrooms: 3

Bathrooms: 2

Foundation: Crawl space, slab, or basement

Materials List Available: Yes

Price Category: B

Images provided by designer/architect.

If you admire the exterior features of this home — the L-shaped front porch, nested gables, and transom lights — you'll love its interior.

Features:

- Ceiling Height: Ceilings are 9-ft. high to enhance this home's spacious feeling.

- Living Room: A fireplace creates a cozy feeling in this open, spacious room.

- Dining Room: Decorative columns grace the transition between this room and the living room.

- Kitchen: This open kitchen features a serving bar, a large pantry, and access to the back deck.

- Laundry: The washer and dryer are housed in a large utility closet to minimize noise.

- Master Suite: A designer window, vaulted ceiling, and walk-in closet make the bedroom luxurious, and the garden tub and shower make the private bath a true retreat.

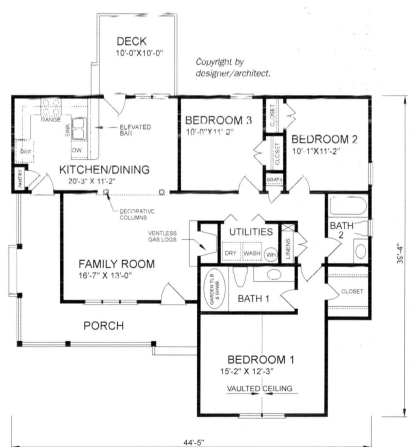

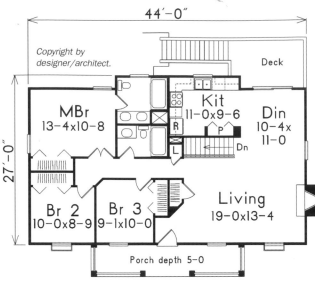

Plan #321022

Dimensions: 44' W x 27' D

Levels: 1

Square Footage: 1,140

Bedrooms: 3

Bathrooms: 2

Foundation: Basement

Materials List Available: Yes

Price Category: B

Images provided by designer/architect.

SMARTtip

Basement Moldings

Keep moldings simple in a basement with lower ceilings. Elaborate moldings around the ceiling or floor can shorten the height of the room.

Plan #321023

Dimensions: 39'8" W x 41' D

Levels: 1

Square Footage: 1,092

Bedrooms: 3

Bathrooms: 1½

Foundation: Basement

Materials List Available: Yes

Price Category: B

Images provided by designer/architect.

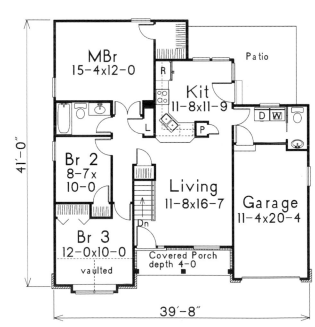

Copyright by designer/architect.

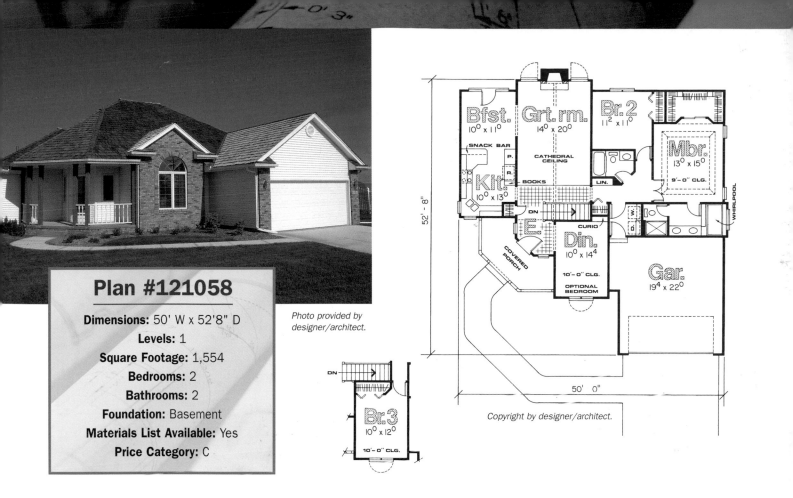

Plan #121058

Dimensions: 50' W x 52'8" D

Levels: 1

Square Footage: 1,554

Bedrooms: 2

Bathrooms: 2

Foundation: Basement

Materials List Available: Yes

Price Category: C

Photo provided by designer/architect.

Copyright by designer/architect.

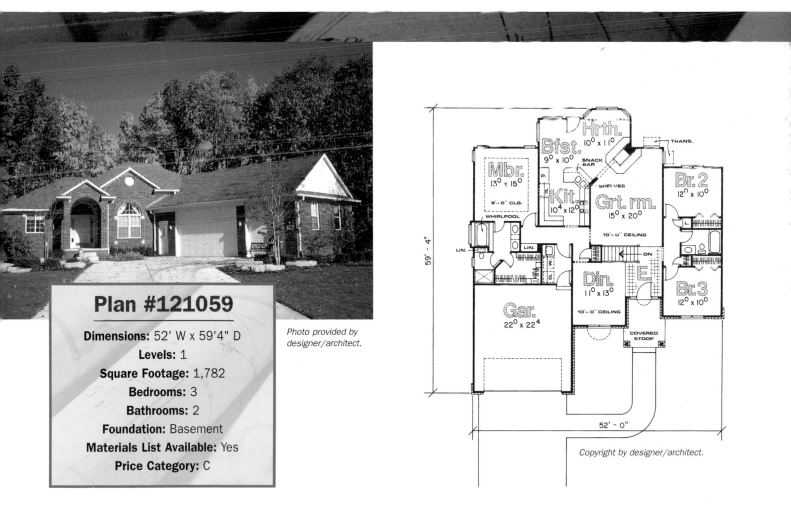

Plan #121059

Dimensions: 52' W x 59'4" D

Levels: 1

Square Footage: 1,782

Bedrooms: 3

Bathrooms: 2

Foundation: Basement

Materials List Available: Yes

Price Category: C

Photo provided by designer/architect.

Copyright by designer/architect.

Plan #161001

Dimensions: 67'2" W x 47' D

Levels: 1

Square Footage: 1,782

Bedrooms: 3

Bathrooms: 2

Foundation: Basement

Materials List Available: Yes

Price Category: C

Images provided by designer/architect.

An all-brick exterior displays the solid strength that characterizes this gracious home.

Features:

- Gathering Area: A feeling of spaciousness permeates this gathering area, created by the foyer, great room, and dining room. Multiple windows provide natural light that dances along a sloped ceiling, spilling onto decorative columns and a fireplace.

- Breakfast Area: A continuation of the sloped ceiling leads to this breakfast area, where French doors open to a screened porch.

- Kitchen: An abundance of cabinets and counter space are the hallmarks of this large kitchen, with its easy access to a spacious laundry room and storage area.

- Master Suite: A tray ceiling and spacious walk-in closet in the master bedroom, along with a whirlpool tub and double-bowl vanity in the bathroom, enable you to pamper yourself.

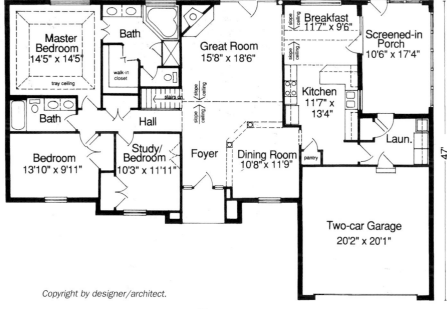

Copyright by designer/architect.

Rear Elevation

Left Side Elevation

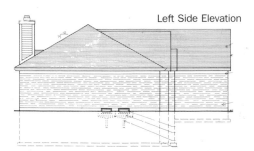

Right Side Elevation

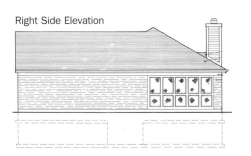

Front View

Great Room / Foyer

Plan #221024

Dimensions: 43' W x 40' D

Levels: 2

Square Footage: 1,732

Main Level Sq. Ft.: 1,289

Upper Level Sq. Ft.: 544

Bedrooms: 3

Bathrooms: 2½

Foundation: Basement

Materials List Available: No

Price Category: C

Illustration provided by designer/architect.

If your family loves contemporary split-level designs and large rooms with an open feeling, this is the home of their dreams.

Features:

• Living Room: A vaulted ceiling adds dimension to this large room, which is open to the dining room.

• Dining Room: Vaulted ceilings here and in the adjacent kitchen add to the spacious feeling. Sliding glass doors that open to the backyard make a practical pathway for the children.

• Family Room: This huge room features a fireplace for cozy comfort on chilly nights.

• Master Suite: A tray ceiling, walk-in closet, and private bath make this upstairs suite a joy.

• Bonus Room: Finish this 18-ft. x 29-ft.-9-in. space on the lower level as a home office or game room.

• Bedrooms: Both bedrooms have good closet space and share a full bath off the hallway.

Main Level Floor Plan

Copyright by designer/architect.

Basement Level Floor Plan

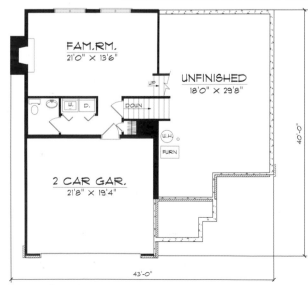

Plan #271030

Dimensions: 56' W x 45' D
Levels: 2
Square Footage: 1,926
Main Level Sq. Ft.: 1,490
Upper Level Sq. Ft.: 436
Bedrooms: 3
Bathrooms: 2½
Foundation: Basement
Materials List Available: Yes
Price Category: D

Photo provided by designer/architect.

This traditional home's main-floor master suite is hard to resist, with its inviting window seat and delightful bath.

Features:

• **Master Suite:** Just off from the entry foyer, this luxurious oasis is entered through double doors, and offers an airy vaulted ceiling, plus a private bath that includes a separate tub and shower, dual-sink vanity, and walk-in closet.

• **Great Room:** This space does it all in style, with a breathtaking wall of windows and a charming fireplace.

• **Kitchen:** A cooktop island makes dinnertime tasks a breeze. You'll also love the roomy pantry. The adjoining breakfast room, with its deck access and built-in desk, is sure to be a popular hangout for the teens.

• **Secondary Bedrooms:** Two additional bedrooms reside on the upper floor and allow the younger family members a measure of desired—and necessary—privacy.

Main Level Floor Plan

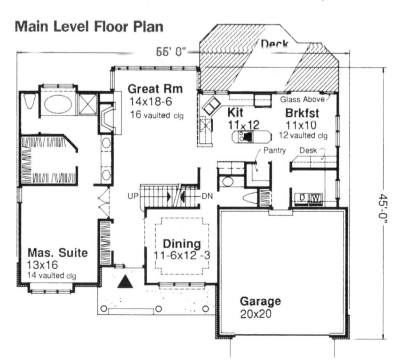

Upper Level Floor Plan

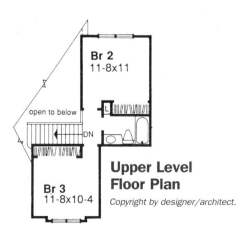

Copyright by designer/architect.

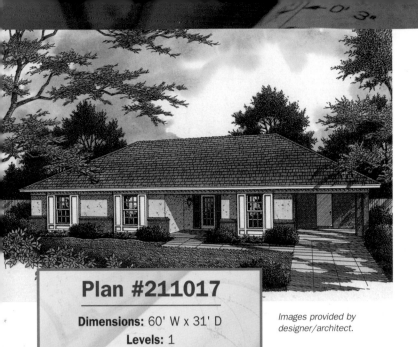

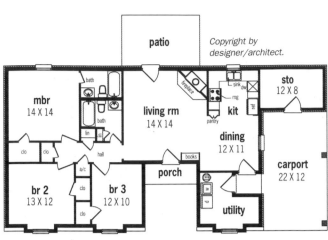

Copyright by designer/architect.

patio

mbr
14 X 14

bath

bath

lin

clo | clo

living rm
14 X 14

kit

sink | dw

rng

ref

sto
12 X 8

dining
12 X 11

carport
22 X 12

hall

a/c

clo

books

porch

br 2
13 X 12

clo

br 3
12 X 10

clo

utility

Plan #211017

Dimensions: 60' W x 31' D

Levels: 1

Square Footage: 1,212

Bedrooms: 3

Bathrooms: 2

Foundation: Slab

Materials List Available: No

Price Category: B

Images provided by designer/architect.

SMARTtip

Adding Trim Accessories

Consider adding plinth and corner blocks to door and window casings. These relatively inexpensive elements add a decorative flourish to wall openings, bringing depth and richness to an interior space.

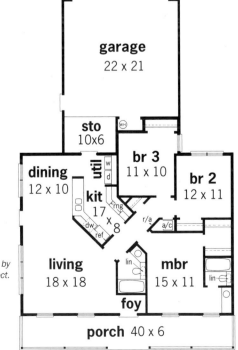

garage
22 x 21

sto
10x6

WH

br 3
11 x 10

dining
12 x 10

util

w
d

kit
17
x
8

rng

br 2
12 x 11

dw
ref

r/a

a/c

living
18 x 18

lin

mbr
15 x 11

lin

foy

porch 40 x 6

Plan #211018

Dimensions: 40' W x 64' D

Levels: 1

Square Footage: 1,266

Bedrooms: 3

Bathrooms: 2

Foundation: Crawl space

Materials List Available: Yes

Price Category: B

Images provided by designer/architect.

Copyright by designer/architect.

Plan #211020

Dimensions: 54' W x 44'6" D

Levels: 1

Square Footage: 1,346

Bedrooms: 3

Bathrooms: 2

Foundation: Slab

Materials List Available: Yes

Price Category: B

Images provided by designer/architect.

Copyright by designer/architect.

Plan #211021

Dimensions: 61' W x 35' D

Levels: 1

Square Footage: 1,375

Bedrooms: 3

Bathrooms: 2

Foundation: Slab

Materials List Available: Yes

Price Category: B

Images provided by designer/architect.

Copyright by designer/architect.

SMARTtip

Creating Built-up Cornices

Combine various base, crown, and cove moldings to create an elaborate cornice that is both imaginative and tasteful. Use the pattern throughout your home to establish a unique architectural element having the appearance of being professionally designed.

Images provided by designer/architect.

Plan #321008

Dimensions: 57' W x 52'2" D

Levels: 1

Square Footage: 1,761

Bedrooms: 4

Bathrooms: 2

Foundation: Basement

Materials List Available: Yes

Price Category: C

One look at the roof dormers and planter boxes that grace the outside of this ranch, and you'll know that the interior is planned for comfortable family living.

Features:

- **Great Room:** A vaulted ceiling in this room points up its generous dimensions. Put a grouping of chairs near the fireplace to take advantage of the cozy spot it creates in chilly weather.

- **Kitchen:** Open to the great room, this kitchen has been planned for convenience. It features a pass-through to the dining area for easy serving when you've got a crowd to feed.

- **Master Bedroom:** A vaulted ceiling here makes you feel especially pampered, and the walk-in closet and amenity-filled bath add to that feeling.

- **Additional Bedrooms:** Great closet space characterizes all the rooms in this home, making it easy for children of any age to keep it organized and tidy.

Copyright by designer/architect.

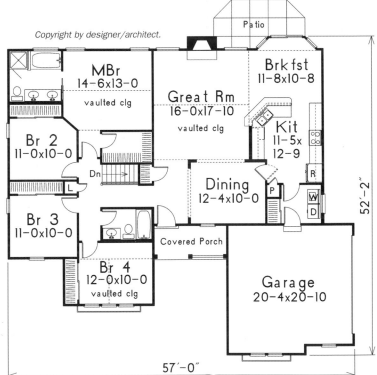

SMARTtip

Hanging Wallpaper

Use liner paper to smooth out a damaged wall and to provide uniform support for expensive paper.

Illustration provided by designer/architect.

Plan #291002

Dimensions: 62'8" W x 38'4" D

Levels: 1

Square Footage: 1,550

Bedrooms: 3

Bathrooms: 2

Foundation: Basement

Materials List Available: No

Price Category: C

This comfortable Southwestern style ranch house will fit perfectly into any setting.

Features:

• **Ceiling Height:** 8 ft. unless otherwise noted.

• **Front Porch:** This scalloped front porch offers plenty of room for enjoying a cool summer breeze.

• **Foyer:** Upon entering this impressive foyer you'll be greeted by a soaring space encompassing the living room and dining room.

• **Living/Dining Area:** This combined living room and dining room has a handsome fireplace as its focal point. When dinner is served, guests will flow casually into the dining area.

• **Kitchen:** Take your cooking up a notch in this terrific kitchen. It features a 42-in.-high counter that will do double-duty as a snack bar for family meals and a wet bar for entertaining.

• **Master Suite:** This master retreat is separated from the other bedrooms and features an elegant vaulted ceiling. The dressing area has a compartmentalized bath and a walk-in closet.

Rear View

Copyright by designer/architect.

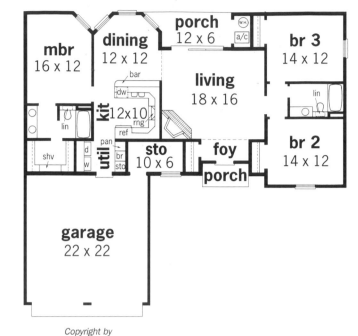

Images provided by designer/architect.

Copyright by designer/architect.

Plan #211026

Dimensions: 56' W x 50' D

Levels: 1

Square Footage: 1,415

Bedrooms: 3

Bathrooms: 2

Foundation: Slab

Materials List Available: Yes

Price Category: B

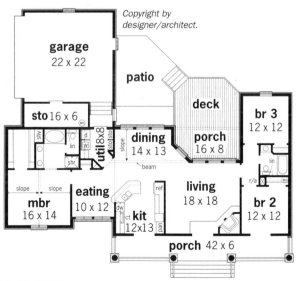

Illustration provided by designer/architect.

Plan #211029

Dimensions: 68' W x 60' D

Levels: 1

Square Footage: 1,672

Bedrooms: 3

Bathrooms: 2

Foundation: Crawl space

Materials List Available: Yes

Price Category: C

SMARTtip

Ponds

If a pond or small body of water already exists on your property, arrange your garden elements to take advantage of it. Build a bridge over it to connect it to other areas of the garden. If there's a dock already in place, make use of it for an instant midday picnic for one.

Plan #211032

Dimensions: 77' W x 32' D

Levels: 1

Square Footage: 1,751

Bedrooms: 4

Full Baths: 2

Foundation: Slab

Materials List Available: Yes

Price Category: C

Images provided by designer/architect.

SMARTtip

Using a Laser Level

Pick a central location for the laser from which the projected beam will reach all the walls involved in the project. This is the easiest way to check existing floors and ceilings for level.

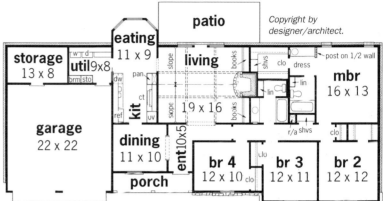

Copyright by designer/architect.

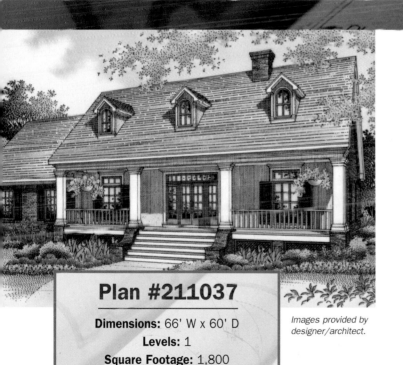

Plan #211037

Dimensions: 66' W x 60' D

Levels: 1

Square Footage: 1,800

Bedrooms: 3

Bathrooms: 2

Foundation: Crawl space

Materials List Available: Yes

Price Category: D

Images provided by designer/architect.

Copyright by designer/architect.

SMARTtip

Reflected Light in the Bathroom

The addition of a large mirror can bring reflected light into a small bathroom, adding the illusion of space without the expense of renovation.

Plan #291001

Dimensions: 62'8" W x 38'4" D

Levels: 1

Square Footage: 1,550

Bedrooms: 3

Bathrooms: 2

Foundation: Basement

Materials List Available: No

Price Category: C

A handsome porch with Greek Revival details greets visitors to this Early-American style home.

Features:

- Ceiling Height: 8 ft. unless otherwise noted.

- Foyer: Upon entering this foyer you'll be struck by the space provided by the vaulted ceiling in the dining room, living room, and kitchen.

- Dining Room: This dining room is perfectly suited for formal dinner parties as well as less formal family meals.

- Decks: Two rear decks are conveniently accessible from the master bedroom, kitchen, and living room.

- Kitchen: You'll enjoy cooking in this well-designed kitchen, which features an eating area that is perfect for informal family meals.

- Master Bedroom: This master retreat is separated from the other bedrooms for additional privacy. It features an elegant vaulted ceiling and is graced with a dressing area, private bath, and walk-in closet.

Photo provided by designer/architect.

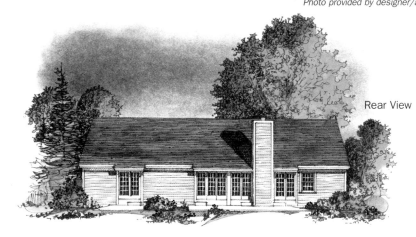

Rear View

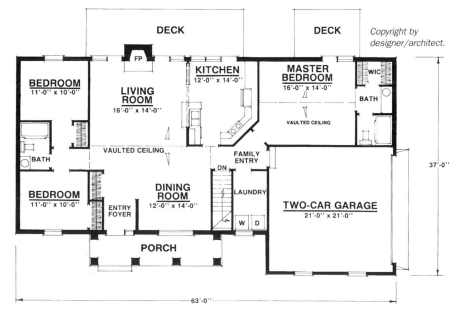

Copyright by designer/architect.

Plan #281011

Dimensions: 50' W x 54' D

Levels: 1

Square Footage: 1,314

Bedrooms: 3

Bathrooms: 2

Foundation: Basement

Materials List Available: Yes

Price Category: B

Images provided by designer/architect.

This attractive ranch home takes advantage of views at both the front and rear.

Features:

- Ceiling Height: 8 ft.
- Porch: This large, inviting porch welcomes your guests and provides shade for the big living-room window on hot summer days.
- Living Room: This large main living area has plenty of room for entertaining and family activities.
- Dining Room: This room can accommodate large dinner parties. It's located near the living room and the kitchen for convenient entertaining.
- Deck: Family and friends will enjoy stepping out on this large covered sun deck that is accessible from the living room, dining room, and kitchen.
- Master Suite: You'll enjoy retiring at the end of the day to this luxurious master suite, which features its own walk-in closet and bathroom.

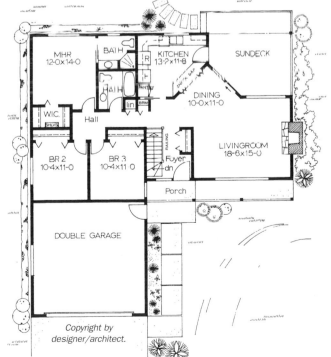

Copyright by designer/architect.

Rear Elevation

SMARTtip

Rag-Rolling Off

Paint Tip: Work with a partner. One person can roll on the glaze while the other lifts it off with the rag in a rhythmic pattern of even, steady strokes.

Plan #211024

Dimensions: 61' W x 44' D

Levels: 1

Square Footage: 1,418

Bedrooms: 3

Bathrooms: 2

Foundation: Slab

Materials List Available: Yes

Price Category: B

Images provided by designer/architect.

Copyright by designer/architect.

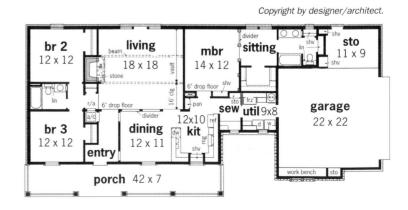

Plan #211030

Dimensions: 75' W x 37' D

Levels: 1

Square Footage: 1,600

Bedrooms: 3

Bathrooms: 2

Foundation: Slab

Materials List Available: Yes

Price Category: C

Images provided by designer/architect.

SMARTtip

Brackets in Window Treatments

Although it is rarely noticed, a bracket plays an important role in supporting rods and poles. If a treatment rubs against a window frame, an extension bracket solves the problem. It projects from the wall at an adjustable length, providing enough clearance. A hold-down bracket anchors a cellular shade or a blind to the bottom of a door, preventing the treatment from moving when the door is opened or closed.

Copyright by designer/architect.

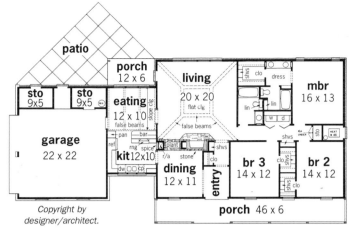

porch 46 x 6

Copyright by designer/architect.

Plan #211036

Dimensions: 80' W x 40' D
Levels: 1
Square Footage: 1,800
Bedrooms: 3
Bathrooms: 2
Foundation: Slab
Materials List Available: Yes
Price Category: D

Images provided by designer/architect.

SMARTtip

Dimmer Switches

You can dim lights just slightly to extend lamp life and save energy, and there will be very little perceptible change in light level. For instance, dimming the light to 50 percent will be perceived as though the light were only dimmed to 70 percent. Therefore, there is no dramatic dilation or constriction of the eye due to light level change.

Plan #251003

Dimensions: 42' W x 41'9" D
Levels: 1
Square Footage: 1,393
Bedrooms: 3
Bathrooms: 2
Foundation: Crawl space, slab
Materials List Available: Yes
Price Category: B

Images provided by designer/architect.

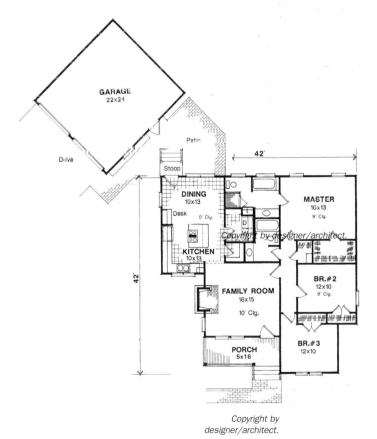

Copyright by designer/architect.

Plan #161007

Dimensions: 66'4" W x 43'10" D

Levels: 1

Square Footage: 1,611

Bedrooms: 3

Bathrooms: 2

Foundation: Slab

Materials List Available: Yes

Price Category: C

Images provided by designer/architect.

A lovely front porch and an entry with side-lights invite you to experience the impressive amenities offered in this exceptional ranch home.

Features:

- **Great Room:** Grand openings, featuring columns from the foyer to this great room and continuing to the bayed dining area, convey an open, spacious feel. The fireplace and matching windows on the rear wall of the great room enhance this effect.

- **Kitchen:** This well-designed kitchen offers convenient access to the laundry and garage. It also features an angled counter with ample space and an abundance of cabinets.

- **Master Suite:** This deluxe master suite contains many exciting amenities, including a lavishly appointed dressing room and a large walk-in closet.

- **Porch:** Sliding doors lead to this delightful screened porch for relaxing summer interludes.

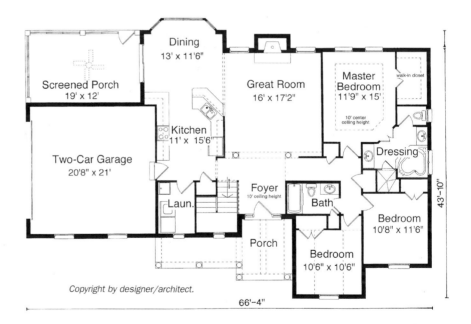

Copyright by designer/architect.

Rear Elevation

Plan #131041

Dimensions: 42' W x 45' D
Levels: 2
Square Footage: 1,679
Main Level Sq. Ft.: 1,134
Upper Level Sq. Ft.: 545
Bedrooms: 3
Bathrooms: 2½
Foundation: Crawl space, slab, or basement
Materials List Available: Yes
Price Category: D

Illustrations provided by designer/architect.

This rustic-looking two-story cottage includes contemporary amenities for your total comfort.

Features:

- **Great Room:** With a 9-ft.-4-in.-high ceiling, this large room makes everyone feel at home. A fireplace with raised hearth and built-in niche for a TV will encourage the whole family to gather here on cool evenings, and sliding glass doors leading to the rear covered porch make it an ideal entertaining area in mild weather.

- **Kitchen:** When people aren't in the great room, you're likely to find them here, because the convenient serving bar welcomes casual dining, and this room also opens to the p porch.

- **Master Suite:** Relax at the end of the day in this room, with its 9-ft.-4-in.-high ceiling and walk-in closet, or luxuriate in the private bath with whirlpool tub and dual-sink vanity.

- **Optional Basement:** This area can include a tuck-under two-car garage if you desire it.

Main Level Floor Plan

Upper Level Floor Plan

Great Room

Copyright by designer/architect.

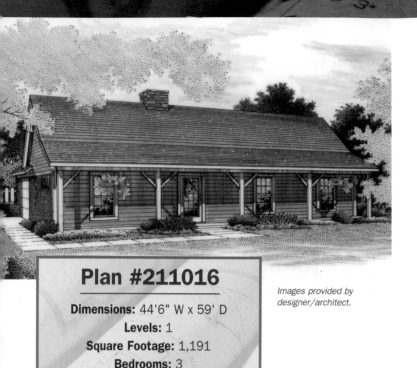

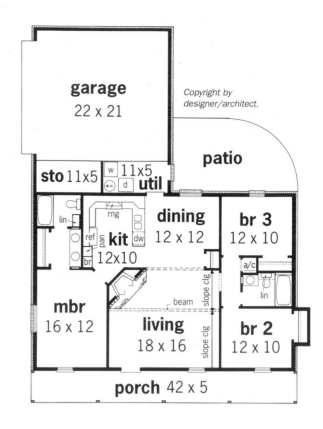

Copyright by designer/architect.

garage 22 x 21

patio

sto 11x5

w 11x5

util

d

dining 12 x 12

br 3 12 x 10

kit 12x10

ref pan

dw

lin

rng

br

a/c

lin

mbr 16 x 12

beam

slope clg

living 18 x 16

slope clg

br 2 12 x 10

porch 42 x 5

Plan #211016

Images provided by designer/architect.

Dimensions: 44'6" W x 59' D

Levels: 1

Square Footage: 1,191

Bedrooms: 3

Bathrooms: 2

Foundation: Slab

Materials List Available: Yes

Price Category: B

SMARTtip

Hose for Dishwasher

Most dishwashers come with a discharge hose. If the unit you buy does not have one, you'll need to supply the hose. Appliance supply stores may have what you need, but if they don't, automotive heater hose is a reasonable substitute. It can handle prolonged exposure to heat and detergent.

Plan #211019

Images provided by designer/architect.

Dimensions: 73' W x 37' D

Levels: 1

Square Footage: 1,395

Bedrooms: 3

Bathrooms: 2

Foundation: Slab

Materials List Available: Yes

Price Category: B

Copyright by designer/architect.

mbr 14 x 13

knee space

shv

living 18 x 17

stone

patio

beam

wood box

w d

lin

shvs

sto

shvs

br 2 12 x 11

br 3 12 x 11

a/c

post w/rail

foy

dining 12 x 11

kit 12x10

drop clg

ref

rng

garage 21 x 21

bar

dw

porch 42 x 7

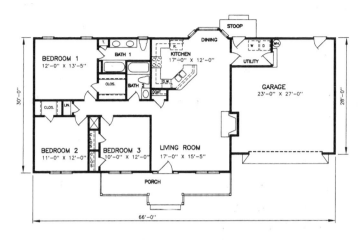

Images provided by designer/architect.

Copyright by designer/architect.

Plan #341005

Dimensions: 66' W x 30' D

Levels: 1

Square Footage: 1,334

Bedrooms: 3

Bathrooms: 2

Foundation: Crawl space, slab, or basement

Materials List Available: Yes

Price Category: B

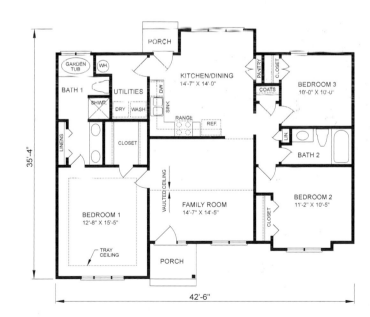

Images provided by designer/architect.

Copyright by designer/architect.

Plan #341010

Dimensions: 42'6" W x 35'4" D

Levels: 1

Square Footage: 1,261

Bedrooms: 3

Bathrooms: 2

Foundation: Crawl space, slab, or basement

Materials List Available: Yes

Price Category: B

Plan #121064

Dimensions: 44' W x 40' D
Levels: 2
Square Footage: 1,846
Main Level Sq. Ft.: 919
Upper Level Sq. Ft.: 927
Bedrooms: 4
Bathrooms: 2½
Foundation: Basement
Materials List Available: Yes
Price Category: D

Photo provided by designer/architect.

You'll love the features and design in this compact but amenity-filled home.

Features:

• Entry: A balcony overlooks this two-story entry, where a plant shelf tops the coat closet.

• Great Room: A trio of tall windows points up the large dimensions of this room, which is sure to be the hub of your home. Arrange the furniture to create a cozy space around the fireplace, or leave it open to the room.

• Kitchen: You'll love to work in this well-designed kitchen area.

• Master Suite: On the second floor, this master suite features a tiered ceiling and two walk-in closets. In the bath, you'll find a double vanity, whirlpool tub, and separate shower.

Main Level Floor Plan

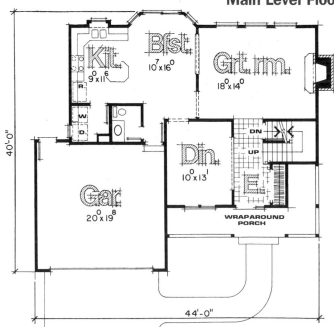

Upper Level Floor Plan

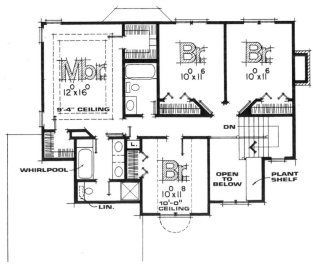

Copyright by designer/architect.

Photo provided by designer/architect.

Plan #121066

Dimensions: 46' W x 41'5" D
Levels: 2
Square Footage: 2,078
Main Level Sq. Ft.: 1,113
Upper Level Sq. Ft.: 965
Bedrooms: 4
Bathrooms: 2½
Foundation: Basement
Materials List Available: Yes
Price Category: D

This lovely home has an unusual dignity, perhaps because its rooms are so well-proportioned and thoughtfully laid out.

Features:

- **Family Room:** This room is sunken, giving it an unusually cozy, comfortable feeling. Its abundance of windows let natural light stream in during the day, and the fireplace warms it when the weather's chilly.

- **Dining Room:** This dining room links to the parlor beyond through a cased opening.

- **Parlor:** A tall, angled ceiling highlights a large, arched window that's the focal point of this room.

- **Breakfast Area:** A wooden rail visually links this bayed breakfast area to the family room.

- **Master Suite:** A roomy walk-in closet adds a practical touch to this luxurious suite. The bath features a skylight, whirlpool tub, and separate shower.

Main Level Floor Plan

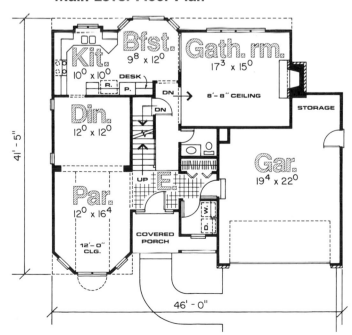

Upper Level Floor Plan

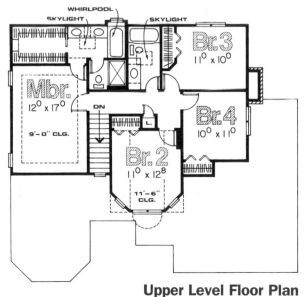

Copyright by designer/architect.

Plan #341018

Dimensions: 53'6" W x 35' D

Levels: 1

Square Footage: 1,191

Bedrooms: 3

Bathrooms: 2

Foundation: Crawl space, slab, or basement

Materials List Available: Yes

Price Category: B

Images provided by designer/architect.

Copyright by designer/architect.

Plan #341012

Dimensions: 43'2" W x 33'6" D

Levels: 1

Square Footage: 1,316

Bedrooms: 3

Bathrooms: 2

Foundation: Crawl space, slab, or basement

Materials List Available: Yes

Price Category: B

Images provided by designer/architect.

Copyright by designer/architect.

Plan #341021

Dimensions: 40' W x 35' D

Levels: 1

Square Footage: 1,208

Bedrooms: 3

Bathrooms: 2

Foundation: Crawl space, slab, or basement

Materials List Available: Yes

Price Category: B

Images provided by designer/architect.

Copyright by designer/architect.

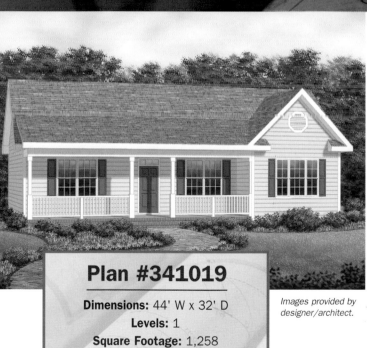

Plan #341019

Dimensions: 44' W x 32' D

Levels: 1

Square Footage: 1,258

Bedrooms: 3

Bathrooms: 2

Foundation: Crawl space, slab, or basement

Materials List Available: Yes

Price Category: B

Images provided by designer/architect.

Copyright by designer/architect.

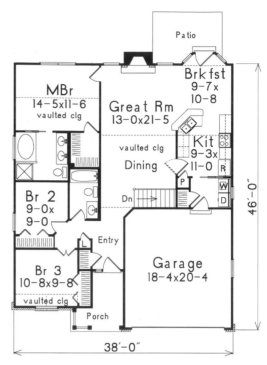

Plan #321033

Dimensions: 38' W x 46' D

Levels: 1

Square Footage: 1,268

Bedrooms: 3

Bathrooms: 2

Foundation: Basement

Materials List Available: Yes

Price Category: B

Images provided by designer/architect.

Copyright by designer/architect.

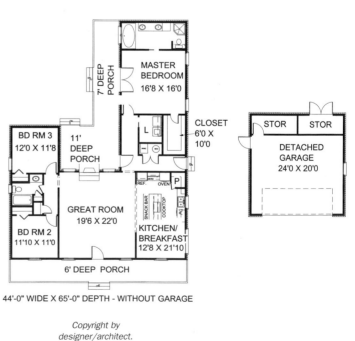

Plan #191002

Dimensions: 44' W x 65' D

Levels: 1

Square Footage: 1,716

Bedrooms: 3

Bathrooms: 2

Foundation: Crawl space, slab

Materials List Available: No

Price Category: C

Images provided by designer/architect.

44'-0" WIDE X 65'-0" DEPTH - WITHOUT GARAGE

Copyright by designer/architect.

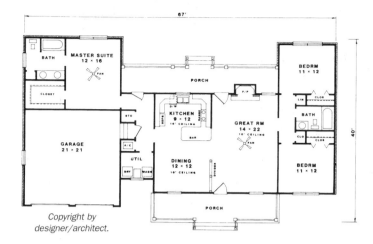

Copyright by designer/architect.

Plan #171002

Dimensions: 67' W x 40' D

Levels: 1

Square Footage: 1,458

Bedrooms: 3

Bathrooms: 2

Foundation: Slab, crawl space

Materials List Available: Yes

Price Category: B

Images provided by designer/architect.

SMARTtip

Accent Landscape Lighting

Accent highlights elements in your landscape. It creates ambiance and helps integrate the garden with the deck. Conventional low-voltage floodlights are excellent for creating effects such as wall grazing, silhouetting, and uplighting.

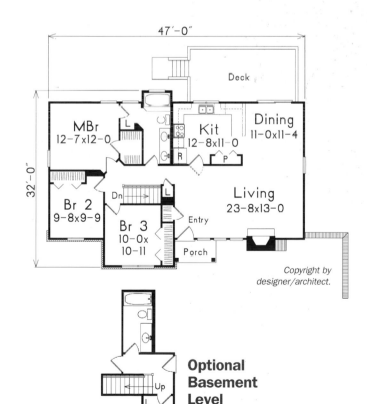

Copyright by designer/architect.

Optional Basement Level Floor Plan

Plan #321024

Dimensions: 47' W x 32' D

Levels: 1

Square Footage: 1,403

Bedrooms: 3

Bathrooms: 1-2

Foundation: Daylight basement

Materials List Available: Yes

Price Category: B

Images provided by designer/architect.

Plan #131043

Dimensions: 65'8" W x 43'10" D
Levels: 2
Square Footage: 1,945
Main Level Sq. Ft.: 1,375
Upper Level Sq. Ft.: 570
Bedrooms: 3
Bathrooms: 2½
Foundation: Crawl space, slab, or basement
Materials List Available: Yes
Price Category: E

Illustration provided by designer/architect.

This home will delight you with its three dormers and half-round transom windows, which give a nostalgic appearance, and its amenities and conveniences that are certainly contemporary.

Features:

• Porch: This covered porch forms the entryway.

• Great Room: Enjoy the fireplace in this large, comfortable room, which is open to the dining area. A French door here leads to the

covered porch at the rear of the house.

• Kitchen: This large, country-style kitchen has a bayed nook, and oversized breakfast bar, and pass-through to the rear porch to simplify serving and make entertaining a pleasure.

• Master Suite: A tray ceiling sets an elegant tone for this room, and the bay window adds to it. The large walk-in closet is convenient, and the bath is sumptuous.

• Bedrooms: These comfortable rooms have convenient access to a bath.

Main Level Floor Plan

Upper Level Floor Plan

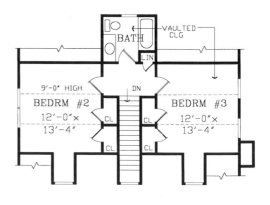

Copyright by designer/architect.

Plan #161006

Dimensions: 78'6" W x 47'7" D

Levels: 1

Square Footage: 1,755

Bedrooms: 3

Bathrooms: 2

Foundation: Slab

Materials List Available: Yes

Price Category: C

Images provided by designer/architect.

This enchanting, family-friendly home combines a solid brick exterior with an arched window, front porch, and three-car garage.

Features:

- **Great Room:** The 10-ft. ceiling complements the grand first impression created by the warm and friendly fireplace, which is flanked by matching French doors.

- **Kitchen:** In this functional kitchen, you can enjoy sitting at the bar or in the spacious dining area, with its angled bay and view of a delightful rear porch.

- **Master Bedroom:** Whether beginning your day or relaxing at its end, enjoy the comfort and luxury of the lavishly equipped bath and large walk-in closet.

- **Additional Bedrooms:** A full bath is easily accessible from both rooms which feature ample closet space.

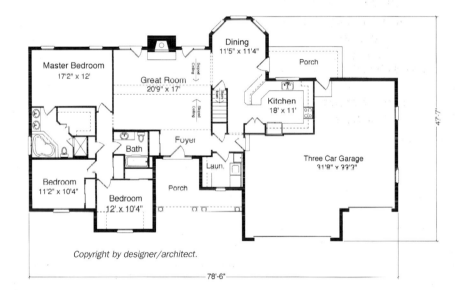

Copyright by designer/architect.

Rear Elevation

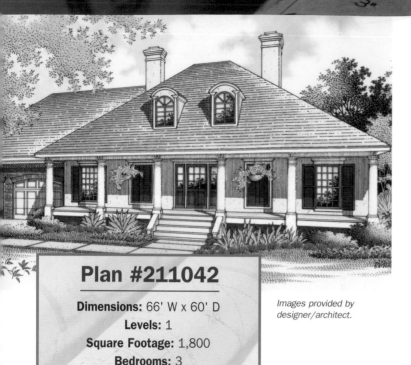

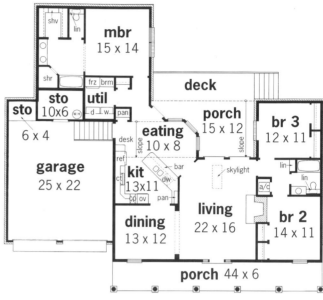

Plan #211042

Dimensions: 66' W x 60' D
Levels: 1
Square Footage: 1,800
Bedrooms: 3
Bathrooms: 2
Foundation: Crawl space
Materials List Available: Yes
Price Category: D

Images provided by designer/architect.

Copyright by designer/architect.

Plan #321021

Dimensions: 80' W x 42' D
Levels: 1
Square Footage: 1,708
Bedrooms: 3
Bathrooms: 2
Foundation: Basement
Materials List Available: Yes
Price Category: C

Images provided by designer/architect.

SMARTtip

Planning a Safe Children's Room

Keep safety in mind when planning a child's room. Make sure that there are covers on electrical outlets, guard rails on high windows, sturdy screens in front of radiators, and gates blocking any steps. Other suggestions include safety hinges for chests and nonskid backing for rugs.

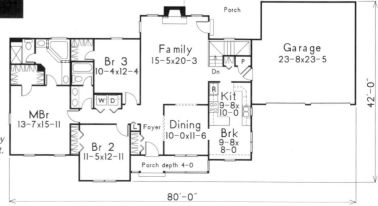

Copyright by designer/architect.

Plan #151059

Dimensions: 41'10" W x 53' D

Levels: 1

Square Footage: 1,382

Bedrooms: 3

Bathrooms: 2

Foundation: Crawl space, slab, with basement option for fee

Materials List Available: Yes

Price Category: B

Images provided by designer/architect.

Copyright by designer/architect.

Plan #151054

Dimensions: 67' W x 54'10" D

Levels: 1

Square Footage: 1,746

Bedrooms: 3

Bathrooms: 2

Foundation: Crawl space, slab, with basement option for fee

Materials List Available: Yes

Price Category: C

Images provided by designer/architect.

Copyright by designer/architect.

SMARTtip

Mixing and Matching Windows

Windows, both fixed and operable, are made in various styles and shapes. While mixing styles should be carefully avoided, a variety of interesting window sizes and shapes may nevertheless be combined to achieve symmetry, harmony, and rhythm on the exterior of a home.

Photo provided by designer/architect.

Plan #211069

Dimensions: 58' W x 42' D
Levels: 1½
Square Footage: 1,600
Main Level Sq. Ft.: 1,136
Upper Level Sq. Ft.: 464
Bedrooms: 3
Bathrooms: 2
Foundation: Crawl space
Materials List Available: Yes
Price Category: C

Enjoy the large front porch on this traditionally styled home when it's too sunny for the bugs, and use the screened back porch at dusk and dawn.

Features:

• Living Room: Call this the family room if you wish, but no matter what you call it, expect friends and family to gather here, especially when the fireplace gives welcome warmth.

• Kitchen: You'll love the practical layout that pleases everyone from gourmet chefs to beginning cooks.

• Master Suite: Positioned on the main floor to give it privacy, this suite has two entrances for convenience. You'll find a large walk-in closet here as well as a dressing room that includes a separate vanity and mirror makeup counter.

• Storage Space: The 462-sq.-ft. garage is roomy enough to hold two cars and still have space to store tools, out-of-season clothing, or whatever else that needs a dry, protected spot.

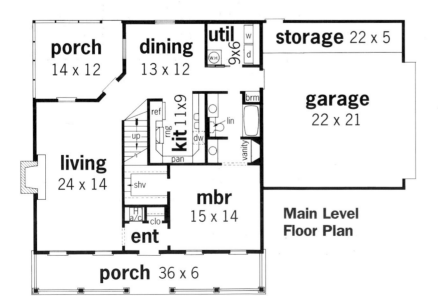

Main Level Floor Plan

Upper Level Floor Plan

Copyright by designer/architect.

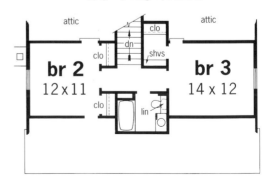

Photo provided by designer/architect.

Plan #131001

Dimensions: 72'4" W x 32'4" D
Levels: 1
Square Footage: 1,615
Bedrooms: 3
Bathrooms: 2
Foundation: Basement, crawl space, or slab
Materials List Available: Yes
Price Category: D

Copyright by designer/architect.

Cathedral ceilings and illuminating skylights add drama and beauty to this practical ranch house.

Features:

Ceiling Height: 8 ft.

- Front Porch: Watch the rain in comfort from the covered front porch.

- Foyer: The stone-tiled foyer flows into the living areas.

- Living Room: Oriented towards the front of the house, the living room opens to the dining room and shares a lovely three-sided fireplace with the family room.

- Family Room: Conveniently located to share the fireplace with the living room, this room is bright and cheery thanks to its skylights as well as the sliding glass doors that open onto the rear patio.

- Kitchen: An island makes this sunny room both efficient and attractive.

- Breakfast Nook: Located just off the kitchen, this area can serve double-duty as a spot for kitchen visitors to sit.

- Dining Room: The open design between the dining and living rooms adds to the spacious feeling that the cathedral ceiling creates in this area.

- Laundry Room: This area opens from the kitchen for convenience.

- Master Suite: A walk-in closet makes this room practical, but the master bathroom with a skylight, dual-sink vanity, soaking tub, and separate shower makes it luxurious.

- Bedrooms: The two additional bedrooms share a bathroom.

Plan #321002

Dimensions: 72' W x 28' D
Levels: 1
Square Footage: 1,400
Bedrooms: 3
Bathrooms: 2
Foundation: Basement, crawl space
Materials List Available: Yes
Price Category: B

If you're looking for a well-designed compact home with contemporary amenities, this could be the home of your dreams.

Features:

• Porch: Just the right size for some rockers and a swing, this porch could become your outdoor living area when the weather is fine.

• Living Room: A vaulted ceiling adds to the spacious feeling in this room, where friends and family are sure to gather.

• Kitchen: This space-saving design, in combination with the ample counter and cabinet space, makes cooking a pleasure.

• Utility Room: This large room is fitted with cabinets for extra storage space. You'll find storage space in the large garage, too.

• Master Bedroom: This room is somewhat secluded for privacy, making it an ideal place for some quiet time at the end of the day.

Images provided by designer/architect.

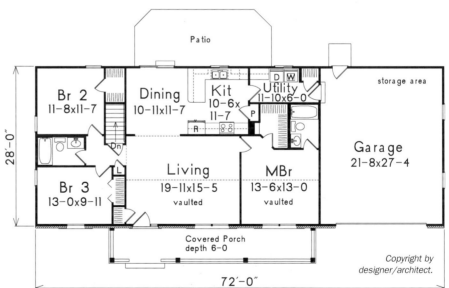

Copyright by designer/architect.

SMARTtip
Fabric Draping Ability

Test a fabric's draping ability by looking at a large piece in a fabric store. Gather at least two to three yards of material, holding one end in your hand. Check how it drapes. Does it fall into folds easily? Also look at the pattern when it is gathered. Does the design become lost in the folds? Ask a salesclerk or a friend to hold the fabric, and look at it from a few feet away.

Plan #101014

Dimensions: 52' W x 28' D
Levels: 2
Square Footage: 1,598
Main Level Sq. Ft.: 812
Upper Level Sq. Ft.: 786
Bedrooms: 3
Bathrooms: 2½
Foundation: Slab, crawl space
Materials List Available: No
Price Category: C

Illustration provided by designer/architect.

This lovely Victorian home has a perfect balance of ornamental features and modern amenities.

Features:

- Ceiling Height: 8 ft. unless otherwise noted.
- Foyer: An impressive beveled glass-front door invites you into this roomy foyer.
- Kitchen: This bright and open kitchen offers an abundance of counter space to make cooking a pleasure.

- Breakfast Room: You'll enjoy plenty of informal family meals in this sunny and open spot next to the kitchen.
- Family Room: The whole family will be attracted to this handsome room. A full-width bay window adds to the Victorian charm.
- Master Suite: This dramatic suite features a multi-faceted vaulted ceiling and his and her closets and vanities. A separate shower and 6-ft. garden tub complete the lavish appointments.

Main Level Floor Plan

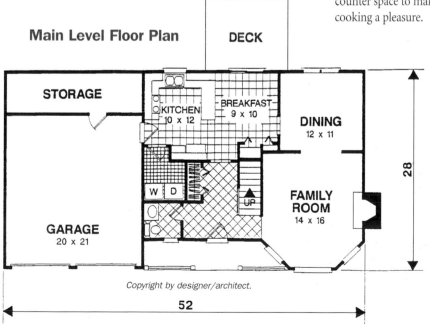

Copyright by designer/architect.

Upper Level Floor Plan

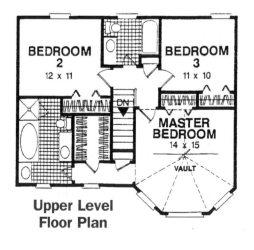

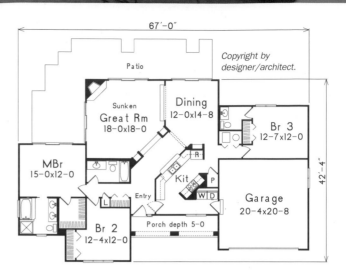

Copyright by
designer/architect.

Plan #321026

Dimensions: 67' W x 42'4" D

Levels: 1

Square Footage: 1,712

Bedrooms: 3

Bathrooms: 2½

Foundation: Crawl space

Materials List Available: Yes

Price Category: C

Images provided by designer/architect.

SMARTtip

Deck Design with Computers

Consider using a computer-aided design (CAD) program to plan your deck. Some programs let you see three-dimensional views of your design complete with railings, stairs, planters, hot tubs, and the surrounding landscaping.

Plan #231004

Dimensions: 44' W x 37'6" D

Levels: 1

Square Footage: 1,463

Bedrooms: 2

Bathrooms: 2

Foundation: Crawl space

Materials List Available: No

Price Category: A

Images provided by designer/architect.

Copyright by
designer/architect.

Plan #171007

Dimensions: 62' W x 44' D

Levels: 2

Square Footage: 1,650

Main Level Sq. Ft.: 1,097

Upper Level Sq. Ft.: 553

Bedrooms: 3

Bathrooms: 2

Foundation: Slab, crawl space

Materials List Available: Yes

Price Category: C

Images provided by designer/architect.

Main Level Floor Plan

Upper Level Floor Plan

Copyright by designer/architect.

Plan #251007

Dimensions: 71' W x 42'6" D

Levels: 2

Square Footage: 1,597

Main Level Sq. Ft.: 982

Upper Level Sq. Ft.: 615

Bedrooms: 4

Bathrooms: 2½

Foundation: Basement

Materials List Available: Yes

Price Category: C

Images provided by designer/architect.

Main Level Floor Plan

Upper Level Floor Plan

Copyright by designer/architect.

Plan #321064

Dimensions: 34' W x 47' D

Levels: 2

Square Footage: 1,769

Main Level Sq. Ft.: 1,306

Upper Level Sq. Ft.: 463

Bedrooms: 3

Bathrooms: 2

Foundation: Basement

Materials List Available: Yes

Price Category: C

Images provided by designer/architect.

You'll love the way that this spacious A-frame home, with its distinctive interior design, complements any site.

Features:

• Living Room: With an elegant cathedral ceiling and a handsome fireplace, this room makes an ideal spot for entertaining in every season.

• Kitchen: The "U-shape" of this kitchen and adjoining dining area create a warm welcome for friends and family. This an ideal work spot, thanks to the thoughtful layout and ample counter and cabinet space.

• Master Suite: A sloped ceiling gives drama to this secluded suite. A walk-in closet adds practicality, and the amenities in the private bath provide the luxury that will make this area a true retreat.

• Secondary Bedrooms: The secondary bedrooms have large double closets for convenient storage space as well as access to natural lighting from their well-positioned windows.

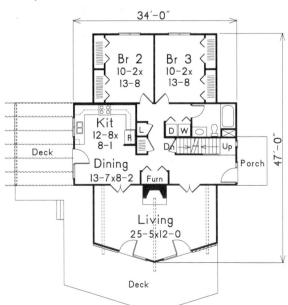

Main Level Floor Plan

Copyright by designer/architect.

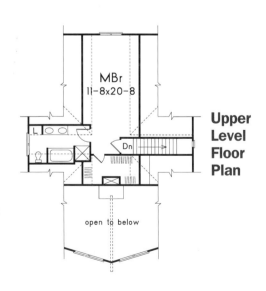

Upper Level Floor Plan

Plan #161003

Dimensions: 60' W x 47' D

Levels: 1

Square Footage: 1,508

Bedrooms: 3

Bathrooms: 2

Foundation: Slab

Materials List Available: Yes

Price Category: C

Images provided by designer/architect.

Multiple gables and a cozy front porch invite you to this enchanting one-story home.

Features:

- **Great Room:** This bright and cheery room features a sloped ceiling and fireplace. The great room is designed for convenience, with easy access to the foyer and dining area, creating the look and feel of a home much larger than its actual size.

- **Dining Area:** Adjacent to the great room, this dining area has multiple windows and angles that add light and dimension.

- **Kitchen:** This spacious kitchen is designed for easy work patterns with an abundance of counter and cabinet space. It also features a snack bar.

- **Master Bedroom:** Designed for step-saving convenience, this master bedroom includes a compartmented bath, double-bowl vanity, and large walk-in closet.

Copyright by designer/architect.

Rear Elevation

Plan #181143

Dimensions: 38' W x 36'4" D

Levels: 1

Square Footage: 1,056

Bedrooms: 2

Bathrooms: 1

Foundation: Full basement with walkout

Materials List Available: Yes

Price Category: B

Images provided by designer/architect.

Copyright by designer/architect.

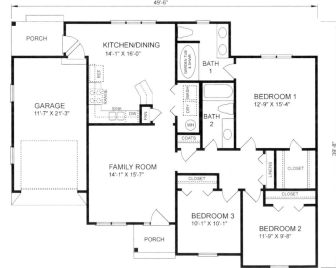

Plan #341024

Dimensions: 49'6" W x 39'8" D

Levels: 1

Square Footage: 1,310

Bedrooms: 3

Bathrooms: 2

Foundation: Crawl space, slab, or basement

Materials List Available: Yes

Price Category: B

Images provided by designer/architect.

Copyright by designer/architect.

Images provided by designer/architect.

Plan #341034

Dimensions: 50' W x 38'2" D

Levels: 1

Square Footage: 1,445

Bedrooms: 3

Bathrooms: 2

Foundation: Crawl space, slab, or basement

Materials List Available: Yes

Price Category: B

Copyright by designer/architect.

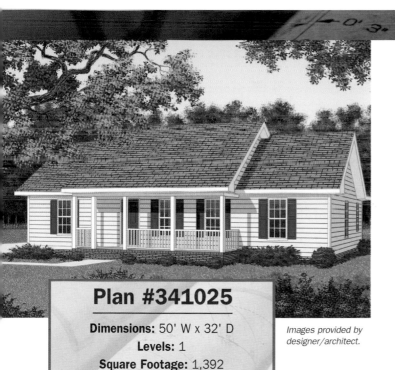

Images provided by designer/architect.

Plan #341025

Dimensions: 50' W x 32' D

Levels: 1

Square Footage: 1,392

Bedrooms: 3

Bathrooms: 2

Foundation: Crawl space, slab, or basement

Materials List Available: Yes

Price Category: B

Copyright by designer/architect.

Family Kitchens

From every standpoint, the importance of the kitchen and its design cannot be underestimated. The heart of the home beats in the kitchen. There's the hum of the refrigerator, the whir of the food processor, the crunch of the waste-disposal unit, and the bubbling of dinner simmering on the stove. These are the reassuring sounds of a home in action. The kitchen is also a warehouse, a communications center, a place to socialize, and the hub of family life. According to industry studies, 90 percent of American families eat some or all of their meals in the kitchen. It is also the command center where household bills are paid and vacations are planned. The kitchen is even a playroom at times. Emotions, as well as tasks, reside here. When you were little, this is where you could find mom whenever you needed her. It's where the cookies were kept. When other rooms were cold and empty, the kitchen was a place of warmth and companionship. It is from the kitchen that the family sets off into the day. And it is to the kitchen that they return at nightfall.

The Great Room Concept

Today, the family life that was once contained by the kitchen is spilling into an adjoining great room. Usually a large, open room, great rooms and kitchens are often considered part of the same space. It is here where the family gathers to watch TV, share meals, and do homework. In short, great rooms/kitchens are the new heart of the home and the places where families do most of their living. In most designs, a kitchen and great room are separated by a snack counter, an island, or a large pass-through.

Kitchen Layouts That Work

The basic layout of your kitchen will depend on the home design you choose. Look for aisles that have at least 39 inches between the front of the cabinets and appliances or an opposite-facing island. If it's possible, a clearance of 42 inches is better. And given more available space, a clear-

Large kitchen/great rooms, below, are now considered the true heart of the family home.

In large kitchens, opposite, look for plenty of counter and storage space, but insist on compact, efficient work areas.

ance of 48 to 49 inches is ideal. It means that you can open the dishwasher to load or unload it, and someone will still be able to walk behind you without doing a side-to-side shuffle or a crab walk. It also means that two people can work together in the same area. Any more than 49 inches, and the space is too much and involves a lot of walking back and forth. Fifty-four inches, for example, is too big a stretch. In large kitchens, look for balance; the work areas should have generous proportions, but to be truly efficient they should be compact and well designed.

Food Prep Areas and Surfaces. In many families, much of the food preparation takes place between the sink and the refrigerator. When you think of the work triangle, think of how much and how often you use an appliance. For example, sinks are generally used the most, followed by the refrigerator. The use of the cooktop is a matter of personal habit. Some families use it everyday, others use it sporadically. How close does it really need to be in relation to

the sink and refrigerator? Make your primary work zone the link between the sink and the refrigerator; then make the cooktop a secondary zone that's linked to them.

Cabinets Set the Style

Cabinets are the real furniture of a kitchen, making their selection both an aesthetic and functional choice. They are also likely to account for the largest portion of the budget.

Laminate. There are different brands and grades of plastic laminate, but cabinets made from this material generally are the least expensive you can buy. For the most part, they are devoid of detail and frameless, so don't look for raised panels, moldings, or inlaid beads on plastic laminate cabinets.

Although the surface is somewhat vulnerable (depending on the quality) to scratches and chips, plastic laminate cabinets can be refaced relatively inexpensively. Laminates come in a formidable range of

colors and patterns. Some of the newer speckled and patterned designs, which now even include denim and canvas, not only look great but won't show minor scratches and scars.

Wood. Wood cabinets offer the greatest variety of type, style, and finish. Framed cabinets (the full frame across the face of the cabinets may show between the doors) are popular for achieving a traditional look, but they are slightly less roomy inside. That's because you lose the width of the frame, which can be as much as an inch on each side. Frameless cabinets have full overlay doors and drawer fronts. With frameless cabinets, you gain about 2 inches of interior space per cabinet unit. Multiply that by the number of cabinet doors or drawer units you have, and add it up. It's easy to see that if space is at a premium, choose the frameless or full-overlay type. Besides, most cabinet companies now offer enough frameless styles to give you a traditional look in cabinetry, if that's your style.

Be creative with storage, above. Here a tall cabinet tops a drawer unit that holds dish towels and tablecloths.

A great room, below, works best when a well-defined kitchen area flows effortlessly into the living area.

The Decorative Aspect of Cabinets

While the trend in overall kitchen style is toward more decorative moldings and carvings, the trend in cabinet doors is toward simpler designs. Plain panels, for instance, are now more popular than raised panels. They allow you to have more decoration elsewhere. Ornamentation is effective when it is used to provide a focal point over a hood, fridge, or sink. Instead of installing a single crown profile, you might create a three- or four-piece crown treatment, or add a carving of grapevines, acanthus leaves, or another decorative motif. In the traditional kitchen, add them, but sparingly.

Finishes. Of all of the choices you will need to make regarding wood cabinets, the selection of the finish may be the hardest. Wood can be stained, pickled, painted, or oiled. Your selection will be determined in part by whether you order stock or custom cabinets. Finishing options on stock cabinets are usually limited, and variations are offered as an upgrade. Translation: more money. Try working with the manufacturer's stock cabinets. It not only costs less but also speeds up the process. There is usually a reason why manufacturers offer certain woods in certain choices: it's because those choices work best with other elements in the room.

Wood Stains. Today, stains that are close to natural wood tones are popular, particularly natural wood finishes. Cherry is quickly becoming the number-one wood in the country. Pickled finishes, very popular in the early 1990s, are now looking dated. Some woods, particularly oak, have more grain than others. Some, such as maple, are smoother. And others, such as birch, dent more easily. The quality and inherent characteristics of the wood you choose will help determine whether it is better to stain, pickle, or paint. For staining, you need a good-quality clear wood. Pickling, because it has pigment in the stain, masks more of the grain but is still translucent. Because paint completely covers the grain, painted wood cabinets are usually made of lesser-quality paint-grade wood.

Painted Wood. Paint gives wood a smooth, clean finish. You can paint when you want a change or if the finish starts to show wear. This comes at no small expense, though, because the painter will have to sand the surfaces well before applying several coats of paint. If you choose painted cabinets, be sure to obtain a small can of the exact same paint from your kitchen vendor. There is usually a charge for this, but it allows you to do small touch-ups yourself, ridding your cabinets of particularly hideous scars without a complete repainting. While in theory the color choice for painted cabinets is infinite, manufacturers generally offer four shades of white and a few other standard color options from which to choose.

Pickled Wood. Pickled cabinets fall midway between full-grain natural cabinets and painted ones. Pickling is a combination of stain and paint, allowing some of the grain to show. It subdues the strongest patterns, while it covers over the lesser ones. The degree depends on your choice and on the options available from the manufacturer.

Hardware. Handles are easier to maneuver than knobs. Advocates of universal design, which takes into consideration the capabilities of all people—young and old, with and without physical limitations—recommend them. Knobs do not work easily for children or elderly people with arthritis. A handle with a backplate will keep fingerprints off the cabinet door.

Fitting Cabinets into Your Layout

This calls for attention to the kitchen layout. In specifying cabinets, first let common sense and budget be your guide. Kitchen geography can help you determine how much storage you need and where it should be. Mentally divide your kitchen into zones: food preparation, food consumption, and so on. And don't forget about the nonfood areas. Do you see yourself repotting plants or working on a hobby in the kitchen? You'll need work space and cabinet space for those extra activities.

A kitchen workhorse, the island, is not new to kitchen design. It's as old as the solid, slightly elevated, central table of medieval kitchens in England. But where that table was a work surface, today's island can hold cabinets, a sink, a cooktop, a beverage refrigerator, and it can serve to divide areas of the kitchen.

How Tall Is Too Tall?

Upper cabinets are typically 12 inches deep; base, or lower, cabinets are 24 inches deep. With the exception of a desk unit, standard base cabinets are always the same height, 36 inches. Although most people prefer clean lines and planes as much as possible, some circumstances call for variations in the height of lower cabinets. There may be an often-used area where you want a countertop at which you can work while seated, for example.

Upper cabinets come in two or three standard heights: 30, 36, and 42 inches. The 30-inch ones look short; 36-inch cabinets look standard, and 42-inch ones can look too tall if your ceiling is not unusually high. In general, there is a slight up-charge for 30-inch cabinets and a big jump in price for 42-inch units. Order another size and you will pay double-custom prices. But you don't need to. For greater variation, install upper cabinets at varying heights. The old standard was to install 30-inch upper cabinets under a soffit—the often,

but not always, boxed-in area just under the ceiling and above the wall cabinets. Now, unless you have very tall ceilings, soffits are practically obsolete. Provided you have standard-height, 8-foot ceilings, the way to go now seems to be 36-inch cabinets with the remaining space of 6 inches or so filled with decorative trim up to the ceiling. It is a nicer, more refined look than cabinets that extend all the way to the ceiling, unless you prefer something contemporary and totally sleek and without ornament.

Size and Space. You don't want a massive bank of cabinets, either. Add up the dimensions wherever you're considering wall units. The counter is 36 inches high; backsplashes typically range from 15 to 17 inches. So with 36-inch-high upper cabinets, we're talking 7½ feet in all, 8 feet if you chose 42-inch-high wall units. Your own size can help determine which ones to choose. Determine what's comfortable by measuring your reach. A petite person will lose access to the top third of a cabinet. An inch or two can make a very big difference.

Also, be sure that the small appliances you keep on the countertop fit under the wall cabinets. Having them sit at the front edge of a countertop is an accident waiting to happen. A lot of people who have "appliance garages" discovered this. Whenever they pulled out the appliance, which places it nearer the counter's edge, they watched their mixer or coffeemaker tumble to the floor.

Often people need extra storage, so they extend the cabinets up to the ceiling. This provides the added extra storage space, but it can only be reached by a step stool. An open soffit above the upper cabinets provides just as much space for oversize, infrequently used objects, and it is equally accessible by stepladder. Plus it can be both a display area and perfect home for hard-to-store items: pitchers, trays, salad bowls, vases, collectibles, platters, covered servers, and so forth.

Light, natural wood finishes, left, are a popular cabinet choice.

Kitchen offices, left, are becoming increasingly popular. This desk and office storage matches the kitchen cabinets.

Just remember to allow plenty of room for air to circulate around the TV.

Kitchen Storage Solutions

There are many storage options that are extremely useful. At the top of the list is a spice drawer or rack attached to an upper cabinet or door. Both drawer and door spice racks are offered as factory options when you order cabinets, or you can retrofit them into existing cabinets. They provide visible access to all spices, so you don't end up with three tins of cinnamon, nine jars of garlic salt, four tiny bottles of vanilla, and no red pepper.

Lazy Susans. These rotating trays make items in the back of corner cabinets accessible. Consider adding inexpensive, plastic lazy Susans in a small upper cabinet. They will make the seasonings and cooking items you use everyday easily accessible.

Pie-cut door attachments can provide the same accessibility as a lazy Susan. Your choice depends on how much and what kind of storage you need. If a corner cabinet is home to sodas, chips, and cooking materials, install a pie-cut. A lazy Susan is more stable, best for pots, bowls, and larger, heavier objects.

The Kitchen Desk

Consider whether you will actually sit at a kitchen desk. Many people don't. Instead, they use it as the family message center and generally stand or perch on a stool. An additional, taller counter simply introduces more clutter to a room that is already overburdened with paraphernalia. And forget a desk-high cabinet, too. Instead use a standard counter-height cabinet to streamline whenever and wherever you can in the room.

Think about outfitting the desk area with a phone and answering machine and a corkboard for notes, your family's social schedule, invitations, and reminders. If you have room, a file drawer makes sense for storing school and business papers that

need to be easy to retrieve. Also, if you don't have a separate study, and there's room, the kitchen may be a place to keep the family computer. Not only will you likely be using it more in the future for household record-keeping, but you can also help the kids with their homework and monitor their Internet use. In those cases, it makes sense to add a desk for comfort.

A Niche for the TV. Many people also want a TV in the kitchen. Plan for it. Who wants to see the back of the set or look at cords stretching across work areas, atop the refrigerator or the stove? Space and an outlet can be built into the lower portion of a well-placed wall cabinet or an open unit.

Pullouts, Rollouts, and Dividers.

Pullout fittings maximize the use of very narrow spaces. There are just two options for these areas: vertical tray-storage units or pullout pantries. You can find a 12-inch-wide base cabinet that is a pullout pantry with storage for canned goods and boxed items.

Pullout racks for cabinets and lid-rack dividers for drawers are also available from some cabinet suppliers. They are handy, but if you have enough cabinet storage space, the best thing is to store pots and pans with the lids on them in a couple of large cabinets.

Rollout cabinets are great and offer a lot of flexibility. They are adjustable to accommodate bulky countertop appliances and

Pullout cutting boards, above left, increase usable counter space.

Accessories for tall, narrow cabinets, left, home in handy for storing cookie sheets and trays.

Decorative molding, above, can enhance any cabinet. Most manufacturers offer a variety of molding options.

Knife, Towel, and Bread Storage. If you want a place to store knives, use slotted storage on a countertop. Frequently islands have false backs because they are deeper than base cabinets. Slots for knives can be cut into the area of the countertop that covers the void behind the base cabinet.

You can obtain all these storage options at the time you buy your cabinets. But you don't have to and may not even want to until you see how you really end up using your kitchen. A carpenter or handyman can often make them or install off-the-shelf units. Think outside of the box. We get in a rut; it is hard to be objective. Ask friends where they keep their kitchen stuff, and analyze every aspect of how you use your kitchen. Store things at point of use, such as leftover containers and sandwich bags near the refrigerator; mixing bowls and carving knives near the sink.

stock pots, and they can save a lot of steps and banging around.

You can also divide a base cabinet vertically into separate parts. Some of the vertical spaces are further subdivided horizontally—good places for storing cutting boards, cookie trays, baking tins, and big glass baking dishes.

Other Organizers

Buy cutlery drawers carefully. They are often too big and too clumsy, and they fail to take advantage of the full interior of the drawer. They are as bad as bookshelves spread too far apart. Consider cutlery dividers that are almost no wider than a spoon, with separate sections for teaspoons, cereal spoons, breakfast and dinner knives, lunch forks, dinner forks, and serving pieces. Add to this a section for miscellaneous utensils such as spoons for iced tea, chopsticks, and so on. Drawer dividers should be adjustable in case your needs, or your cutlery, change.

Plan #101004

Dimensions: 55'8" W x 56'6" D

Levels: 1

Square Footage: 1,787

Bedrooms: 3

Bathrooms: 2

Foundation: Slab, crawl space, basement

Materials List Available: No

Price Category: C

Illustration provided by designer/architect.

This carefully designed ranch provides the feel and features of a much larger home.

Features:

- Ceiling Height: 9 ft. unless otherwise noted.

- Foyer: Guests will step up onto the inviting front porch and into this foyer, with its impressive 11-ft. ceiling.

- Dining Room: Open to the entry and to its left is this elegant dining room, perfect for entertaining or informal family gatherings.

- Family Room: This family gathering place features an 11-ft. ceiling to enhance its sense of spaciousness.

- Kitchen: This intelligently designed kitchen has an open plan. A breakfast bar and a serving bar are features that add to its convenience.

- Master Suite: This suite is loaded with amenities, including a double-step tray ceiling, direct access to the screened porch, a sitting room, deluxe bath, and his and her walk-in closets.

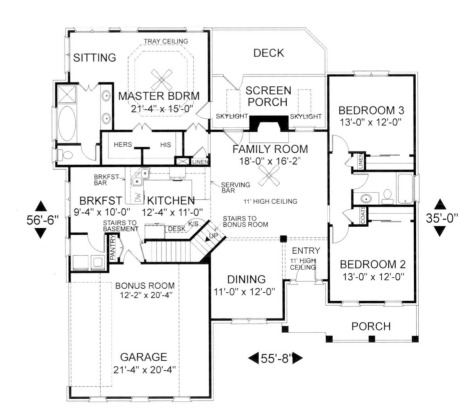

Copyright by designer/architect.

Plan #171001

Dimensions: 44' W x 41' D

Levels: 1

Square Footage: 1,277

Bedrooms: 3

Bathrooms: 2

Foundation: Crawl space, slab, or basement

Materials List Available: Yes

Price Category: B

Images provided by designer/architect.

You'll love this design if you're looking for a compact ranch with rustic, country styling and plenty of well designed family areas.

Features:

- **Porch:** Set a couple of rockers and containers of blooming plants and fragrant herbs on this lovely front porch.

- **Great Room:** A substantial fireplace is the focal point of this large room. Fill it with a dried floral bouquet in summer, and gather chairs around its warmth in winter.

- **Dining Room:** This room adjoins the great room for easy entertaining in any season and opens to the large screened porch for summer parties.

- **Kitchen:** With good counter space and an open layout, this kitchen is built for efficiency.

- **Master Bedroom:** Split from the other two bedrooms for privacy, this quiet retreat features a large walk-in closet and lovely window area.

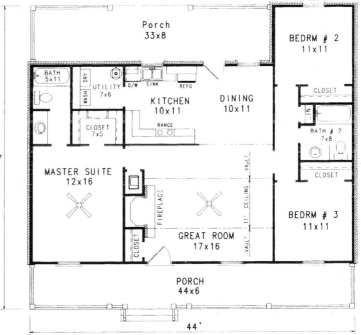

Copyright by designer/architect.

Plan #321057

Dimensions: 38' W x 39'4" D

Levels: 2

Square Footage: 1,524

Main Level Sq. Ft.: 951

Upper Level Sq. Ft.: 573

Bedrooms: 3

Bathrooms: 2½

Foundation: Basement

Materials List Available: Yes

Price Category: C

Images provided by designer/architect.

Main Level Floor Plan

Living 17-8x12-0

MBr 12-4x15-4

Kit 10-6x 10-6

Dining 10-6x9-10

Garage 19-4x20-4

Porch

Patio

38'-0"

39'-4"

Upper Level Floor Plan

Copyright by designer/architect.

Br 2 17-8x12-0

Br 3 10-6x13-0

open to below

Plan #321060

Dimensions: 36' W x 46'8" D

Levels: 2

Square Footage: 1,575

Main Level Sq. Ft.: 802

Upper Level Sq. Ft.: 773

Bedrooms: 3

Bathrooms: 2½

Foundation: Basement

Materials List Available: Yes

Price Category: C

Images provided by designer/architect.

Main Level Floor Plan

36'-0"

46'-8"

Kit 9-0x11-7

Brkfst 10-0x11-0

Dining 12-0x11-0

Living 15-7x14-4

Garage 19-4x20-4

Upper Level Floor Plan

Copyright by designer/architect.

MBr 12-0x14-8 vaulted clg

Br 2 12-0x11-0

Br 3 12-0x11-3 vaulted clg

plant shelf

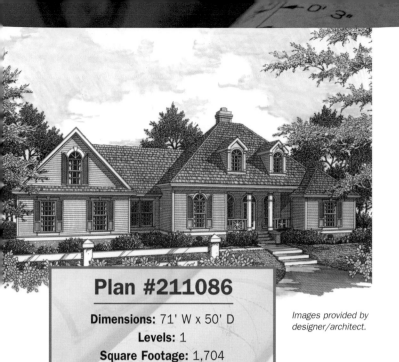

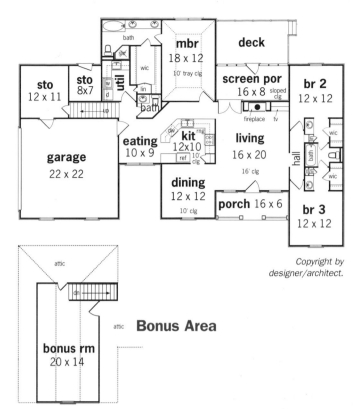

Images provided by designer/architect.

Copyright by designer/architect.

Bonus Area

Plan #211086

Dimensions: 71' W x 50' D

Levels: 1

Square Footage: 1,704

Bedrooms: 3

Bathrooms: 2½

Foundation: Crawl space

Materials List Available: Yes

Price Category: C

Images provided by designer/architect.

Copyright by designer/architect.

Plan #121056

Dimensions: 48' W x 50' D

Levels: 1

Square Footage: 1,479

Bedrooms: 2

Bathrooms: 2

Foundation: Basement

Materials List Available: Yes

Price Category: B

Optional Third Bedroom Floor Plan

Plan #341033

Dimensions: 57' W x 32'3" D

Levels: 1

Square Footage: 1,297

Bedrooms: 3

Bathrooms: 2

Foundation: Crawl space, slab, or basement

Materials List Available: Yes

Price Category: B

Images provided by designer/architect.

Copyright by designer/architect.

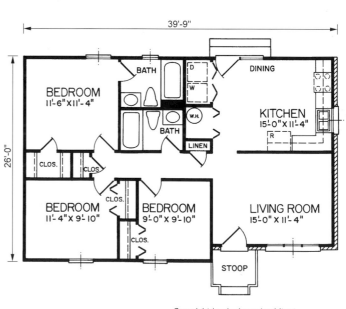

Plan #341026

Dimensions: 39'9" W x 26' D

Levels: 1

Square Footage: 1,009

Bedrooms: 3

Bathrooms: 2

Foundation: Crawl space, slab, or basement

Materials List Available: Yes

Price Category: B

Images provided by designer/architect.

Copyright by designer/architect.

Plan #341029

Dimensions: 49' W x 57' D

Levels: 1

Square Footage: 1,737

Bedrooms: 3

Bathrooms: 2

Foundation: Crawl space, slab, or basement

Materials List Available: Yes

Price Category: C

Images provided by designer/architect.

Copyright by designer/architect.

BEDROOM 2
15'-0" X 11'-5"

BATH 1

BEDROOM 1
13'-9" X 15'-0"

CLOSET

CLOS.

D.

W.

BATH 2

KITCHEN
15'-5" X 15'-9"

REF

ISLAND

D.W.

SCREENED PORCH

CLOSET

BEDROOM 3
11'-5" X 10'-9"

LIN

COATS

W.H.

PANTRY

DINING AREA

DECK

GREAT ROOM
29'-2" X 14'-9"

VAULTED CEILING

COVERED DECK

DECK

57'-0"

49'-0"

Plan #341028

Dimensions: 40' W x 32' D

Levels: 1

Square Footage: 1,248

Bedrooms: 3

Bathrooms: 2

Foundation: Crawl space, slab, or basement

Materials List Available: Yes

Price Category: B

Images provided by designer/architect.

Copyright by designer/architect.

DECK

MASTER BEDROOM
11'-5" X 13'-5"

BATH 1

W

D

KITCHEN / DINING
16'-8" X 13'-5"

PANTRY

SINKS

D.W.

BA. 2

UTILITY

WH

REF.

RANGE

CLOSET

LIN

COATS

LIVING ROOM
15'-9" X 15'-5"

BEDROOM 2
12'-7" X 10'-0"

CLOSET

BEDROOM 3
10'-4" X 10'-5"

PORCH

32'-0"

40'-0"

Plan #161015

Dimensions: 55'4" W x 40'4" D

Levels: 2

Square Footage: 1,768

Main Level Sq. Ft.: 960

Upper Level Sq. Ft.: 808

Bedrooms: 3

Bathrooms: 2½

Foundation: Slab

Materials List Available: No

Price Category: C

Images provided by designer/architect.

One look at this dramatic exterior—a 12-ft. high entry with a transom and sidelights, multiple gables, and an impressive box window—you'll fall in love with this home.

Features:

- **Foyer:** This 2-story area announces the grace of this home to everyone who enters it.

- **Great Room:** A natural gathering spot, this room is sunken to set it off from the rest of the house. The 12-ft. ceiling adds a spacious feeling, and the access to the rear porch makes it ideal for friends and family.

- **Kitchen:** The kids will enjoy the snack bar and you'll love the adjoining breakfast room with its access to the rear porch.

- **Master Suite:** A whirlpool in the master bath and walk-in closets in the bedroom spell luxury.

- **Laundry Area:** Two large closets are so handy that you'll wonder how you ever did without them.

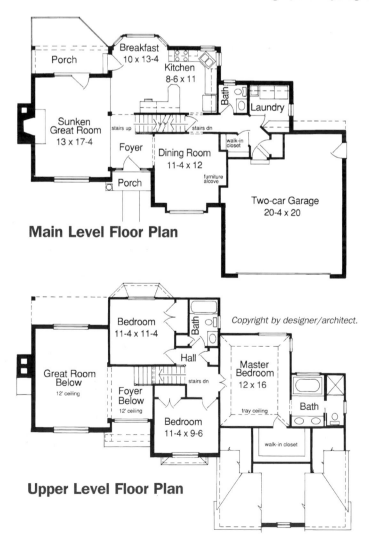

Main Level Floor Plan

Upper Level Floor Plan

Copyright by designer/architect.

Plan #131004

Dimensions: 59'4" W x 35'8" D
Levels: 1
Square Footage: 1,097
Bedrooms: 3
Bathrooms: 2
Foundation: Basement, crawl space, or slab
Materials List Available: Yes
Price Category: C

Images provided by designer/architect.

You'll love the extra features you'll find in this charming but easy-to-build ranch home.

Features:

- Porch: This full-width porch is graced with impressive round columns, decorative railings, and ornamental moldings.

- Living Room: Just beyond the front door, the living room entrance has a railing that creates the illusion of a hallway. The 10-ft. tray ceiling makes this room feel spacious.

- Dining Room: Flowing from the living room, this room has a 9-ft.-high stepped ceiling and leads to sliding glass doors that open to the large rear patio.

- Kitchen: This kitchen is adjacent to the dining room for convenience and has a large island for efficient work patterns.

- Master Suite: Enjoy the privacy in this bedroom with its private bathroom.

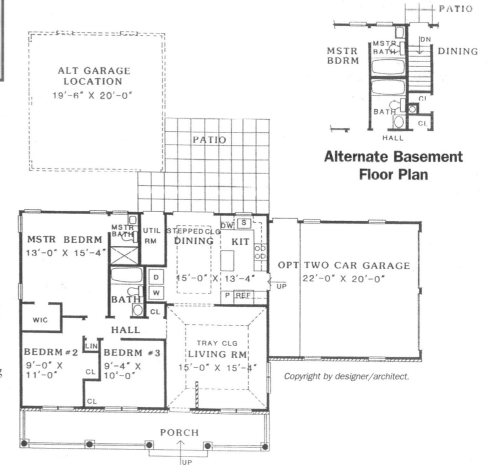

Alternate Basement Floor Plan

Copyright by designer/architect.

Images provided by designer/architect.

Plan #341031

Dimensions: 50' W x 50' D

Levels: 1

Square Footage: 1,400

Bedrooms: 3

Bathrooms: 2

Foundation: Crawl space, slab, or basement

Materials List Available: Yes

Price Category: B

Copyright by designer/architect.

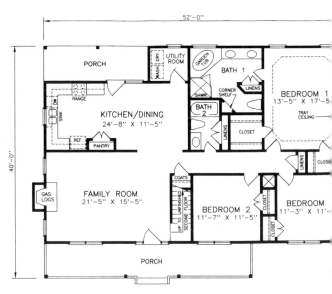

Images provided by designer/architect.

Plan #341030

Dimensions: 52' W x 40' D

Levels: 1

Square Footage: 1,660

Bedrooms: 3

Bathrooms: 2

Foundation: Crawl space, slab, or basement

Materials List Available: Yes

Price Category: C

Copyright by designer/architect.

Plan #341027

Dimensions: 54' W x 55'10" D

Levels: 1

Square Footage: 1,657

Bedrooms: 3

Bathrooms: 2

Foundation: Crawl space, slab, or basement

Materials List Available: Yes

Price Category: C

Images provided by designer/architect.

Copyright by designer/architect.

Plan #341032

Dimensions: 76' W x 38' D

Levels: 1

Square Footage: 1,528

Bedrooms: 3

Bathrooms: 2

Foundation: Crawl space, slab, or basement

Materials List Available: Yes

Price Category: C

Images provided by designer/architect.

Copyright by designer/architect.

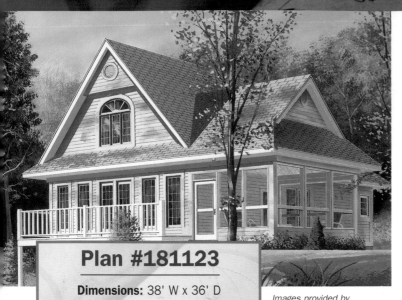

Main Level Floor Plan

Images provided by designer/architect.

Plan #181123

Dimensions: 38' W x 36' D

Levels: 2

Square Footage: 1,482

Main Level Sq. Ft.: 895

Upper Level Sq. Ft.: 587

Bedrooms: 2

Bathrooms: 1½

Foundation: Full basement with walkout

Materials List Available: Yes

Price Category: B

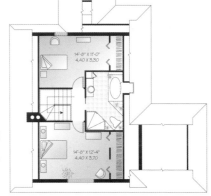

Upper Level Floor Plan

Copyright by designer/architect.

Images provided by designer/architect.

Main Level Floor Plan

Copyright by designer/architect.

Plan #181107

Dimensions: 32'4" W x 24'4" D

Levels: 3

Square Footage: 1,879

Lower Level Sq. Ft.: 790

Main Level Sq. Ft.: 790

Upper Level Sq. Ft.: 299

Bedrooms: 3

Bathrooms: 2

Foundation: Daylight basement

Materials List Available: Yes

Price Category: D

Basement Level Floor Plan

Upper Level Floor Plan

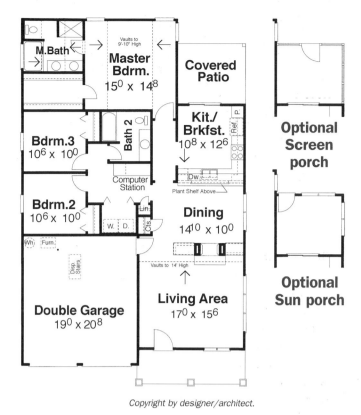

Images provided by designer/architect.

Plan #141004

Dimensions: 48' W x 29' D

Levels: 1

Square Footage: 1,514

Bedrooms: 3

Bathrooms: 2

Foundation: Slab, basement

Materials List Available: No

Price Category: C

Copyright by designer/architect.

Images provided by designer/architect.

Plan #341022

Dimensions: 58'4" W x 31'10" D

Levels: 1

Square Footage: 1,281

Bedrooms: 3

Bathrooms: 2

Foundation: Crawl space, slab, or basement

Materials List Available: Yes

Price Category: B

Copyright by designer/architect.

Plan #101016

Dimensions: 31'2" W x 42' D

Levels: 2

Square Footage: 1,985

Main Level Sq. Ft.: 1,009

Upper Level Sq. Ft.: 976

Bedrooms: 3

Bathrooms: 2½

Foundation: Slab, crawl space, or basement

Materials List Available: No

Price Category: D

Illustration provided by designer/architect.

This delightful Victorian-style home has a compact footprint that is perfect for narrow lots.

Features:

• Ceiling Height: 9 ft. unless otherwise noted.

• Family Room: From the entry you'll step into this inviting family room. Family and friends alike will be drawn to the room's warming fireplace. A set of French doors leads out to a porch.

• Dining Room: Pass through another set of French doors from the family room into this elegant dining room.

• Deck: Yet another set of French doors from the living room lead to this enormous deck.

• Kitchen: Food preparation will be a pleasure, thanks to the 3-ft. x 5-ft. island that you'll find in this bright and airy open kitchen.

• Breakfast Area: This bayed breakfast area has a fourth set of French doors that leads to the deck.

• Master Suite: This master bedroom has a 9-ft.-6-in. tray ceiling and a 7-ft. x 11-ft. walk-in closet.

Main Level Floor Plan

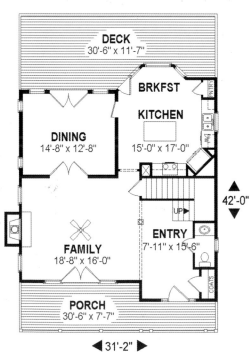

Upper Level Floor Plan

Copyright by designer/architect.

Illustration provided by designer/architect.

Plan #141009

Dimensions: 44' W x 34' D

Levels: 2

Square Footage: 1,683

Main Level Sq. Ft.: 797

Upper Level Sq. Ft.: 886

Bedrooms: 3

Bathrooms: 2½

Foundation: Basement, crawl space or slab

Materials List Available: No

Price Category: C

A full front porch combined with brick, wood siding, and metal roofing create a visually interesting facade.

Features:

• Ceiling Height: 8 ft. unless otherwise noted.

• Foyer: Guests will be greeted with a sense of spaciousness in this two-story entrance, with its dramatic angled staircase.

• Living Area: This large area is designed to accommodate formal gatherings as well as more intimate family get-togethers.

• Kitchen: You'll love the corner window above the sink. It's perfect for an indoor kitchen herb garden.

• Breakfast Area: Just off the kitchen, this breakfast area is the perfect spot for informal family dining. There's a private bathroom just off this area.

• Master Bath: This luxurious bath boasts a garden tub, his and her vanities, and a commode closet, features usually associated with larger homes.

Main Level Floor Plan

Sundeck 16-0 x 12-0

Brkfst. 8-0 x 9-6

Kitchen 9-4 x 11-8

Living Area 18-0 x 11-8

Stor. 5-6 x 12-0

Dining 11-0 x 13-4

Open Foyer 8-4 x 11-10

Double Garage 19-8 x 21-4

Porch

Upper Level Floor Plan

M. Bath

Bdrm. 3 13-0 x 9-6

Master Bdrm. 15-6 x 11-0

Bth. 2

Open Foyer

Bdrm. 2 13-0 x 9-6

Copyright by designer/architect.

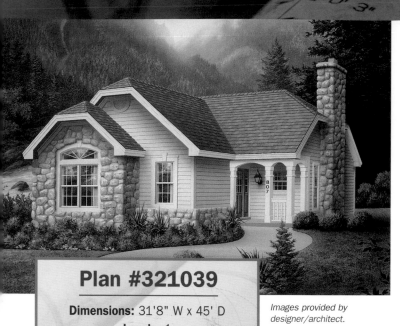

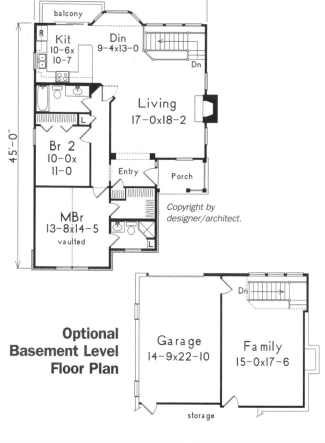

31'-8"

balcony

Kit
10-6x
10-7

Din
9-4x13-0

Dn

Living
17-0x18-2

Br 2
10-0x
11-0

MBr
13-8x14-5
vaulted

Entry

Porch

45'-0"

L

L

Copyright by designer/architect.

Images provided by designer/architect.

Plan #321039

Dimensions: 31'8" W x 45' D

Levels: 1

Square Footage: 1,231

Bedrooms: 2

Bathrooms: 2

Foundation: Basement

Materials List Available: Yes

Price Category: B

Optional Basement Level Floor Plan

Dn

Garage
14-9x22-10

Family
15-0x17-6

storage

68'

CLOSET

SHWR   SEAT

MASTER
SUITE
13x19

Copyright by designer/architect.

WHIRLPOOL

BATH

CLOSET

TRAY CEILING

PORCH

BEDRM.
12x12

CLOSET

GARAGE
21x22

STOR

A/C

REFG D/W

KIT
12x15

SINK

RANGE

GREAT RM.
16x17

TRAY CEILING

BATH

CLOSET

BEDRM.
12x12

UTILITY

DRY WASH

COLONIAL
COLUMN

DINING
12x12

1/2 WALL

FOYER

STUDY
9x8

50'

9' CEILINGS TYPICAL

PORCH

Images provided by designer/architect.

Plan #171009

Dimensions: 68' W x 50' D

Levels: 1

Square Footage: 1,771

Bedrooms: 3

Bathrooms: 2

Foundation: Slab, crawl space

Materials List Available: Yes

Price Category: C

SMARTtip

Deck Awnings

Awnings come in bright colors. As light filters through, it will cast a hue to anything under the deck. Warm colors, such as red or pink, will create a rosy glow; cool colors, such blues or greens, will enhance the shade.

Plan #171008

Dimensions: 72' W x 40' D
Levels: 1
Square Footage: 1,652
Bedrooms: 3
Bathrooms: 2
Foundation: Slab, crawl space
Materials List Available: Yes
Price Category: C

Images provided by designer/architect.

Copyright by designer/architect.

SMARTtip

Lighting for Decorative Shadows

Use lighting to create decorative shadows. For interesting, undefined shadows, set lights at ground level aiming upward in front of a shrub or tree that is close to a wall. For silhouetting, place lights directly behind a plant or garden statue that is near a wall. In both cases, using a wide beam will increase the effect.

Plan #281009

Dimensions: 46' W x 52' D
Levels: 1
Square Footage: 1,423
Bedrooms: 3
Bathrooms: 2
Foundation: Walk-out basement
Materials List Available: Yes
Price Category: B

Images provided by designer/architect.

Copyright by designer/architect.

Rear Elevation

Plan #141010

Dimensions: 43'4" W x 37' D

Levels: 2

Square Footage: 1,765

Main Level Sq. Ft.: 1,210

Upper Level Sq. Ft.: 555

Bedrooms: 3

Bathrooms: 3

Foundation: Basement

Materials List Available: No

Price Category: C

Images provided by designer/architect.

A Palladian window in a stone gable adds a new twist to a classical cottage design.

Features:

- Ceiling Height: 8 ft. unless otherwise noted.

- Living Area: Dormers open into this handsome living area, which is designed to accommodate gatherings of any size.

- Master Suite: This beautiful master bedroom opens off the foyer. It features a modified cathedral ceiling that makes the front Palladian window a focal point inside as well as out. The master bath offers a dramatic cathedral ceiling over the tub and vanity.

- Balcony: U-shaped stairs lead to this elegant balcony, which overlooks the foyer while providing access to two additional bedrooms.

- Garage: This garage is tucked under the house to improve the appearance from the street. It offers two bays for plenty of parking and storage space.

Copyright by designer/architect.

SMARTtip
Stone Tables

Marble- and stone-topped tables with plants are perfect for use in light-filled rooms. Warmed by the sun during the day, the tabletops catch leaf droppings and can stand up to the splatters of watering cans and plant sprayers.

Plan #161021

Dimensions: 48' W x 38' D

Levels: 2

Square Footage: 1,897

Main Level Sq. Ft.: 1,036

Upper Level Sq. Ft.: 861

Bedrooms: 3

Bathrooms: 2½

Foundation: Slab

Materials List Available: No

Price Category: D

Images provided by designer/architect.

If you're looking for a home where you can create a loving family-life, you'll love this one.

Features:

- Foyer: The view from the foyer through the great room and its rear windows to the back yard gives a spacious feeling to this home.

- Great Room: French doors topped by arched windows add quiet elegance to this room.

- Dining Room: A furniture alcove in this formal room adds convenience.

- Kitchen: Enjoy the extra storage space the pantry provides in this well-designed area.

- Laundry Room: This large room makes even the most complicated laundry jobs a snap.

- Stairs: The split stairs feature a wood rail that leads to a window seat at the top with a balcony that overlooks the great room.

Rear Elevation

Main Level Floor Plan

Upper Level Floor Plan

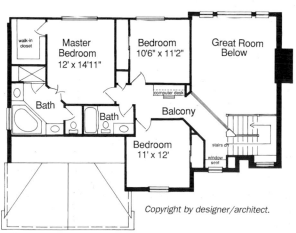

Copyright by designer/architect.

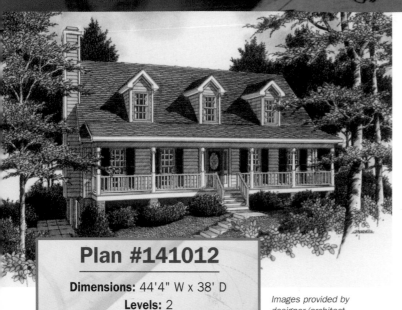

Plan #141012

Dimensions: 44'4" W x 38' D

Levels: 2

Square Footage: 1,870

Main Level Sq. Ft.: 1,159

Upper Level Sq. Ft.: 711

Bedrooms: 3

Bathrooms: 2½

Foundation: Basement

Materials List Available: Yes

Price Category: D

Images provided by designer/architect.

Main Level Floor Plan

Sundeck 16-0 x 12-0

Brkfst. 10-6 x 7-6

Kit. 10-6 x 10-0

Dining 10-10 x 8-10

Lav.

M.Bath

Living Area 20-6 x 13-6

Master Bedroom 17-6 x 14-6

Entry

44-4

38-0

Upper Level Floor Plan

Bdrm.2 15-0 x 14-8

Bdrm.3 14-8 x 15-0

Bth.2

Low Storage

Copyright by designer/architect.

Plan #291010

Dimensions: 68' W x 33' D

Levels: 2

Square Footage: 1,776

Main Level Sq. Ft.: 1,182

Upper Level Sq. Ft.: 594

Bedrooms: 3

Bathrooms: 2½

Foundation: Basement

Materials List Available: No

Price Category: C

Images provided by designer/architect.

Main Level Floor Plan

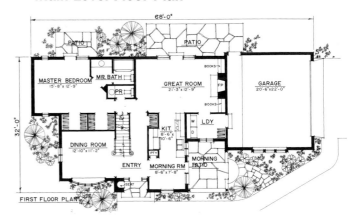

68'-0"

32'-0"

MASTER BEDROOM 15'-8" x 12'-9"

MR. BATH

GREAT ROOM 21'-3" x 12'-9"

GARAGE 20'-6" x 22'-0"

DINING ROOM 12'-10" x 11'-2"

KIT. 8'-6" x 7'-6"

LDY

ENTRY

MORNING RM 8'-6" x 7'-8"

MORNING PATIO

PATIO

PATIO

FIRST FLOOR PLAN

Copyright by designer/architect.

Upper Level Floor Plan

BATH #2

OPEN TO VAULTED CEILING

BEDROOM #2 13'-4" x 14'-4"

BEDROOM #3 11'-0" x 14'-11"

RAILING

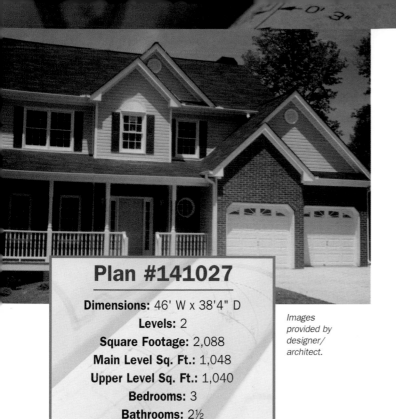

Plan #141027

Dimensions: 46' W x 38'4" D

Levels: 2

Square Footage: 2,088

Main Level Sq. Ft.: 1,048

Upper Level Sq. Ft.: 1,040

Bedrooms: 3

Bathrooms: 2½

Foundation: Basement

Materials List Available: Yes

Price Category: D

Images provided by designer/architect.

Main Level Floor Plan

- Sundeck 21-0 x 12-0
- Kitchen 12-6 x 13-4
- Brkfst. 12-10 x 13-8
- Living Area 20-0 x 13-4
- Dining 13-0 x 14-8
- Open Foyer
- Double Garage 19-8 x 21-4
- Porch
- 38-4
- 46-0

Upper Level Floor Plan

- M.Bath
- Bdrm.3 13-0 x 10-10
- Master Bdrm. 13-0 x 18-6
- Open To Foyer
- Bdrm.2 13-0 x 10-0

Copyright by designer/architect.

Plan #231035

Dimensions: 50' W x 50' D

Levels: 2

Square Footage: 1,954

Main Level Sq. Ft.: 1,508

Upper Level Sq. Ft.: 446

Bedrooms: 3

Bathrooms: 3

Foundation: Crawl space, slab

Materials List Available: No

Price Category: D

Images provided by designer/architect.

Main Level Floor Plan

- Patio
- Kit. 11-6x9
- M.Br. 14x11
- Dining 12x10
- Util.
- Br. 13-6x10
- Family 14x12
- Vaulted Ceiling
- Parlor 11-6x13
- Den 9x10
- Garage 19-6x21-6
- Cov.Porch

Upper Level Floor Plan

- OPEN TO BELOW
- Loft
- Br. 11x12-4

Copyright by designer/architect.

Plan #151010

Dimensions: 38'4" W x 68'6" D

Levels: 1

Square Footage: 1,379

Bedrooms: 3

Bathrooms: 2

Foundation: Crawl, slab

Materials List Available: Yes

Price Category: B

Photo provided by designer/architect.

This French Country home has a spacious great room for friends and family to gather, but you can sneak away to the covered rear porch or patio off the master suite for cozy tête-à-têtes.

Features:

- Entry: Take advantage of the marvelous 10-ft. ceilings to hang groups of potted flowering plants.

- Great Room: This spacious room, with an optional 10-ft. boxed ceiling, is the place to curl up by the gas fireplace on a cold winter night.

- Kitchen: The kitchen includes a bar for casual meals, and is open to the breakfast room.

- Rear Porch: Enjoy leisurely meals on the covered rear porch that you can access from both the master suite and the breakfast room.

- Master Suite: The 10-ft. boxed ceiling in the bedroom and the master bath with a whirlpool tub and separate shower make this suite a luxurious place to end a long day.

Copyright by designer/architect.

Plan #131003

Dimensions: 60' W x 39'10" D
Levels: 1
Square Footage: 1,466
Bedrooms: 3
Bathrooms: 2
Foundation: Basement, crawl space, or slab
Materials List Available: Yes
Price Category: C

Images provided by designer/architect.

Victorian styling adds elegance to this compact and easy-to-maintain ranch design.

Features:

- Ceiling Height: 8 ft.

- Foyer: Bridging between the front door and the great room, this foyer is a surprise feature.

- Great Room: A 10-ft. ceiling adds to the spacious feeling of this room, while the corner fireplace gives it an intimate feeling. Sliding glass doors at the rear of the room open to the backyard.

- Dining Room: This formal room adjoins the great room, allowing guests and family to flow between the rooms.

- Breakfast Room: Turrets add a Victorian feeling to this room that's just off the kitchen and overlooks the front porch.

- Master Suite: Privacy is assured in this suite, which is separated from the main part of the house. A compartmented bath and large walk-in closet add convenience to its beauty.

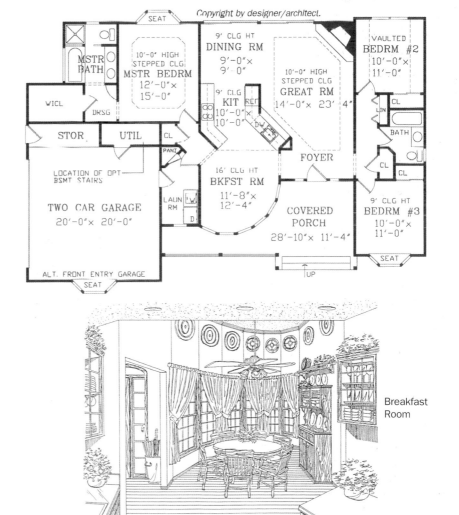

Breakfast Room

Plan #131005

Dimensions: 70' W x 37'4" D
Levels: 1
Square Footage: 1,595
Bedrooms: 3
Bathrooms: 2
Foundation: Basement, crawl space, or slab
Materials List Available: Yes
Price Category: D

SMARTtip

Create a Courtyard

Create a private walled-garden retreat with fences covered by climbing vines. Add height with trellises, and divide spaces with clipped boxwood hedges. Include an (almost) instant patio by digging away an area of sod and then covering it with a layer of sand and landscaping mesh to discourage weeds. Then cover it with pea gravel, and add a garden bench, statuary, and perhaps an antique or two. The result? European ambiance for even the most nondescript suburban yard.

Images provided by designer/architect.

With the finest features of an open design in the main living areas, this home gives privacy where you need it. Best of all, it's wheelchair accessible.

Features:

• Foyer: A high ceiling gives this area real presence and serves to blend it seamlessly with the great room and the dining room.

• Great Room: The open design allows you to use this room as an extension of the dining room or, if you wish, furnish it to create a private reading nook or visually separate media center.

• Breakfast Room: Both this room and the adjacent well-appointed kitchen flow into the rest of the living area. However, access to the rear porch, where you can sit out and enjoy the weather while you eat, distinguishes this room.

• Master Suite: Located in the same wing as the other bedrooms, this suite has a separate entrance and features a vaulted ceiling, three closets, and a compartmented bath.

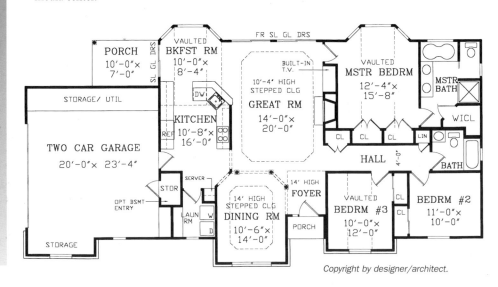

Copyright by designer/architect.

Foyer

Dining Room

Great Room

Living Room

SMARTtip

Natural Trellis

Create a natural rustic trellis that might even, if growing conditions are right, produce its own pretty blooms. Cut and place saplings in the ground as uprights. Then weave old grapevines with smaller saplings for the lattice.

Plan #251008

Dimensions: 44'4" W x 73'2" D

Levels: 2

Square Footage: 1,808

Main Level Sq. Ft.: 1,271

Upper Level Sq. Ft.: 537

Bedrooms: 3

Bathrooms: 2½

Foundation: Basement

Materials List Available: Yes

Price Category: D

Illustration provided by designer/architect.

An elegant front dormer adds distinction to this country home and brings light into the foyer.

Features:

- Ceiling Height: 9 ft. unless otherwise noted.
- Front Porch: A full-length front porch adds to the country charm and provides a relaxing place to sit.

- Foyer: This impressive foyer soars to two stories thanks to the front dormer.
- Dining Room: This dining room has ample space for entertaining. After dinner, guests can step out of the dining room directly onto the rear deck.
- Kitchen: This well-designed kitchen has a double sink. It features a snack bar with plenty of room for impromptu meals.
- Master Bedroom: This distinctive master bedroom features a large-walk-in closet.
- Master Bath: This master bath features walk-in closets in addition to a double vanity and a deluxe tub.

Copyright by designer/architect.

Plan #141013

Dimensions: 64' W x 38'4" D

Levels: 2

Square Footage: 1,936

Main Level Square Footage: 1,312

Second Level Square Footage: 624

Bedrooms: 3

Bathrooms: 2½

Foundation: Basement

Materials List Available: No

Price Category: D

Images provided by designer/architect.

This story-and-a-half design features a welcoming front porch that exudes country style.

Features:

- Ceiling Height: 9 ft. unless otherwise noted.

- Formal Dining Room: Columns add an elegant feel to your formal dining experience. The dining room is open to the foyer and great room for a more spacious feel.

- Master Bedroom: This bedroom is located on first floor separated from other bedrooms for privacy.

- Great Room: This room has a fireplace along with French doors that open to rear sundeck.

- Balcony: This small balcony overlooks the open foyer.

Main Level Floor Plan

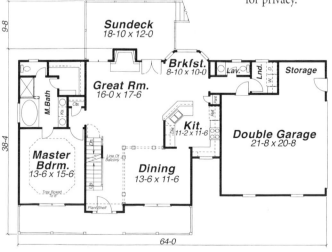

Upper Level Floor Plan

Copyright by designer/architect.

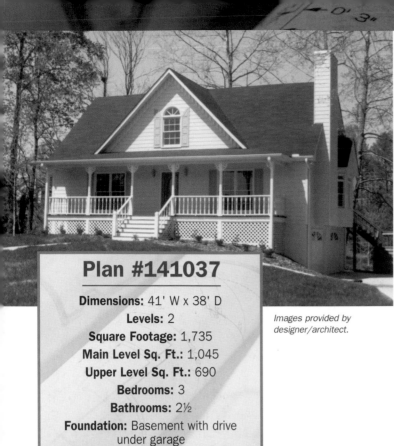

Main Level Floor Plan

Images provided by designer/architect.

Upper Level Floor Plan

Copyright by designer/architect.

Plan #141037

Dimensions: 41' W x 38' D

Levels: 2

Square Footage: 1,735

Main Level Sq. Ft.: 1,045

Upper Level Sq. Ft.: 690

Bedrooms: 3

Bathrooms: 2½

Foundation: Basement with drive under garage

Materials List Available: No

Price Category: C

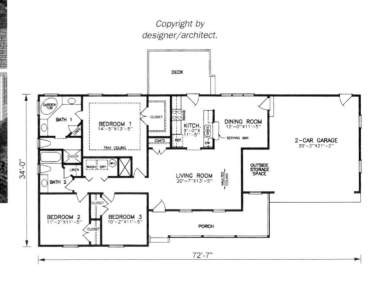

Copyright by designer/architect.

Images provided by designer/architect.

Plan #341023

Dimensions: 72'7" W x 34' D

Levels: 1

Square Footage: 1,469

Bedrooms: 3

Bathrooms: 2

Foundation: Crawl space, slab, or basement

Materials List Available: Yes

Price Category: B

Plan #181094

Dimensions: 50' W x 39' D

Levels: 2

Square Footage: 2,099

Main Level Sq. Ft.: 1,060

Upper Level Sq. Ft.: 1,039

Bedrooms: 4

Bathrooms: 2½

Foundation: Full basement

Materials List Available: Yes

Price Category: D

Images provided by designer/architect.

Main Level Floor Plan

Upper Level Floor Plan

Copyright by designer/architect.

Plan #141023

Dimensions: 38' W x 40' D

Levels: 2

Square Footage: 1,715

Main Level Sq. Ft.: 1,046

Upper Level Sq. Ft.: 669

Bedrooms: 3

Bathrooms: 2½

Foundation: Basement

Materials List Available: Yes

Price Category: C

Images provided by designer/architect.

Main Level Floor Plan

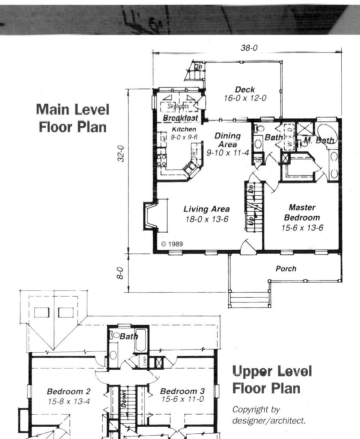

Upper Level Floor Plan

Copyright by designer/architect.

Plan #251001

Dimensions: 61'3" W x 40'6" D
Levels: 1
Square Footage: 1,253
Bedrooms: 3
Bathrooms: 2
Foundation: Crawl space, basement
Materials List Available: Yes
Price Category: B

Illustration provided by designer/architect.

This charming country home has a classic full front porch for enjoying summertime breezes.

Features:

- Ceiling Height: 8 ft.

- Foyer: Guests will walk through the front porch into this foyer, which opens to the family room.

- Screened Porch: A second porch is screened and is located at the rear of the home off the dining room, so your guests can step out for a bit of fresh air after dinner.

- Family Room: Family and friends will be drawn to this large open space, with its handsome fireplace and sloped ceiling.

- Kitchen: This open and airy kitchen is a pleasure in which to work. It has ample counter space and a pantry.

- Master Bedroom: This master bedroom features a large walk-in closet. It has its own master bath with a single vanity, a tub, and a walk-in shower.

- Garage: This attached garage provides plenty of extra storage space, as well as parking for two cars.

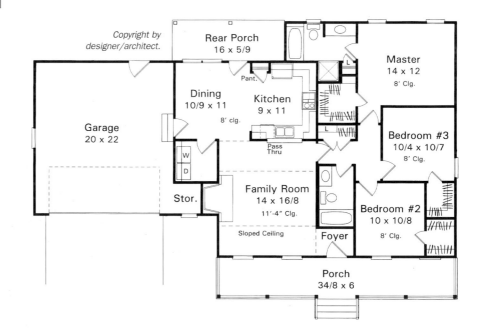

Illustration provided by designer/architect.

Plan #191003

Dimensions: 56' W x 42' D
Levels: 1
Square Footage: 1,785
Bedrooms: 3
Bathrooms: 3
Foundation: Crawl space, slab, or basement
Materials List Available: No
Price Category: C

Enjoy the amenities you'll find in this gracious home, with its traditional Southern appearance.

Features:

- **Great Room:** This expansive room is so versatile that everyone will gather here. A built-in entertainment area with desk makes a great lounging spot, and the French doors topped by transoms open onto the lovely rear porch.

- **Dining Room:** An arched entry to this room helps to create the open feeling in this home.

- **Kitchen:** Another arched entryway leads to this fabulous kitchen, which has been designed with the cook's comfort in mind. It features a downdraft range, many cabinets, a snack bar, and a sunny breakfast area, where the family is sure to gather.

- **Laundry.** A sink, shower, toilet area, and cabinets galore give total convenience in this room.

- **Master Suite:** Enjoy the walk-in closet and bath with toilet room, whirlpool tub, and shower.

Copyright by designer/architect.

56'-0" Width

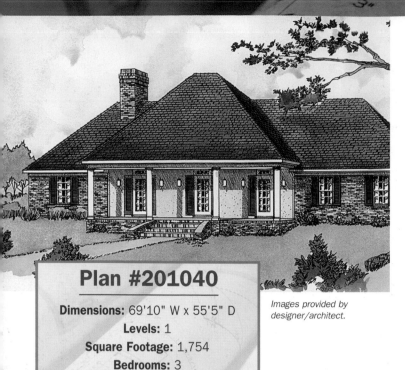

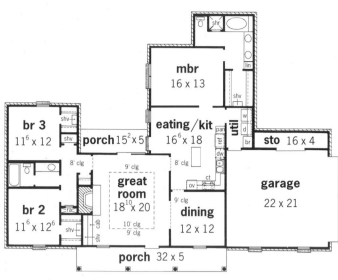

Images provided by designer/architect.

Copyright by designer/architect.

Plan #201040

Dimensions: 69'10" W x 55'5" D

Levels: 1

Square Footage: 1,754

Bedrooms: 3

Bathrooms: 2

Foundation: Crawl space, slab, or basement

Materials List Available: Yes

Price Category: C

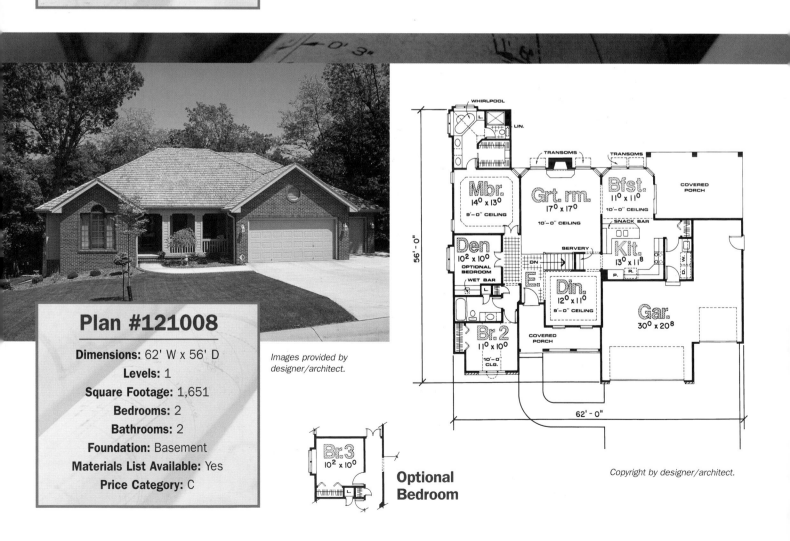

Images provided by designer/architect.

Plan #121008

Dimensions: 62' W x 56' D

Levels: 1

Square Footage: 1,651

Bedrooms: 2

Bathrooms: 2

Foundation: Basement

Materials List Available: Yes

Price Category: C

Optional Bedroom

Copyright by designer/architect.

Plan #341013

Dimensions: 44' W x 34' D

Levels: 1

Square Footage: 1,363

Bedrooms: 3

Bathrooms: 2

Foundation: Crawl space, slab, or basement

Materials List Available: Yes

Price Category: B

Images provided by designer/architect.

The luxurious amenities in this compact, well designed home are sure to delight everyone in the family.

Features:

- Ceiling Height: 9-ft. ceilings add to the spacious feeling created by the open design.

- Family Room: A vaulted ceiling and large window area add elegance to this comfortable room, which will be the heart of this home.

- Dining Area: Adjoining the kitchen, this room features a large bayed area as well as French doors that open onto the back deck.

- Kitchen: This step-saving design will make cooking a joy for everyone in the family.

- Utility Room: Near the kitchen, this room includes cabinets and shelves for extra storage space.

- Master Suite: A triple window, tray ceiling, walk-in closet, and luxurious bath make this area a treat.

Copyright by designer/architect.

Plan #251002

Dimensions: 55'6" W x 64'3" D
Levels: 1
Square Footage: 1,333
Bedrooms: 3
Bathrooms: 2
Foundation: Crawl space, slab
Materials List Available: Yes
Price Category: B

Although compact, this farmhouse has all the amenities for comfortable modern living.

Features:

• Ceiling Height: 8 ft. unless otherwise noted.

• Foyer: This gracious and welcoming foyer opens to the family room.

• Family Room: This inviting family room is designed to accommodate all kinds of family activities. It features a 9-ft. ceiling and a handsome, warming fireplace.

• Kitchen: Cooking in this kitchen is a real pleasure. It includes a center island, so you'll never run out of counter space for food preparation.

• Master Bedroom: This master bedroom features a large walk-in closet and an elegant 9-ft. recessed ceiling.

• Master Bath: This master bath offers a double vanity, a tub, and a walk-in shower.

• Garage: This attached garage provides plenty of extra storage space, as well as parking for two cars.

Images provided by designer/architect.

SMARTtip

Arts and Crafts Style

The heart of this style rests in its earthy connection. The more you can bring nature into it, the more authentic it will be. An easy way to do this is with plants. A bonus is that plants naturally thrive in the bathroom, where they enjoy the humid environment.

Copyright by designer/architect.

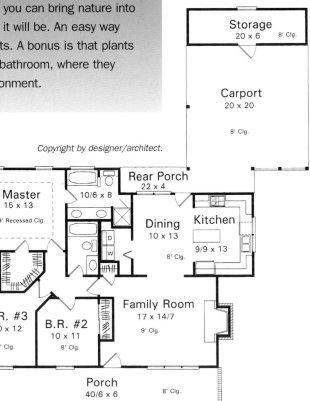

Plan #251004

Dimensions: 50'9" W x 42'1" D
Levels: 1
Square Footage: 1,500
Bedrooms: 3
Bathrooms: 2
Foundation: Crawl space, slab
Materials List Available: Yes
Price Category: C

Images provided by designer/architect.

Combine the old-fashioned appeal of a country farmhouse with all the comforts of modern living.

Features:

- Ceiling Height: 9 ft.
- Foyer: When guests enter this inviting foyer, they will be greeted by a view of the lovely family room.
- Family Room: Usher family and friends into this welcoming family room, where they can warm up in front of the fireplace. The room's 12-ft. ceiling enhances its sense of spaciousness.

- Kitchen: Gather around and keep the cook company at the snack bar in this roomy kitchen. There's still plenty of counter space for food preparation, thanks to the kitchen island.
- Master Bedroom: This elegant master bedroom features a large walk-in closet and a 9-ft. recessed ceiling.
- Master Bath: This master bath includes a double vanity, a tub, and a walk-in shower.
- Garage: This attached garage provides plenty of extra storage space, as well as parking for two cars.

Copyright by designer/architect.

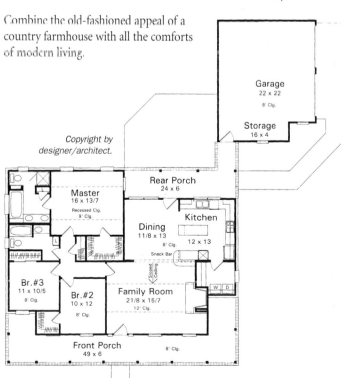

SMARTtip

Shaker Style in Your Bathroom

This warm, likable style fits in perfectly with a country home because of its old-fashioned values. But it blends in well with contemporary interiors, too, because of its clean lines and plain geometric shapes. In fact, adding a few Shaker elements can warm up the sometimes cold look of a thoroughly modern room.

Plan #271012

Dimensions: 48' W x 30' D
Levels: 2
Square Footage: 1,359
Main Level Sq. Ft.: 668
Upper Level Sq. Ft.: 691
Bedrooms: 3
Bathrooms: 2½
Foundation: Basement
Materials List Available: Yes
Price Category: B

Photo provided by designer/architect.

This traditional home blends an updated exterior with a thoroughly modern interior.

Features:

- **Living Room:** This sunny, vaulted gathering room offers a handsome fireplace and open access to the adjoining dining room.
- **Dining Room:** Equally suited to intimate family gatherings and larger dinner parties, this space includes access to a spacious backyard deck.
- **Kitchen/Breakfast Nook:** Smartly joined, these two rooms are just perfect for speedy weekday mornings and lazy weekend breakfasts.
- **Master Suite:** A skylighted staircase leads to this upper-floor masterpiece, which includes a private bath, a walk-in closet, and bright, boxed-out window arrangement.
- **Secondary Bedrooms:** One of these is actually a loft/bedroom conversion, which makes it suitable for expansion space as your family grows.

Main Level Floor Plan

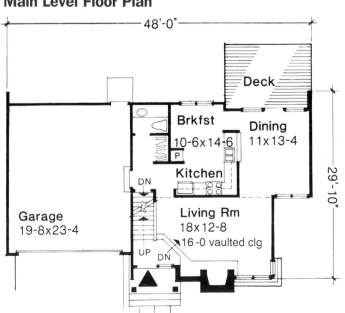

Upper Level Floor Plan

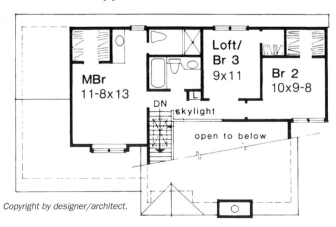

Copyright by designer/architect.

Plan #121085

Dimensions: 42' W x 54' D

Levels: 2

Square Footage: 1,948

Main Level Sq. Ft.: 1,517

Upper Level Sq. Ft.: 431

Bedrooms: 4

Bathrooms: 3

Foundation: Basement

Materials List Available: Yes

Price Category: D

Photo provided by designer/architect.

You'll love the spacious feeling in this home, with its generous rooms and excellent design.

Features:

- **Great Room:** This room is lofty and open, thanks in part to the transom-topped windows that flank the fireplace. However, you can furnish to create a cozy nook for reading or a private spot to watch TV or enjoy some quiet music.

- **Kitchen:** Wrapping counters add an unusual touch to this kitchen, and a pantry gives extra storage area. A snack bar links the kitchen with a separate breakfast area.

- **Master Suite:** A tiered ceiling adds elegance to this area, and a walk-in closet adds practicality. The private bath features a sunlit whirlpool tub, separate shower, and double vanity.

- **Upper-Level Bedrooms:** The upper-level placement is just right for these bedrooms, which share an amenity-filled full bathroom.

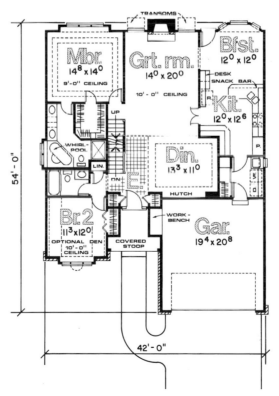

Main Level Floor Plan

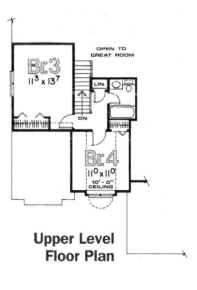

Upper Level Floor Plan

Copyright by designer/architect.

Move-Up Homes

More space. Who doesn't need it? More features. Everyone wants them. More convenience? Every family deserves it. When kids arrive, it's time to invest in a home that has the features and the amenities that you need: a contemporary open layout that suits your casual style of living and entertaining, comfortable common areas where you can spend time together, quiet private retreats where individuals can rest and have time alone, and convenient places to store all of the things that accumulate and clutter the house.

Many families prefer the informality and warmth of a spacious kitchen that is open to a great room, a concept that combines living, dining, and sometimes the kitchen in one large space. Unlike traditional separate rooms, this arrangement lets you keep the kids nearby while you're cooking or paying the bills and they're playing, for example. It's also a comfortable place where the whole family can watch a movie together, gather with friends, or simply relax. When it's time for rest, the ultimate getaway for

Mom and Dad is a master suite, something you're sure to find in almost any new home today. For the kids, it's a room of their own, and a plan this size may come with as many as three or four bedrooms.

With about 1,500 to 2,500 sq. ft. today's family home is just right, especially when you make the most of outdoor areas—porches, patios, and decks.

The modern family home, above, reflects the way people live today, with casual comfort and style.

In this family room, below left, furnishings are relaxed but chic, and colors are warm and welcoming.

Outdoor areas like this spacious front porch, below, or a deck or patio, extend the living space of a home.

Plan #161027

Dimensions: 59'10" W x 37'4" D

Levels: 2

Square Footage: 2,388

Main Level Sq. Ft.: 1,207

Upper Level Sq. Ft.: 1,181

Bedrooms: 4

Bathrooms: 2½

Foundation: Slab

Materials List Available: No

Price Category: E

Images provided by designer/architect.

Double gables, wood trim, an arched window, and sidelights at the entry give elegance to this family-friendly home.

Features:

- **Foyer:** Friends and family will see the angled stairs, formal dining room, living room, and library from this foyer.

- **Family Room:** A fireplace makes this room cozy in the evenings on those chilly days, and multiple windows let natural light stream into it.

- **Kitchen:** You'll love the island and the ample counter space here as well as the butler's pantry. A breakfast nook makes a comfortable place to snack or just curl up and talk to the cook.

- **Master Suite:** Tucked away on the upper level, this master suite provides both privacy and luxury.

- **Additional Bedrooms:** These three additional bedrooms make this home ideal for any family.

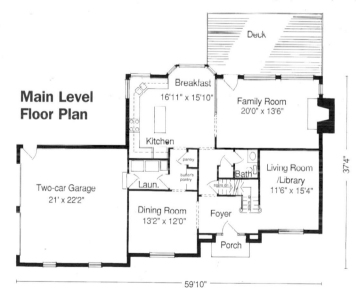

Main Level Floor Plan

Upper Level Floor Plan

Copyright by designer/architect.

Illustration provided by designer/architect.

Plan #241003

Dimensions: 60' W x 58' D
Levels: 1
Square Footage: 2,080
Bedrooms: 3
Bathrooms: 2
Foundation: Slab
Materials List Available: No
Price Category: D

Striking rooflines combine with a stone-and-shingle exterior to give this lovely country home immediate appeal.

Features:

- Great Room: Certain to become a favorite gathering place for friends and family, this great room features a fireplace, bookshelves, and an entertainment center.

- Kitchen: This well-designed kitchen—with ample counter space and cabinets—features a pantry, island, and large breakfast area. It also includes a convenient computer nook, well suited for managing today's complexities.

- Master Suite: Separated for privacy, this master suite features his and her vanities, a corner tub, a separate shower, a large walk-in closet, and a delightful window seat for your relaxing pleasure.

- Garage: Use the extra space in this garage for storage.

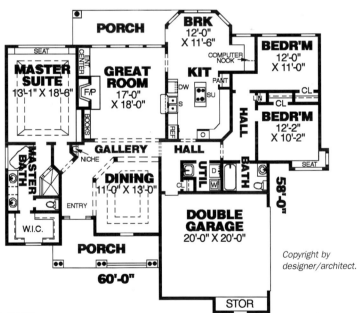

Copyright by designer/architect.

SMARTtip®

Color Basics for Kids' Rooms

Use color effectively to enhance the perception of the space itself. Make a large room feel cozy with warm colors, which tend to advance. Conversely, open up a small room with cool colors or neutrals, which tend to recede. The less-intense version of a color will generally reduce its tendency to advance or recede, as well. Other tricks: Sharp contrasts often have the same impact as a dark color, reducing perceived space. Monochromatic schemes enlarge space. Neutrals of similar value make walls appear to retreat.

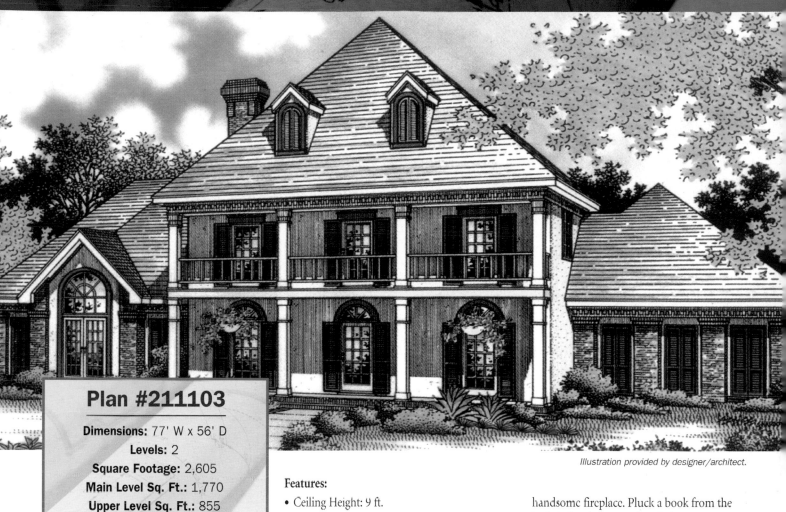

Illustration provided by designer/architect.

Plan #211103

Dimensions: 77' W x 56' D

Levels: 2

Square Footage: 2,605

Main Level Sq. Ft.: 1,770

Upper Level Sq. Ft.: 855

Bedrooms: 4

Bathrooms: 2½

Foundation: Slab

Materials List Available: Yes

Price Category: F

This grand plantation style home has all the amenities you need for gracious modern living.

Features:

- Ceiling Height: 9 ft.

- Kitchen: You'll love cooking in this huge gourmet kitchen. It boasts a large island for plenty of food-preparation space. Linger over coffee and the Sunday paper as you enjoy the sunlight streaming into the breakfast nook.

- Living Room: Family and guests alike will be drawn to this central living room, with its

handsome fireplace. Pluck a book from the built-in bookcases, and settle into your favorite chair for a read by the fire.

- Back Porch: When the weather warms, step through the elegant French doors in the living room and catch a breeze on this back porch.

- Energy-Efficient Structure: Expect lower heating and cooling bills thanks to the 2x6 framing that allows room for more insulation in the walls.

Main Level Floor Plan

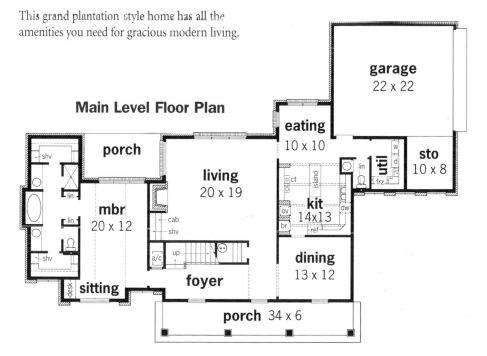

Upper Level Floor Plan

Copyright by designer/architect.

Plan #131030

Dimensions: 51' W x 41'10" D
Levels: 2
Square Footage: 2,470
Main Level Sq. Ft.: 1,290
Upper Level Sq. Ft.: 1,180
Bedrooms: 4
Bathrooms: 2½
Foundation: Crawl space, slab, basement, or walk-out basement
Materials List Available: Yes
Price Category: F

Photos provided by designer/architect.

Master Bedroom

Master Bathroom

Entry

If high ceilings and spacious rooms make you happy, you'll love this gorgeous home.

Features:

- Family Room: An 18-ft. vaulted ceiling that's open to the balcony above, a corner fireplace, and a wall of windows make this room feel special.

- Dining Room: This formal room, which flows into the living room, also opens to the front porch and optional backyard deck.

- Kitchen: A bright breakfast room joins with this kitchen and opens to the backyard deck.

- Master Suite: You'll smile when you see the 11-ft. vaulted ceiling, stunning arched window, and two walk-in closets in the bedroom. A skylight lets natural light into the private bath, with its spa tub, separate shower, and dual-sink vanity.

- Bedrooms: To reach these three charming bedrooms, you'll admire the view into the family room below as you walk along the balcony hall.

Main Level Floor Plan

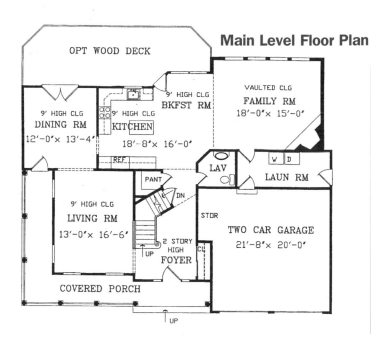

OPT WOOD DECK

9' HIGH CLG
BKFST RM

9' HIGH CLG
DINING RM
12'-0"× 13'-4"

9' HIGH CLG
KITCHEN
18'-8"× 16'-0"

VAULTED CLG
FAMILY RM
18'-0"× 15'-0"

REF

PANT

LAV

W D

LAUN RM

9' HIGH CLG
LIVING RM
13'-0"× 16'-6"

DN

UP

STOR

2 STORY
HIGH
FOYER

CL

TWO CAR GARAGE
21'-8"× 20'-0"

COVERED PORCH

UP

Upper Level Floor Plan

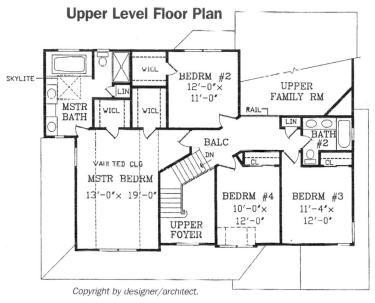

SKYLITE

WICL

LIN

BEDRM #2
12'-0"×
11'-0"

UPPER
FAMILY RM

RAIL

MSTR
BATH

WICL

WICL

LIN

BATH
#2

BALC

DN

CL

CL

VAULTED CLG
MSTR BEDRM
13'-0"× 19'-0"

UPPER
FOYER

BEDRM #4
10'-0"×
12'-0"

BEDRM #3
11'-4"×
12'-0"

Copyright by designer/architect.

Kitchen/Breakfast Area

Dining Room

Living Room

Kitchen/Breakfast Area

Images provided by designer/architect.

Plan #211004

Dimensions: 64' W x 62' D

Levels: 1

Square Footage: 1,828

Bedrooms: 4

Bathrooms: 2

Foundation: Slab, crawl space, basement

Materials List Available: Yes

Price Category: D

This super-energy-efficient home has the curb appeal of a much larger house.

Features:

- Ceiling Height: 9 ft.
- Kitchen: You will love cooking in this bright, airy, and efficient kitchen. It features an angled layout that allows a great view to the outside through a window wall in the breakfast area.
- Breakfast Area: With morning sunlight streaming through the wall of windows in this area, you won't be able to resist lingering over a cup of coffee.
- Rear Porch: This breezy rear porch is designed to accommodate the pleasure of old-fashioned rockers or swings.
- Master Bedroom: Retreat at the end of a long day to this bedroom, which is isolated for privacy yet conveniently located a few steps from the kitchen and utility area.
- Attic Storage: No need to fuss with creaky pull-down stairs. This attic has a permanent stairwell to provide easy access to its abundant storage.

SMARTtip

Resin Furniture

Resin furniture is made of molded plastic. Most resin pieces are quite affordable, but lacquered resin with brass fittings is a high-end item. Resin doesn't corrode and cleans easily, but a scratched finish cannot be repaired. However, lacquered resin can be touched up.

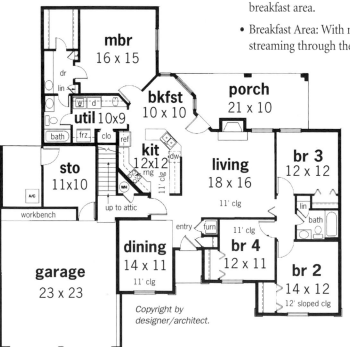

Copyright by designer/architect.

Plan #161025

Dimensions: 63'4" W x 48' D
Levels: 2
Square Footage: 2,738
Main Level Sq. Ft.: 1,915
Upper Level Sq. Ft.: 823
Bedrooms: 4
Bathrooms: 3½
Foundation: Slab
Materials List Available: No
Price Category: F

Images provided by designer/architect.

One look at the octagonal tower, boxed window, and wood-and-stone trim, and you'll know how much your family will love this home.

Features:

- **Foyer:** View the high windows across the rear wall, a fireplace, and open stairs as you come in.

- **Great Room:** Gather in this two-story-high area.

- **Hearth Room:** Open to the breakfast room, it's close to both the kitchen and dining room.

- **Kitchen:** A snack bar and an island make the kitchen ideal for family living.

- **Master Suite:** You'll love the 9-ft. ceiling in the bedroom and 11-ft. ceiling in the sitting area. The bath has a whirlpool tub, double-bowl vanity, and walk-in closet.

- **Upper Level:** A balcony leads to a bedroom with a private bath and 2 other rooms with private access to a shared bath.

Main Level Floor Plan

Upper Level Floor Plan

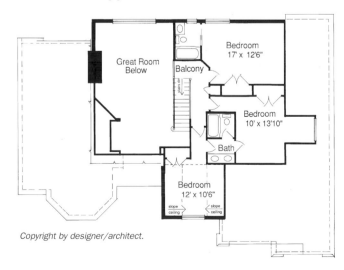

Copyright by designer/architect.

Plan #131046

Dimensions: 68' W x 57'6" D
Levels: 2
Square Footage: 2,245
Main Level Sq. Ft.: 1,720
Upper Level Sq. Ft.: 525
Bedrooms: 3
Bathrooms: 2½
Foundation: Crawl space, slab, or basement
Materials List Available: Yes
Price Category: F

You'll love the mixture of country charm and contemporary amenities in this lovely home.

Features:

• Porch: The covered wraparound porch spells comfort, and the arched windows spell style.

• Great Room: Look up at the 18-ft. vaulted ceiling and the balcony that looks over this room from the upper level, and then notice the wall of windows and the fireplace that's set into a media wall for decorating ease.

• Kitchen: This roomy kitchen is also designed for convenience, thanks to its ample counter space and work island.

• Breakfast Room: The kitchen looks out to this lovely room, with its vaulted ceiling and sliding French doors that open to the rear covered porch.

• Master Bedroom: A 10-ft-ceiling and a dramatic bay window give character to this charming room.

Illustrations provided by designer/architect.

Main Level Floor Plan

Upper Level Floor Plan

Copyright by designer/architect.

Plan #151089

Dimensions: 84' W x 55'6" D
Levels: 1
Square Footage: 1,921
Bedrooms: 3
Bathrooms: 3
Foundation: Crawl space, slab, or basement
Materials List Available: Yes
Price Category: D

Images provided by designer/architect.

If your family loves to combine indoor and outdoor living, this home's fabulous porches and deck space make it perfect.

Features:

- Porches: A huge wraparound front porch, sizable rear porch, and deck that joins them give you space for entertaining or simply lounging.

- Living Room: A fireplace and built-in media center could be the focal points in this large room.

- Hearth Room: Open to both the living room and kitchen, this hearth room also features a fireplace.

- Kitchen: This step-saving kitchen includes ample storage and work space, as well as an angled bar it shares with the hearth room. Atrium doors lead to the rear porch.

- Bonus Upper Level: A large game room and a full bath make this area a favorite with the children.

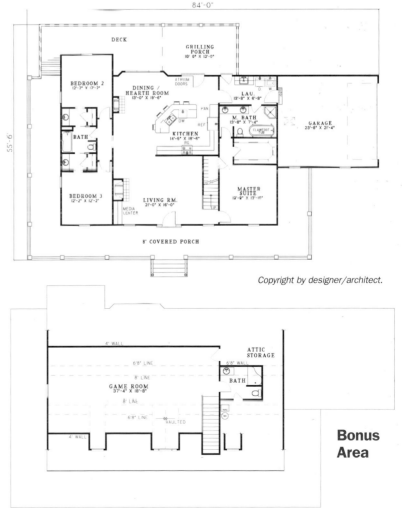

Copyright by designer/architect.

Bonus Area

Images provided by designer/architect.

Plan #301005

Dimensions: 71' W x 42' D
Levels: 1
Square Footage: 1,930
Bedrooms: 3
Bathrooms: 2
Foundation: Crawl space, slab
Materials List Available: Yes
Price Category: D

This home features an old-fashioned rocking-chair porch that enhances the streetscape.

Features:

- Ceiling Height: 8 ft.

- Dining Room: When the weather is warm, guests can step through French doors from this elegant dining room and enjoy a breeze on the rear screened porch.

- Family Room: This family room is a warm and inviting place to gather, with its handsome fireplace and built-in bookcases.

- Kitchen: This kitchen offers plenty of counter space for preparing your favorite recipes. Its U-shape creates a convenient open traffic pattern.

- Master Suite: You'll look forward to retiring at the end of the day in this truly luxurious master suite. The bedroom has a fireplace and opens through French doors to a private rear deck. The bath features a corner spa tub, a walk-in shower, double vanities, and a linen closet.

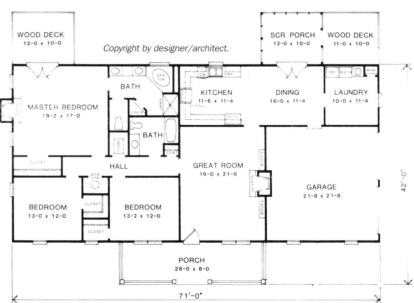

Copyright by designer/architect.

SMARTtip

Light With Shutters

For the maximum the amount of light coming through shutters, use the largest panel possible on the window. Make sure the shutters have the same number of louvers per panel so that all of the windows in the room look unified. However, don't choose a panel that is over 48 inches high, because the shutter becomes unwieldy. Also, any window that is wider than 96 inches requires extra framing to support the shutters.

Plan #301002

Dimensions: 57'2" W x 54'10" D

Levels: 1

Square Footage: 1,845

Bedrooms: 3

Bathrooms: 2½

Foundation: Crawl space, slab

Materials List Available: Yes

Price Category: D

Illustration provided by designer/architect.

Although compact, this home is filled with surprisingly luxurious features.

Features:

• Ceiling Height: 8 ft. unless otherwise noted.

• Front Porch: Guests will be sheltered from the rain by this lovely little porch.

• Foyer: This elegant foyer features a 10-ft. ceiling and is open to the dining room and the rear great room.

• Dining Room: The 10-ft. ceiling from the foyer continues into this spacious dining room.

• Family Room: This family room features a vaulted ceiling and a fireplace with built-in bookcases.

• Kitchen: This kitchen boasts a pantry and plenty of storage and counter space.

• Master Bedroom: This master bedroom includes a cathedral ceiling and two walk-in closets. The master bath has two vanities, a corner spa, and a walk-in closet.

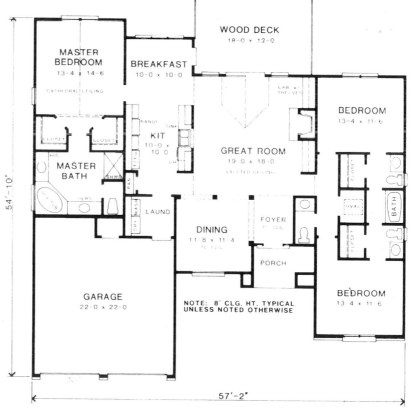

Copyright by designer/architect.

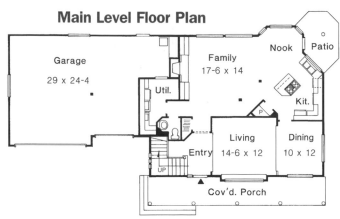

Main Level Floor Plan

Garage
29 x 24-4

Family
17-6 x 14

Nook

Patio

Util.

Kit.

P

Living
14-6 x 12

Dining
10 x 12

Entry

UP

Cov'd. Porch

Illustration provided by designer/architect.

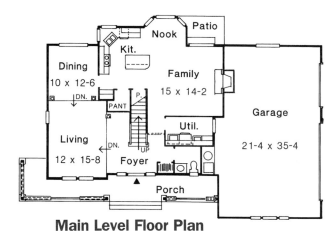

Playroom
13 x 19

DESK

Br #4
10 x 10

M. Br
15 x 14

DESK

LINEN

Br #3
11 x 10

DN.

BALCONY

Br #2
11 x 12

Upper Level Floor Plan

Copyright by designer/architect.

Plan #231013

Dimensions: 71'6" W x 40' D

Levels: 2

Square Footage: 2,780

Main Level Sq. Ft.: 1,200

Upper Level Sq. Ft.: 1,580

Bedrooms: 4

Bathrooms: 3½

Foundation: Crawl space

Materials List Available: No

Price Category: F

Nook

Patio

Kit.

Dining
10 x 12-6

DN.

PANT

Family
15 x 14-2

P.

Garage
21-4 x 35-4

Living
12 x 15-8

DN.

UP

Util.

Foyer

Porch

Main Level Floor Plan

Illustration provided by designer/architect.

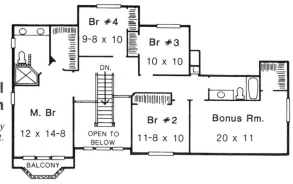

Br #4
9-8 x 10

Br #3
10 x 10

DN.

Upper Level Floor Plan

Copyright by designer/architect.

M. Br
12 x 14-8

OPEN TO BELOW

Br #2
11-8 x 10

Bonus Rm.
20 x 11

BALCONY

Plan #231015

Dimensions: 63' W x 42' D

Levels: 2

Square Footage: 2,360

Main Level Sq. Ft.: 1,054

Upper Level Sq. Ft.: 1,306

Bedrooms: 4

Bathrooms: 2½

Foundation: Crawl space

Materials List Available: No

Price Category: E

Main Level Floor Plan

Illustration provided by designer/architect.

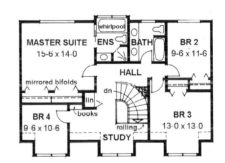

Upper Level Floor Plan

Copyright by designer/architect.

Plan #171017

Dimensions: 84' W x 54' D
Levels: 2
Square Footage: 2,558
Main Level Sq. Ft.: 1,577
Upper Level Sq. Ft.: 981
Bedrooms: 4
Bathrooms: 2½
Foundation: Slab, crawl space
Materials List Available: Yes
Price Category: E

Upper Level Floor Plan

Copyright by designer/architect.

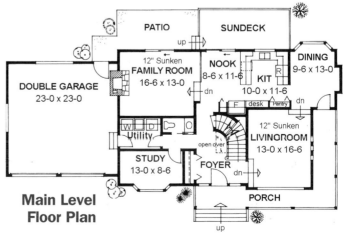

Illustration provided by designer/ architect.

Plan #281003

Dimensions: 71' W x 35' D
Levels: 2
Square Footage: 2,370
Main Level Sq. Ft.: 1,252
Upper Level Sq. Ft.: 1,118
Bedrooms: 4
Bathrooms: 2½
Foundation: Full basement
Materials List Available: Yes
Price Category: E

Main Level Floor Plan

Plan #151018

Dimensions: 69' W x 69'10" D

Levels: 2

Square Footage: 2,755

Main Level Sq. Ft.: 2,406

Upper Level Sq. Ft.: 349

Bedrooms: 3

Bathrooms: 4½

Foundation: Basement, slab, or crawl space

Materials List Available: Yes

Price Category: F

Images provided by designer/architect.

Treasure the countless amenities that make this home ideal for a family and welcoming to guests.

Features:

• Great Room: A gas fireplace and built-in shelving beg for a warm, comfortable decorating scheme.

• Kitchen: An island counter here opens to the breakfast room, and a swinging door leads to the dining room with its formal entry columns.

• Laundry Room: You'll wonder how you ever kept the laundry organized without this room and its built-in ironing board and broom closet.

• Master Suite: Atrium doors to the porch are a highlight of the bedroom, with its two walk-in closets, a corner whirlpool tub with glass blocks, and a separate shower.

• Bedrooms: These large rooms will surely promote peaceful schoolday mornings for the children because each room has both a private bath and a walk-in closet.

Main Level Floor Plan

Upper Level Floor Plan

Copyright by designer/architect.

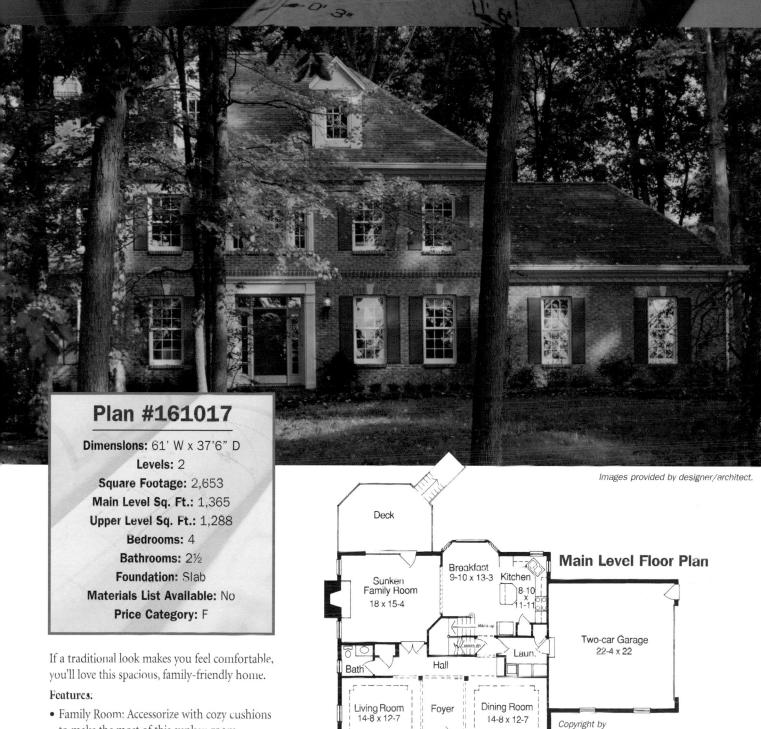

Plan #161017

Dimensions: 61' W x 37'6" D
Levels: 2
Square Footage: 2,653
Main Level Sq. Ft.: 1,365
Upper Level Sq. Ft.: 1,288
Bedrooms: 4
Bathrooms: 2½
Foundation: Slab
Materials List Available: No
Price Category: F

If a traditional look makes you feel comfortable, you'll love this spacious, family-friendly home.

Features:

- **Family Room:** Accessorize with cozy cushions to make the most of this sunken room. Windows flank the fireplace, adding warm, natural light. Doors leading to the rear deck make this room a family "headquarters."

- **Living and Dining Rooms:** These formal rooms open to each other, so you'll love hosting gatherings in this home.

- **Kitchen:** A handy pantry fits well with the traditional feeling of this home, and an island adds contemporary convenience.

- **Master Suite:** Relax in the whirlpool tub in your bath and enjoy the storage space in the two walk-in closets in the bedroom.

Images provided by designer/architect.

Main Level Floor Plan

Copyright by designer/architect.

Upper Level Floor Plan

Plan #201043

Dimensions: 57'10" W x 54'5" D

Levels: 1

Square Footage: 1,887

Bedrooms: 3

Bathrooms: 2

Foundation: Crawl space, slab, or basement

Materials List Available: Yes

Price Category: D

Images provided by designer/architect.

Copyright by designer/architect.

Plan #201044

Dimensions: 74'10" W x 44'4" D

Levels: 1

Square Footage: 1,869

Bedrooms: 3

Bathrooms: 2

Foundation: Crawl space, slab, or basement

Materials List Available: Yes

Price Category: D

Images provided by designer/architect.

SMARTtip

Resin Outdoor Furniture

Resin furniture is made of molded plastic. Most resin pieces are quite affordable, but lacquered resin with brass fittings is a high-end item. Resin doesn't corrode and cleans easily, but a scratched finish cannot be repaired. Lacquered resin can be touched up, however.

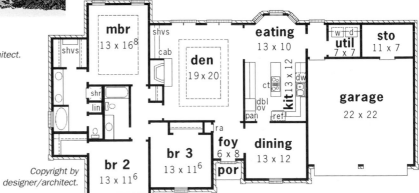

Copyright by designer/architect.

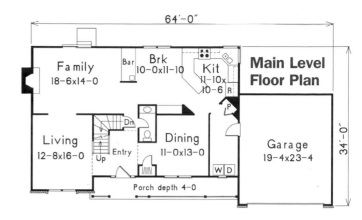

Main Level Floor Plan

64'-0"

34'-0"

Family 18-6x14-0
Bar
Brk 10-0x11-10
Kit 11-10x 10-6
Main Level Floor Plan
Living 12-8x16-0
Entry Up Dn
Dining 11-0x13-0
Garage 19-4x23-4
W D
Porch depth 4-0

Plan #321041

Dimensions: 64' W x 34' D
Levels: 2
Square Footage: 2,286
Main Level Sq. Ft.: 1,283
Upper Level Sq. Ft.: 1,003
Bedrooms: 4
Bathrooms: 2½
Foundation: Basement
Materials List Available: Yes
Price Category: E

Images provided by designer/architect.

Upper Level Floor Plan

Br 4 10-2x 10-8
Br 3 11-7x10-8
MBr 12-8x15-11 vaulted
Dn L
Br 2 12-4x10-8
open to below

Copyright by designer/architect.

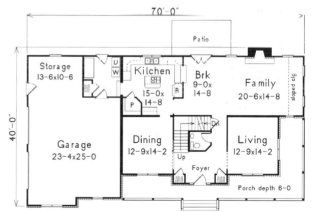

Main Level Floor Plan

70'-0"

40'-0"

Storage 13-6x10-6
Kitchen 15-0x 14-8
Brk 9-0x 14-8
Family 20-6x14-8
Patio
Garage 23-4x25-0
Dining 12-9x14-2
Foyer Up Dn
Living 12-9x14-2
Porch depth 6-0

Plan #321055

Dimensions: 70' W x 40' D
Levels: 2
Square Footage: 2,505
Main Level Sq. Ft.: 1,436
Upper Level Sq. Ft.: 1,069
Bedrooms: 3
Bathrooms: 2½
Foundation: Basement
Materials List Available: Yes
Price Category: E

Images provided by designer/architect.

Upper Level Floor Plan

Copyright by designer/architect.

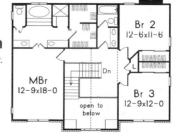

Br 2 12-6x11-6
MBr 12-9x18-0
Dn L
Br 3 12-9x12-0
open to below

Plan #161026

Dimensions: 67'6" W x 63'6" D

Levels: 1

Square Footage: 2,041

Bedrooms: 3

Bathrooms: 2

Foundation: Slab

Materials List Available: No

Price Category: D

Images provided by designer/architect.

You'll love the special features of this home, which has been designed for efficiency and comfort.

Features:

- Foyer: This raised foyer offers a view through the great room and beyond it to the covered deck.

- Great Room: Elegant windows allow versatility — decorate casually or more formally.

- Kitchen: You'll find ample counter space and cabinets in this spacious room, which adjoins the dining room and opens onto the rear yard.

- Library: Curl up on the window seat that wraps around the tower in this quiet spot.

- Laundry Room: A tub makes this large room practical for crafts as well as laundry.

- Master Suite: A vaulted ceiling gives grace to the sitting area, and the garden bath with a walk-in closet and whirlpool tub adds luxury.

Rear Elevation

Main Level Floor Plan

Basement Level Floor Plan

Copyright by designer/architect.

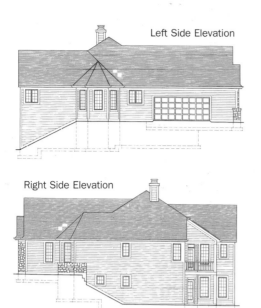

Left Side Elevation

Right Side Elevation

Front View

Living Room

Today's Fireplace Technology

Handsome and romantic, but—drafty. Thirty years ago, you might have described a traditional fireplace in this way. But that was before technological advancements finally made fireplaces more efficient. Now, not only can you expect your fireplace to provide ambiance and warmth, you can relax knowing that your energy dollars aren't going up in smoke. Over the centuries, people had tried to improve the efficiency of the fireplace so that it would generate the maximum heat possible from the wood consumed. But real strides didn't come until the energy crisis of the early 1970s. That's when designers of fireplaces and stoves introduced some significant innovations. Today, fireplaces are not only more efficient, but cleaner and easier to use.

The traditional fireplace is an all-masonry construction, consisting of only bricks and mortar. However, new constructions and reconstructions of masonry fireplaces often include either a metal or a ceramic firebox. This type of firebox has double walls. The space between these walls is where cool air heats up after being drawn in through openings near the floor of the room. The warm air exits through openings near the top of the firebox. Although a metal firebox is more efficient than an all-masonry firebox, it doesn't radiate heat very effectively, and the heat from the fireplace is distributed by convection—that is, the circulation of warmed air. This im–provement in heating capacity comes from the warm air emitted by the upper openings. But that doesn't keep your feet toasty on a cold winter's night—remember, warm air rises.

A more recent development is the ceramic firebox, which is engineered from modern materials such as the type used in kilns. Fires in ceramic fireboxes burn hotter, cleaner, and more efficiently than in all-masonry or metal fireboxes. The main reason is that the back and the walls of a ceramic firebox absorb, retain, and reflect heat effectively. This means that during the time the fire is blazing, more heat radiates into the room than with the other fireboxes. Heat radiation is boosted by the fact that most ceramic units are made with

The warm glow of a realistic-looking modern zero-clearance gas fire, below, can make the hearth the heart of any room in the house.

You'll enjoy a warm glow at the highest efficiency if you use a glass-front wood-burning, opposite, or gas-fueled, below, fireplace insert.

Enhancing the Basics

You can improve the efficiency of any manufactured fireplace, and of masonry and hybrid constructions as well, with a few extras. In a masonry fireplace, a device commonly referred to as a fresh-air intake accessory or an outside air kit may improve performance. A fresh-air accessory makes use of outside air instead of heated room air for combustion, thus improving the fireplace's efficiency. There is another way to make your fireplace more efficient that isn't high tech at all, however. Simply replace the traditional grate or firebasket with a superior design—one that provides greater air circulation and allows a better placement of logs. Another type, a heat-exchanger grate, works with a fan. The device draws in the room's air, re-heats it quickly, and then forces it back into the room.

Capitalizing on Technology

Wood is the traditional fuel for a fireplace, and today's manufactured fireplaces offer designs that make the most out of your cord of hardwood. However, wood is not the only fuel option. In fact, in some places, it's not an option at all. There are manufactured units that offer a choice of natural gas or propane as a fuel source, which heats ceramic logs designed to realistically simulate wood. The fire, complete with glowing embers, is often difficult to distinguish from one burning real wood.

In some areas of the country, fireplace emission regulations have become strict—in places such as much of Colorado and parts of Nevada and California so strict that new construction of wood-burning fireplaces has been outlawed. In these areas, manufactured units using alternative fuels allow homeowners all the benefits of a wood-burning fireplace without the adverse impact on air quality.

Most of the units available today also offer a variety of amenities, including built-in thermostatic control and remote-control devices for turning the fire on and off and regulating heat output.

The Importance of a Clean Sweep

Finally, one of the most important factors in the use of a fireplace or stove is the regular inspection and cleaning of the stovepipe, flue, and chimney. To understand why, remember that the burning of wood results in the combustion of solids as well as combustible gases. However, not everything that goes into the firebox is burned, no matter how efficient the appliance. One of the by-products of wood burning is the dark brown or black tar called creosote, a flammable substance that sticks to the linings of chimney flues.

Although the burning temperature of creosote is high, it can ignite and cause a chimney fire. It may be brief and without apparent damage, but a chimney fire may also be prolonged or intense and result in significant fire and smoke damage or, at worst, the loss of your home if the creosote buildup is great enough. Creosote causes other problems, too. It decreases the inside diameter of stovepipes and flues, causing slower burning. This makes burning less efficient and contributes to further deposits of creosote. In addition, because creosote is acidic, it corrodes mortar, metal, and eventually even stainless-steel and ceramic chimney liners.

To prevent costly and dangerous creosote buildup, have your chimney professionally cleaned by a qualified chimney sweep. How often depends on the amount of creosote deposited during the burning season, and this, in turn, depends largely on how and what kind of wood you burn. Professional sweeps usually recommend at least annual cleaning. Depending on where you live, you'll spend about $150, perhaps less, for a cleaning.

Plan #181151

Dimensions: 50' W x 46' D

Levels: 2

Square Footage: 2,283

Main Level Sq. Ft.: 1,274

Second Level Sq. Ft.: 1,009

Bedrooms: 3

Bathrooms: 2½

Foundation: Basement

Materials List Available: Yes

Price Category: E

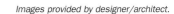

Images provided by designer/architect.

• Kitchen: This efficient and well-designed kitchen has double sinks and offers a separate eating area for those impromptu family meals.

• Master Bedroom: This master retreat has a walk-in closet and its own sumptuous bath.

• Home Office: Whether you work at home or just need a place for the family computer and keeping track of family finances, this home office fills the bill.

Multiple porches, stately columns, and arched multi-paned windows adorn this country home.

Features:

• Ceiling Height: 8 ft. unless otherwise noted.

• Great Room: The second-floor mezzanine overlooks this great room. With its soaring ceiling, this dramatic room is the centerpiece of a spacious and flowing design that is just as suited to entertaining as it is to family life.

• Dining Area: Guests will naturally flow into this dining area when it is time to eat. After dinner they can step directly out onto the porch to enjoy coffee and dessert when the weather is fair.

Main Level Floor Plan

17'-0" X 11'-8"
5,10 X 3,50

9'-8" X 8'-8"
2,90 X 2,60

21'-0" X 20'-8"
6,30 X 6,20

9'-0" X 10'-0"
2,70 X 3,00

10'-0" X 12'-0"
3,00 X 3,60

46'-0"
13,8 m

9'-8" X 9'-4"
2,90 X 2,80

12'-0" X 20'-8"
3,60 X 6,20

50'-0"
15,0 m

Upper Level Floor Plan

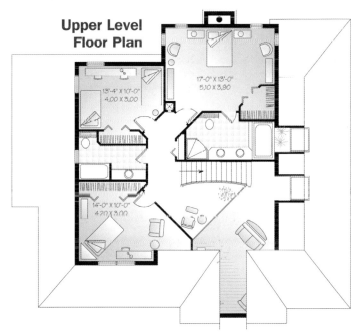

13'-4" X 10'-0"
4,00 X 3,00

17'-0" X 13'-0"
5,10 X 3,90

14'-0" X 10'-0"
4,20 X 3,00

Copyright by designer/architect.

SMARTtip

Coping Chair Rails

If the teeth of your rasp tend to break out thin edges of the cope, try wrapping the rasp with sandpaper to make fine adjustments.

Dining Room

Living Room

Master Bath

Plan #211006

Dimensions: 61' W x 77' D
Levels: 1
Square Footage: 2,177
Bedrooms: 3
Bathrooms: 2
Foundation: Slab, optional basement
Materials List Available: Yes
Price Category: D

Images provided by designer/architect.

This traditional home with a stucco exterior is distinguished by its 9-ft. ceilings throughout and its sleek, contemporary interior.

Features:

- **Living Room:** A series of arched openings that surround this room adds strong visual interest. Settle down by the fireplace on cold winter nights.

- **Dining Room:** Step up to enter this room with a raised floor that sets it apart from other areas.

- **Kitchen:** Ideal for cooking as well as casual socializing, this kitchen has a stovetop island and a breakfast bar.

- **Master Suite:** The sitting area in this suite is so big that you might want to watch TV here or make it a study. In the bath, you'll find a skylight above the angled tub with a mirror surround and well-placed plant ledge.

- **Rear Porch:** This 200-sq.-ft. covered porch gives you plenty of space for entertaining.

SMARTtip

DECK Furniture Style

Mix-and-match tabletops, frames, and legs are stylish. Combine materials such as glass, metal, wood, and mosaic tiles.

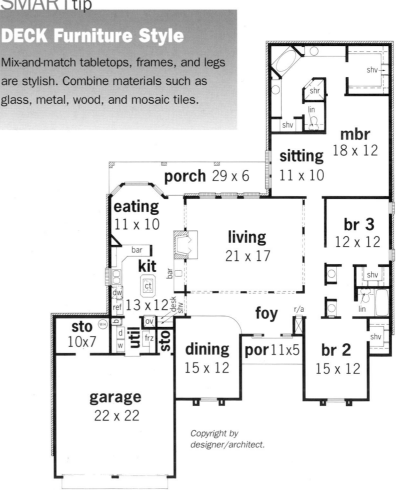

Copyright by designer/architect.

Plan #211009

Dimensions: 72' W x 60' D
Levels: 1
Square Footage: 2,396
Bedrooms: 4
Bathrooms: 2
Foundation: Slab
Materials List Available: Yes
Price Category: E

Beautiful arched windows lend a luxurious feeling to the exterior of this one-story home.

Features:

- Ceiling Height: 9 ft. unless otherwise noted.

- Entry: Guests will be greeted by a dramatic 12-ft. ceiling in this elegant foyer.

- Living Room: The 12-ft. ceiling continues through the foyer into this inviting living room. Everyone will feel welcomed by the crackling fire in the handsome fireplace.

- Covered Porch: When the weather is warm, invite guests to step out of the living room directly into this covered porch.

- Kitchen: This bright and cheery kitchen is designed for the way we live today. It includes a pantry and an angled eating bar that will see plenty of impromptu family meals.

- Energy-Efficient Walls: All the outside walls are framed with 2x6 lumber instead of 2x4. The extra thickness makes room for more insulation to lower your heating and cooling bills.

Images provided by designer/architect.

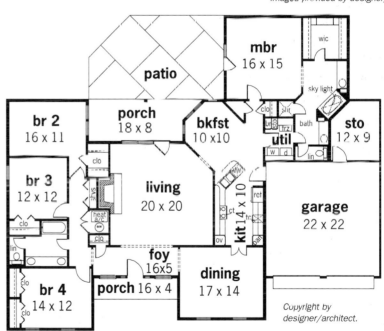

Copyright by designer/architect.

SMARTtip

Ornaments in a Garden

Placement is everything with ornaments in a garden. Some elements are best sitting by themselves. Others are better when they are part of a cohesive whole, perhaps placed in the greenery at a corner or flanking a structure.

Plan #191009

Dimensions: 62' W x 76' D

Levels: 1

Square Footage: 2,172

Bedrooms: 4

Bathrooms: 2

Foundation: Crawl space, slab

Materials List Available: No

Price Category: D

Illustration provided by designer/architect.

This charming home is equally attractive in a rural or a settled area, thanks to its classic lines.

Features:

- Porches: Covered front and back porches emphasize the comfort you'll find in this home.

- Great Room: A tray ceiling gives elegance to this spacious room, where everyone is sure to gather. A fireplace makes a nice focal point, and French doors open onto the rear covered porch.

- Dining Room: Arched openings give distinction to this room, where it's easy to serve meals for the family or host a large group.

- Kitchen: You'll love the cooktop island, walk-in pantry, wall oven, snack bar, and view out of the windows in the adjoining breakfast area.

- Master Suite: The large bedroom here gives you space to spread out and relax, and the bath includes a corner whirlpool tub, shower, and dual sinks. An 8-ft. x 10-ft. walk-in closet is off the bath.

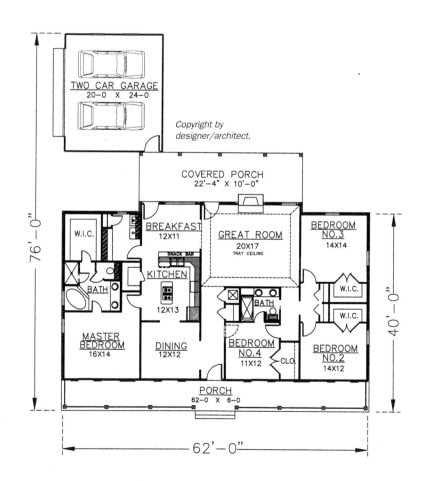

Plan #171011

Dimensions: 55' W x 61'4" D
Levels: 1
Square Footage: 2,069
Bedrooms: 3
Bathrooms: 2
Foundation: Slab, crawl space
Materials List Available: Yes
Price Category: D

Images provided by designer/architect.

This home combines the charm of a country cottage with all the modern amenities.

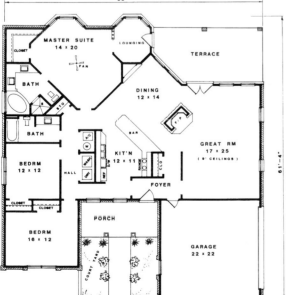

Copyright by designer/architect.

Features:

- Ceiling Height: 9 ft. unless otherwise noted.
- Front Porch: Watch the sun set, read a book, or just relax on this spacious front porch.
- Foyer: This gracious foyer has two closets and opens to the formal dining room and the study.
- Dining Room: This big dining room works just as well for family Sunday dinner as it does for entertaining guests on Saturday night.

- Family Room: This inviting family room features an 11-ft. ceiling, a paddle fan, and a corner fireplace.
- Kitchen: This smart kitchen includes lots of counter space, a built-in desk, and a breakfast bar.
- Master Bedroom: This master bedroom is separate from the other bedrooms for added privacy. It includes a paddle fan.
- Master Bath: This master bath has two vanities, walk-in closets, a deluxe tub, and a walk-in shower.

SMARTtip

Types of Paintbrush Bristles

Nylon Bristles. These are most suitable for latex paint, although they can also be used with solvent-based paint.

Natural Bristles. Also called "China bristle," natural bristle brushes are preferred for use with solvent-based paints and varnishes because they tend to hold more paint and generally brush out to a smoother looking finish. Natural bristle brushes should not be used with latex paint. The water in the paint will cause the bristles to expand and ruin the brush.

Choosing Brushes. When buying a brush, check for thick, resilient bristles that are firmly held in place. Be sure, also, to get the proper type brush for the job.

Plan #151004

Dimensions: 64'8" W x 62'1" D

Levels: 1

Square Footage: 2,158

Bedrooms: 4

Bathrooms: 2½

Foundation: Basement, slab, crawl space

Materials List Available: Yes

Price Category: D

Photo provided by designer/architect.

You'll love the spacious feeling in this comfortable home designed for a family.

Features:

- Foyer: A 10-ft. ceiling greets you in this home.

- Great Room: A 10-ft. ceiling complements this large room, with its fireplace, built-in cabinets, and easy access to the rear covered porch.

- Dining Room: The 9-ft. boxed ceiling in this large room helps to create a beautiful formal feeling.

- Kitchen: The island in this kitchen is open to the breakfast room for true convenience.

- Breakfast Room: Morning light will stream through the bay window here.

- Master Suite: A 9-ft. pan ceiling adds a distinctive note to this room with access to the rear porch. In the bath, you'll find a whirlpool tub, separate shower, double vanities, and two walk-in closets.

Copyright by designer/architect.

Plan #121051

Dimensions: 64' W x 44' D
Levels: 1
Square Footage: 1,808
Bedrooms: 3
Bathrooms: 2½
Foundation: Basement
Materials List Available: Yes
Price Category: D

Photo provided by designer/architect.

You'll love the way that natural light pours into this home from the gorgeous windows you'll find in room after room.

Features:

- **Great Room:** You'll notice the bayed, transom-topped window in the great room as soon as you step into this lovely home. A wet-bar makes this great room a natural place for entertaining, and the see-through fireplace makes it cozy on chilly days and winter evenings.

- **Kitchen:** This well-designed kitchen will be a delight for everyone who cooks here, not only because of the ample counter and cabinet space but also because of its location in the home.

- **Master Suite:** Angled ceilings in both the bedroom and the bathroom of this suite make it feel luxurious, and the picturesque window in the bedroom gives it character. The bath includes a corner whirlpool tub where you'll love to relax at the end of the day.

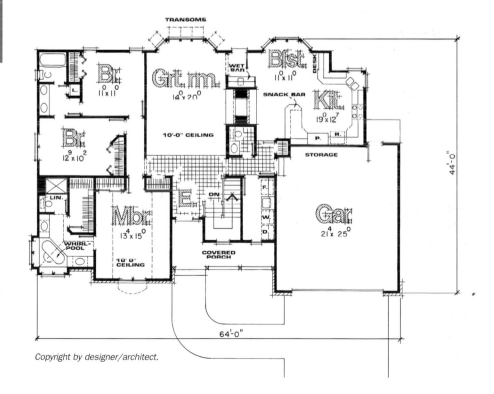

Copyright by designer/architect.

Plan #141028

Dimensions: 48' W x 36'4" D

Levels: 2

Square Footage: 2,215

Main Level Sq. Ft.: 1,075

Upper Level Sq. Ft.: 1,140

Bedrooms: 4

Bathrooms: 3

Foundation: Basement

Materials List Available: Yes

Price Category: E

Photo provided by designer/architect.

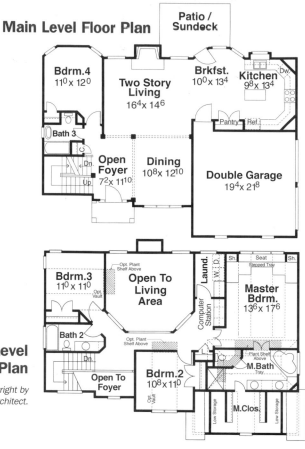

Main Level Floor Plan

Patio / Sundeck

Bdrm.4 11⁰ x 12⁰

Two Story Living 16⁴ x 14⁶

Brkfst. 10⁰ x 13⁴

Kitchen 9⁸ x 13⁴

Bath 3

Open Foyer 7² x 11¹⁰

Dining 10⁸ x 12¹⁰

Double Garage 19⁴ x 21⁸

Pantry   Ref.

Bdrm.3 11⁰ x 11⁰

Open To Living Area

Laund. W.D.

Master Bdrm. 13⁶ x 17⁶

Computer Station

Bath 2

Bdrm.2 10⁸ x 11⁰

Open To Foyer

M.Bath

M.Clos.

Upper Level Floor Plan

Copyright by designer/architect.

Plan #141029

Dimensions: 55' W x 42' D

Levels: 2

Square Footage: 2,289

Main Level Sq. Ft.: 1,382

Upper Level Sq. Ft.: 907

Bedrooms: 4

Bathrooms: 2½

Foundation: Basement

Materials List Available: Yes

Price Category: E

Photo provided by designer/architect.

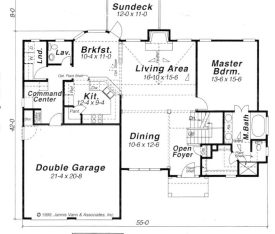

Main Level Floor Plan

Sundeck 12-0 x 11-0

Lnd.   Lav.

Brkfst. 10-4 x 11-0

Living Area 16-10 x 15-6

Master Bdrm. 13-6 x 15-6

Command Center

Kit. 12-4 x 9-4

Pant.

Dining 10-6 x 12-6

Open Foyer

M.Bath

Double Garage 21-4 x 20-8

© 1999, Jannis Vann & Associates, Inc.

55-0

42-0

8-0

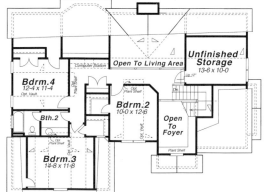

Upper Level Floor Plan

Unfinished Storage 13-6 x 10-0

Computer Station

Open To Living Area

Bdrm.4 12-4 x 11-4

Bdrm.2 10-0 x 12-6

Bth.2

Open To Foyer

Bdrm.3 14-8 x 11-8

Copyright by designer/architect.

Plan #141031

Dimensions: 58'4" W x 30' D

Levels: 2

Square Footage: 2,367

Main Level Sq. Ft.: 1,025

Upper Level Sq. Ft.: 1,342

Bedrooms: 4

Bathrooms: 2½

Foundation: Basement

Materials List Available: No

Price Category: E

Main Level Floor Plan

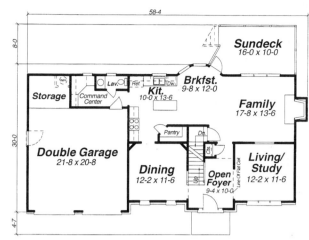

Photo provided by designer/architect.

Upper Level Floor Plan

Copyright by designer/architect.

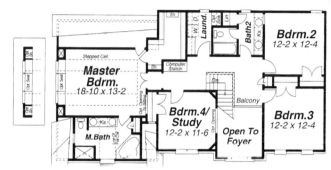

Plan #141032

Dimensions: 52' W x 44' D

Levels: 2

Square Footage: 2,476

Main Level Sq. Ft.: 1,160

Upper Level Sq. Ft.: 1,316

Bedrooms: 4

Bathrooms: 2½

Foundation: Basement

Materials List Available: Yes

Price Category: E

Main Level Floor Plan

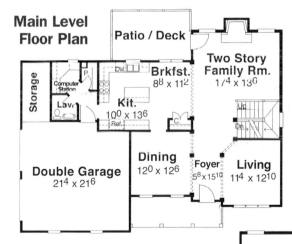

Photo provided by designer/architect.

Upper Level Floor Plan

Copyright by designer/architect.

Plan #131032

Dimensions: 69'2" W x 46' D
Levels: 2
Square Footage: 2,455
Main Level Sq. Ft.: 1,499
Upper Level Sq. Ft.: 956
Bedrooms: 4
Bathrooms: 3
Foundation: Crawl space, slab, or basement
Materials List Available: Yes
Price Category: F

Photos provided by designer/architect.

If you love Victorian styling, you'll be charmed by the ornate, rounded front porch and the two-story bay that distinguish this home.

Features:

- **Living Room:** You'll love the 13-ft. ceiling in this room, as well as the panoramic view it gives of the front porch and yard.

- **Kitchen:** Sunlight streams into this room, where an angled island with a cooktop eases both prepping and cooking.

- **Breakfast Room:** This room shares an eating bar with the kitchen, making it easy for the family to congregate while the family chef is cooking.

- **Guest Room:** Use this lovely room on the first level as a home office or study if you wish.

- **Master Suite:** The dramatic bayed sitting area with a high ceiling has an octagonal shape that you'll adore, and the amenities in the private bath will soothe you at the end of a busy day.

Rear View

Upper Level Floor Plan

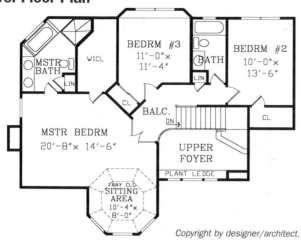

MSTR BATH

WICL

LIN

MSTR BEDRM
20'-8" x 14'-6"

BEDRM #3
11'-0" x 11'-4"

CL

BALC.
DN

BATH

LIN

BEDRM #2
10'-0" x 13'-6"

CL

UPPER FOYER

PLANT LEDGE

TRAY CLG.
SITTING AREA
10'-4" x 8'-0"

Copyright by designer/architect.

Main Level Floor Plan

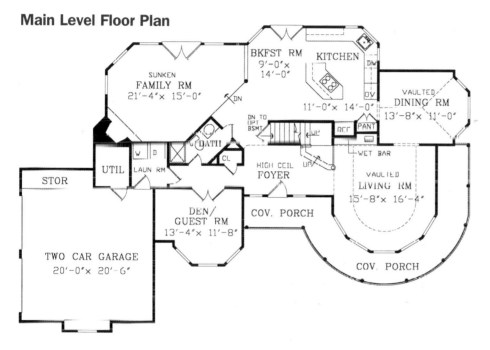

SUNKEN
FAMILY RM
21'-4" x 15'-0"

DN

BKFST RM
9'-0" x 14'-0"

KITCHEN

DW

OV

11'-0" x 14'-0"

VAULTED
DINING RM
13'-8" x 11'-0"

DN TO OPT BSMT

UP

REF

PANT

WET BAR

VAULTED
LIVING RM
15'-8" x 16'-4"

BATH

W   D

UTIL

LAUN RM

CL

HIGH CEIL
FOYER

UP

STOR

DEN/
GUEST RM
13'-4" x 11'-8"

COV. PORCH

TWO CAR GARAGE
20'-0" x 20'-6"

COV. PORCH

Dining Room

Living Room

Kitchen

Breakfast

Foyer

Plan #171003

Dimensions: 69' W x 64' D

Levels: 1

Square Footage: 2,098

Bedrooms: 4

Bathrooms: 3

Foundation: Slab, crawl space

Materials List Available: Yes

Price Category: D

Illustration provided by designer/architect.

Copyright by designer/architect.

Plan #171010

Dimensions: 76' W x 61' D

Levels: 1

Square Footage: 1,972

Bedrooms: 3

Bathrooms: 2

Foundation: Slab, crawl space

Materials List Available: Yes

Price Category: D

Illustration provided by designer/architect.

Copyright by designer/architect.

SMARTtip®

Testing Grill Hoses for Leaks

Hoses on gas grills can develop leaks. To check the hose on your gas grill, brush soapy water over it. If you see any bubbles, turn off the gas valve and disconnect the tank. Then replace the hose.

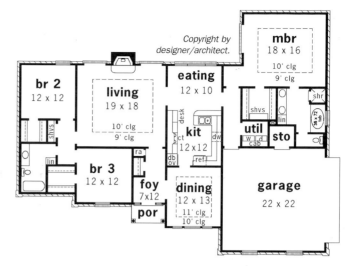

Copyright by designer/architect.

mbr 18 x 16 · 10' clg · 9' clg

br 2 12 x 12

living 19 x 18 · 10' clg · 9' clg

eating 12 x 10

shvs · lin · shr · 36 x 72 sh

br 3 12 x 12

desk · **kit** 12 x 12 · dw · db ov · ref

util w/d cab

sto

foy 7x12

dining 12 x 13 · 11' clg · 10' clg

garage 22 x 22

por

Plan #201053

Dimensions: 65'10" W x 51'10" D
Levels: 1
Square Footage: 1,959
Bedrooms: 3
Bathrooms: 2
Foundation: Crawl space, slab, or basement
Materials List Available: Yes
Price Category: D

Images provided by designer/architect.

SMARTtip
Choosing Awning Colors

When choosing a color for your awning, instead of blending with the landscape or house, you can pick one that contrasts its surroundings. This will draw attention to a handsome deck.

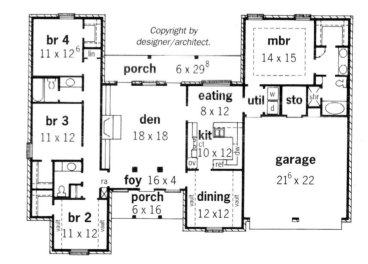

br 4 11 x 12⁶

Copyright by designer/architect.

mbr 14 x 15

porch 6 x 29⁸

br 3 11 x 12

den 18 x 18

eating 8 x 12

util w/d

sto shr

kit 10 x 12 · dw · ref · ov

foy 16 x 4

garage 21⁶ x 22

br 2 11 x 12

ra · **porch** 6 x 16

dining 12 x 12

Plan #201054

Dimensions: 67'10" W x 49'10" D
Levels: 1
Square Footage: 1,987
Bedrooms: 4
Bathrooms: 2½
Foundation: Crawl space, slab, or basement
Materials List Available: Yes
Price Category: D

Images provided by designer/architect.

SMARTtip
Reed Porch Furniture

Reed furniture comes in wicker, rattan, or bamboo. Favored for its decorative appeal and comfort, reed furniture needs some protection from the elements if it is to last. For easy care, check out synthetic look-alikes.

Plan #121020

Dimensions: 64' W x 46' D
Levels: 2
Square Footage: 2,480
Main Level Sq. Ft.: 1,369
Upper Level Sq. Ft.: 1,111
Bedrooms: 4
Bathrooms: 3
Foundation: Basement
Materials List Available: Yes
Price Category: E

Photo provided by designer/architect.

Tapered columns and an angled stairway give this home a classical style.

Features:

• Ceiling Height: 8 ft.

• Living Room: Just off the dramatic two-story entry is this distinctive living room, with its tapered columns, transom-topped windows, and boxed ceiling.

• Formal Dining Room: The tapered columns, transom-topped windows, and boxed ceiling found in the living room continue into this gracious dining space.

• Family Room: Located on the opposite side of the house from the living room and dining room, the family room features a beamed ceiling and fireplace framed by windows.

• Kitchen: An island is the centerpiece of this convenient kitchen.

• Master Suite: Upstairs, a tiered ceiling and corner windows enhance the master bedroom, which is served by a pampering bath.

Main Level Floor Plan

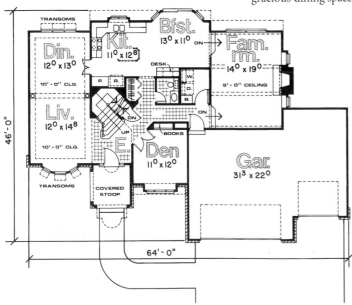

Upper Level Floor Plan

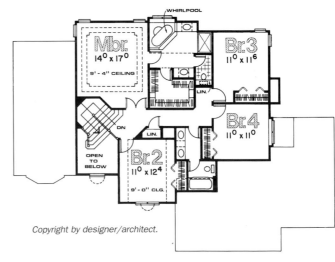

Copyright by designer/architect.

Plan #211005

Dimensions: 68' W x 64' D
Levels: 1
Square Footage: 2,000
Bedrooms: 3
Bathrooms: 2
Foundation: Slab
Materials List Available: Yes
Price Category: D

A brick veneer exterior complements the columned porch to make this a striking home.

SMARTtip

Do-It-Yourself Ponds

To avoid disturbing utility lines, contact your utility companies before doing any digging. Locate a freestanding container pond on your deck near an existing (GFCI) outlet. For an in-ground pond, have an electrician run a buried line and install a GFCI outlet near the pond so you can plug in a pump or fountain.

Images provided by designer/architect.

Features:

- Ceiling Height: 9 ft. unless otherwise noted.

- Living Room: From the front porch, the foyer unfolds into this expansive living room. Family and friends will be drawn to the warmth of the living room's cozy fireplace.

- Formal Dining Room: This elegant room is designed for dinner parties of any size.

- Kitchen: Located between the formal dining room and the dinette, the kitchen can serve formal meals as easily as quick family repasts.

- Master Suite: There's plenty of room to unwind at the end of a long day in the huge master bedroom. Luxuriate in the private bath, with its spa tub, separate shower, dual sinks, and two walk-in closets.

- Home Office: The home office, accessible from the master bedroom, is the perfect quiet spot to work, study, or pay the bills.

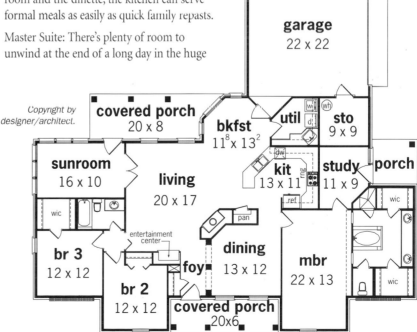

Plan #211047

Dimensions: 74'6" W x 50' D

Levels: 1

Square Footage: 2,009

Bedrooms: 3

Bathrooms: 2

Foundation: Slab

Materials List Available: Yes

Price Category: D

Images provided by designer/architect.

SMARTtip

Saw Setup

If you're using a new saw, it's tempting to plug it in and start cutting. But you should take the time to read the owner's manual, including the safety precautions.

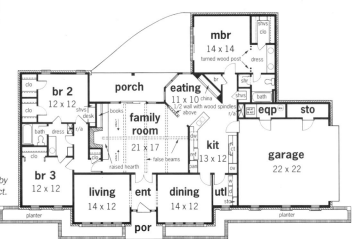

Copyright by designer/architect.

Plan #211051

Dimensions: 58' W x 71' D

Levels: 1

Square Footage: 2,123

Bedrooms: 3

Bathrooms: 2½

Foundation: Crawl space

Materials List Available: Yes

Price Category: D

Images provided by designer/architect.

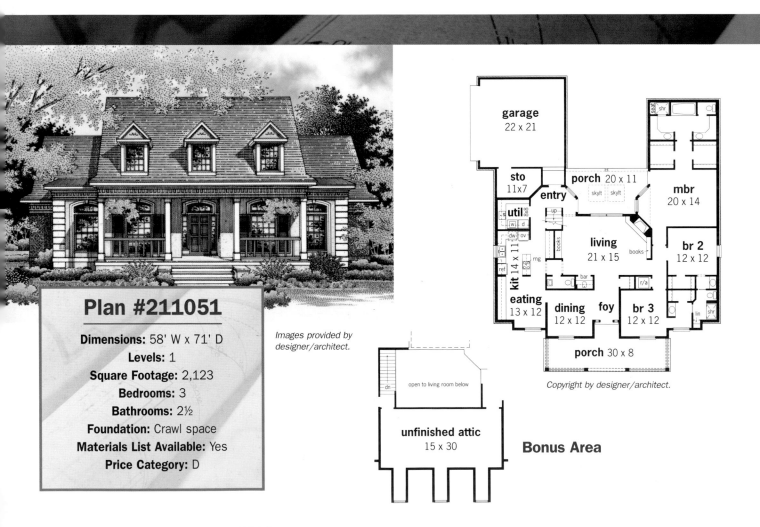

Copyright by designer/architect.

Bonus Area

Plan #251006

Dimensions: 65'5" W x 59'11" D

Levels: 1

Square Footage: 1,849

Bedrooms: 3

Bathrooms: 2

Foundation: Crawl space

Materials List Available: Yes

Price Category: D

Images provided by designer/architect.

Copyright by designer/architect.

Porch 12/4 x 14/3 — Vaulted Ceiling

Master 18 x 14 — Recessed Ceiling

Breakfast 12/4 x 10/8 — 9' Ceiling

Br. #2 12 x 11 — 9' Ceiling

Family Room 20 x 15/3 — 11'-7" Ceiling

Kitchen 14/4 x 9/8

Utility 9/8 x 8/10

Foyer 8/8 x 11/7

Dining 13/4 x 11/7 — 11'-7" Ceiling

Garage 24 x 24

Br. #3 12 x 11 — 9' Ceiling

Porch 11/4 x 6

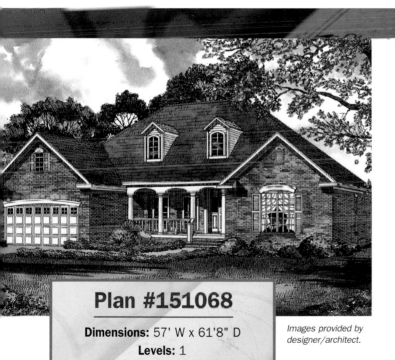

Plan #151068

Dimensions: 57' W x 61'8" D

Levels: 1

Square Footage: 1,880

Bedrooms: 4

Bathrooms: 2

Foundation: Crawl space, slab, or basement

Materials List Available: Yes

Price Category: D

Images provided by designer/architect.

Copyright by designer/architect.

57' 0"

61' 8"

GRILLING PORCH 27'-0" X 10'-0"

BREAKFAST ROOM 9' 11" 11 8' 7"

MASTER SUITE 13'-7" X 15'-0" 10' BOXED CEILING

GREAT ROOM 16'-0" X 17'-8" 10' BOXED CEILING

BEDROOM 2 11'-2" X 10'-6"

KITCHEN 9'-11" X 14'-9"

8" COLUMNS

BEDROOM 3 10'-0" X 10'-4"

M. BATH 13'-7" X 11'-8"

DINING ROOM 12'-6" X 12'-4" 10' CEILING

FOYER 8'-0" X 10'-4" 10' CEILING

BATH

LAU.

BEDROOM 4 13'-6" X 12'-4"

GARAGE 19'-4" X 19'-6"

7' COVERED PORCH 10' CEILING

OPTIONAL SIDE LOAD

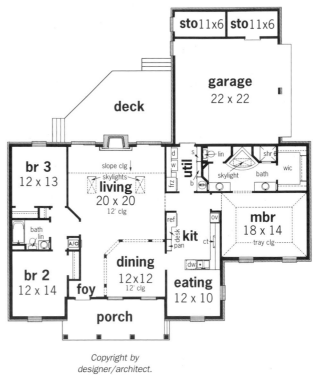

Plan #211046

Dimensions: 62' W x 68' D

Levels: 1

Square Footage: 1,936

Bedrooms: 3

Bathrooms: 2

Foundation: Crawl space

Materials List Available: Yes

Price Category: D

Images provided by designer/architect.

Copyright by designer/architect.

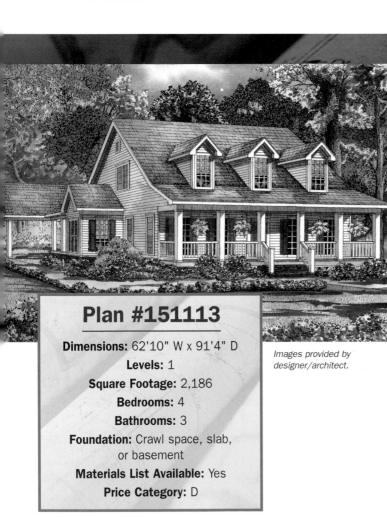

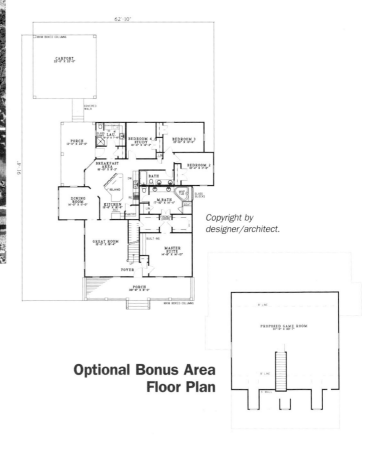

Plan #151113

Dimensions: 62'10" W x 91'4" D

Levels: 1

Square Footage: 2,186

Bedrooms: 4

Bathrooms: 3

Foundation: Crawl space, slab, or basement

Materials List Available: Yes

Price Category: D

Images provided by designer/architect.

Copyright by designer/architect.

Optional Bonus Area Floor Plan

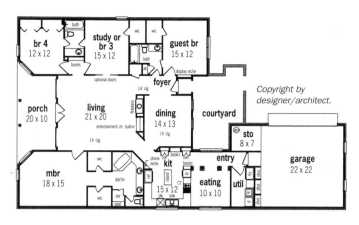

Plan #211057

Dimensions: 50' W x 86' D

Levels: 1

Square Footage: 2,366

Bedrooms: 4

Bathrooms: 3

Foundation: Slab

Materials List Available: No

Price Category: E

Images provided by designer/architect.

Copyright by designer/architect.

SMARTtip

Using a Hand Miter Box

Because hand-powered miter boxes generally are much lighter than electric-powered models, you need to clamp them securely to a workbench to avoid shifting that could alter the cut.

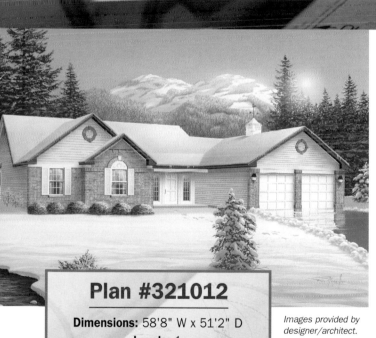

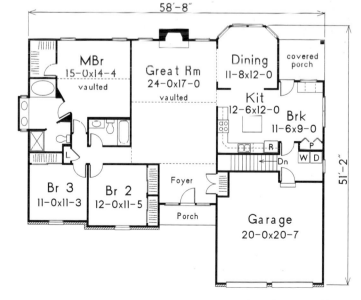

Plan #321012

Dimensions: 58'8" W x 51'2" D

Levels: 1

Square Footage: 1,882

Bedrooms: 3

Bathrooms: 2

Foundation: Basement

Materials List Available: Yes

Price Category: D

Images provided by designer/architect.

Copyright by designer/architect.

Plan #121083

Dimensions: 72' W x 45'4" D

Levels: 2

Square Footage: 2,695

Main Level Sq. Ft.: 1,881

Upper Level Sq. Ft.: 814

Bedrooms: 4

Bathrooms: 3½

Foundation: Basement

Materials List Available: Yes

Price Category: F

Photo provided by designer/architect.

You'll love this home for its soaring entryway ceiling and well-designed layout.

Features:

- **Entry:** A balcony from the upper level looks down into this two-story entry, which features a decorative plant shelf.
- **Great Room:** Comfort is guaranteed in this large room, with its built-in bookcases framing a lovely fireplace and trio of transom-topped windows along one wall.
- **Living Room:** Save both this formal room and the formal dining room, both of which flank the entry, for guests and special occasions.
- **Kitchen:** This convenient work space includes a gazebo-shaped breakfast area where friends and family will gather at any time of day.

Main Level Floor Plan

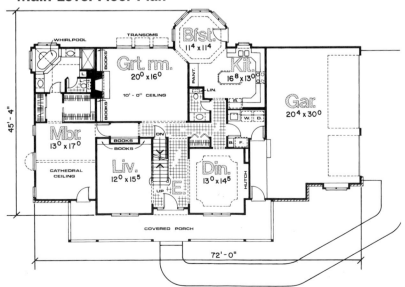

Upper Level Floor Plan

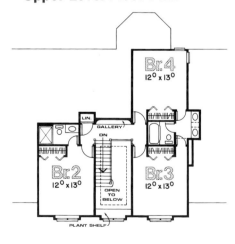

Copyright by designer/architect.

Plan #121097

Dimensions: 58' W x 42'8" D

Levels: 2

Square Footage: 2,417

Main Level Sq. Ft.: 1,162

Upper Level Sq. Ft.: 1,255

Bedrooms: 4

Bathrooms: 2½

Foundation: Basement

Materials List Available: Yes

Price Category: E

This design is ideal if you're looking for a home that will be easy to expand through the years.

Features:

- **Entry:** A balcony from the upper level overlooks this two-story entryway.

- **Study:** Add French doors to make this bayed room an expansion of the family room.

- **Family Room:** This room is positioned so that friends and family will congregate here.

- **Dining Room:** A built-in serving cabinet from the kitchen makes serving meals a pleasure.

- **Kitchen:** A roll-away butcher-block island, full pantry, and snack bar add convenience.

- **Breakfast Area:** Patio doors in this bayed area lead to a private porch where you'll love to dine.

- **Unfinished area:** Use this area for storage or future expansion.

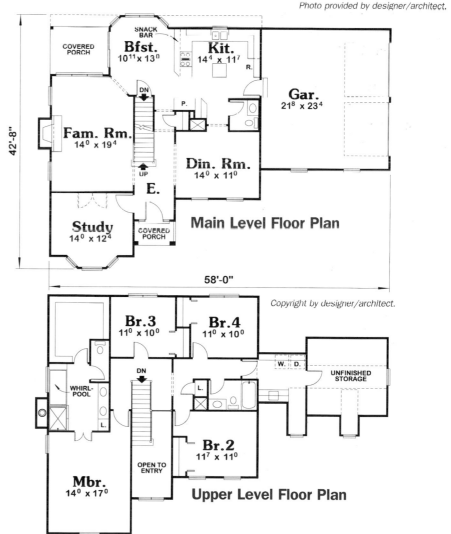

Photo provided by designer/architect.

Copyright by designer/architect.

Main Level Floor Plan

Upper Level Floor Plan

Plan #241001

Dimensions: 65' W x 56'3" D

Levels: 1

Square Footage: 2,350

Bedrooms: 3

Bathrooms: 2½

Foundation: Slab

Materials List Available: No

Price Category: E

Images provided by designer/architect.

Classic, traditional rooflines combine with arched windows to draw immediate attention to this lovely three-bedroom home.

Features:

- **Great Room:** The foyer introduces you to this impressive great room, with its grand 10-ft. ceiling and handsome fireplace.

- **Kitchen:** Certain to become the hub of such a family-oriented home, this spacious kitchen, which adjoins the breakfast area and a delightful sunroom, features an abundance of counter space, a pantry, and a convenient eating bar.

- **Master Suite:** You will enjoy the privacy and comfort of this master suite, which features a whirlpool tub, split vanities, and a separate shower.

- **Study:** Adjourn to the front of the house, and enjoy the quiet confines of this private study with built-in bookshelves to work, read, or just relax.

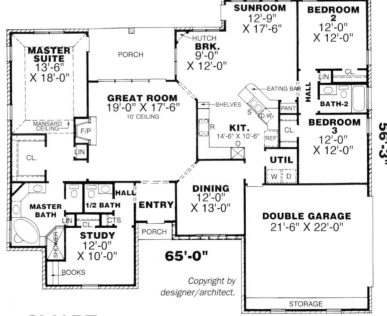

Copyright by designer/architect.

SMARTtip

Kitchen Counters

Make use of counter inserts to help with the cooking chores. For example, ceramic tiles inlaid in a laminate counter create a heat-proof landing zone near the range. A marble or granite insert is tailor-made for pastry chefs. And a butcher-block inlay is a great addition to the food prep area.

Plan #321006

Dimensions: 76' W x 45' D

Levels: 1, optional lower

Square Footage: 1,977

Optional Basement Level Sq. Ft.: 1,416

Bedrooms: 4

Bathrooms: 2½

Foundation: Basement

Materials List Available: Yes

Price Category: D

This design is ideal if you're looking for a home with space to finish as your family and your budget grow.

Features:

- **Great Room:** A vaulted ceiling in this room sets an elegant tone that the gorgeous atrium windows pick up and amplify.

- **Atrium:** Elegance marks the staircase here that leads to the optional lower level.

- **Kitchen:** Both experienced cooks and beginners will appreciate the care that went into the design of this step-saving kitchen, with its ample counter space and generous cabinets.

- **Master Suite:** Enjoy the luxuries you'll find in this suite, and revel in the quiet that the bedroom can provide.

- **Lower Level:** Finish the 1,416 sq. ft. here to create a family room, two bedrooms, two bathrooms, and a study.

Illustration provided by designer/architect.

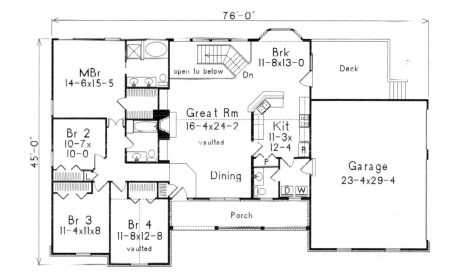

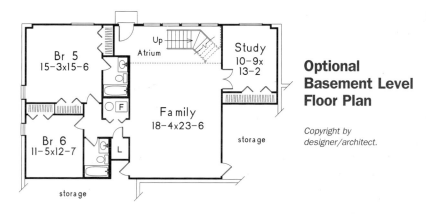

Optional Basement Level Floor Plan

Copyright by designer/architect.

Images provided by
designer/architect.

Copyright by designer/architect.

Plan #321030

Dimensions: 61' W x 51' D

Levels: 1

Square Footage: 2,029

Bedrooms: 4

Bathrooms: 2

Foundation: Basement

Materials List Available: Yes

Price Category: D

SMARTtip

Measuring Angles

A sure-fire way to accurately measure the wall-frame acute angle is to cut a piece of scrap lumber to emulate the angle, and then measure it.

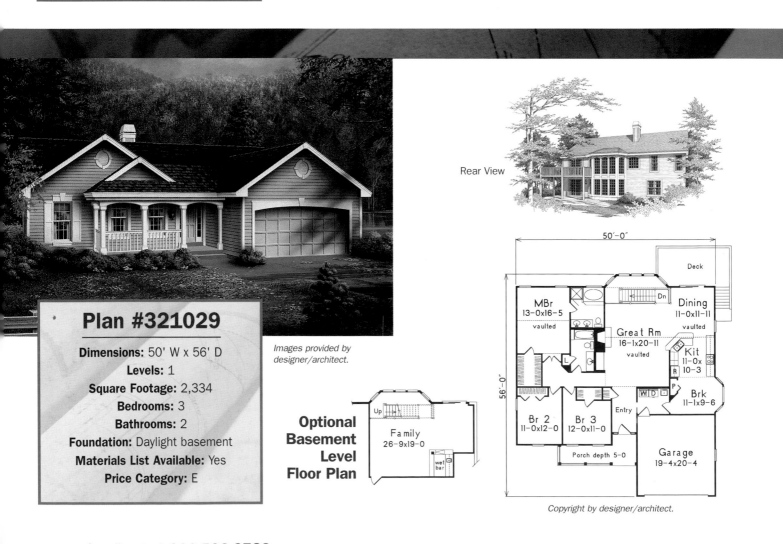

Rear View

Images provided by
designer/architect.

Plan #321029

Dimensions: 50' W x 56' D

Levels: 1

Square Footage: 2,334

Bedrooms: 3

Bathrooms: 2

Foundation: Daylight basement

Materials List Available: Yes

Price Category: E

Optional Basement Level Floor Plan

Copyright by designer/architect.

Copyright by
designer/architect.

Plan #321020

Dimensions: 58' W x 47'6" D

Levels: 1

Square Footage: 1,882

Bedrooms: 4

Bathrooms: 2

Foundation: Basement

Materials List Available: Yes

Price Category: D

*Images provided by
designer/architect.*

Plan #291003

Dimensions: 42'4" W x 73'4" D

Levels: 1

Square Footage: 1,890

Bedrooms: 3

Bathrooms: 2

Foundation: Crawl space

Materials List Available: No

Price Category: D

*Images provided by
designer/architect.*

Copyright by designer/architect.

Plan #121075

Dimensions: 57'4" W x 30' D

Levels: 2

Square Footage: 2,345

Main Level Sq. Ft.: 1,000

Upper Level Sq. Ft.: 1,345

Bedrooms: 4

Bathrooms: 3½

Foundation: Basement

Materials List Available: Yes

Price Category: E

Photo provided by designer/architect.

Imagine owning a home with a Colonial-styled exterior and a practical, amenity-filled interior with both formal and informal areas.

Features:

- **Family Room:** This room will be the heart of your home. A bay window lets you create a special nook for reading or quiet conversation, and a fireplace begs for a circle of comfortable chairs or soft cushions around it.

- **Living Room:** Connected to the family room by a set of French doors, you can use this room for formal entertaining or informal family fun.

- **Kitchen:** This kitchen has been designed for efficient work patterns. However, the snack bar that links it to the breakfast area beyond also invites company while the cook is working.

- **Master Suite:** Located on the second level, this suite features an entertainment center, a separate sitting area, built-in dressers, two walk-in closets, and a whirlpool tub.

Main Level Floor Plan

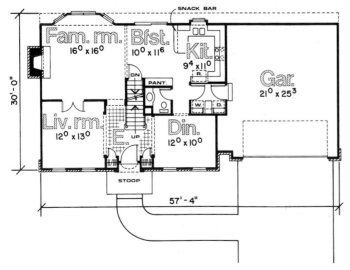

Upper Level Floor Plan

Copyright by designer/architect.

Photo provided by designer/architect.

Plan #121052

Dimensions: 56' W x 70' D

Levels: 1

Square Footage: 2,093

Bedrooms: 4

Bathrooms: 2

Foundation: Basement

Materials List Available: Yes

Price Category: D

You'll love this one story home with all the amenities that usually go with a larger home with more levels.

Features:

- Entry: As you enter this home, you'll have a long view into the great room, letting you feel welcome right away.

- Great Room: Enjoy the fireplace in this large room during cool evenings, and during the day, bask in the sunlight streaming through the arched windows that flank the fireplace.

- Den: French doors from the great room open into this room that features a spider-beamed ceiling.

- Kitchen: An island, pantry, and built-in desk make this kitchen a versatile work space. It includes a lovely breakfast area, too, that opens into the backyard.

- Master Suite: This secluded suite features an angled ceiling in the private bathroom.

Copyright by designer/architect.

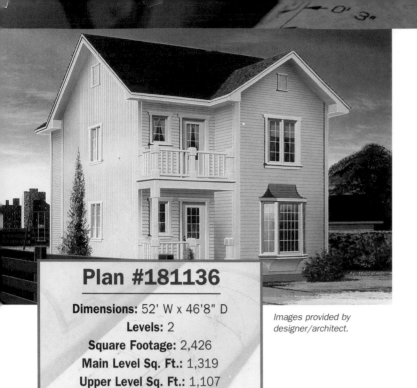

Main Level Floor Plan

9'-0" X 11'-4"
2,70 X 3,40

11'-8" X 10'-0"
3,50 X 3,00

11'-4" X 13'-4"
3,40 X 4,00

32'-0"
9,6 m

22'-0"
6,6 m

9'-0" X 10'-0"
2,70 X 3,00

11'-4" X 9'-8"
3,40 X 2,90

9'-4" X 6'-8"
2,80 X 2,00

11'-4" 10'-8"
3,40 X 3,20

Upper Level Floor Plan

Images provided by designer/architect.

Copyright by designer/architect.

Plan #181136

Dimensions: 52' W x 46'8" D

Levels: 2

Square Footage: 2,426

Main Level Sq. Ft.: 1,319

Upper Level Sq. Ft.: 1,107

Bedrooms: 3

Bathrooms: 1½

Foundation: Full basement

Materials List Available: Yes

Price Category: E

Plan #141030

Dimensions: 38' W x 32' D

Levels: 2

Square Footage: 2,323

Main Level Sq. Ft.: 1,179

Upper Level Sq. Ft.: 1,144

Bedrooms: 4

Bathrooms: 2½

Foundation: Basement

Materials List Available: Yes

Price Category: E

Images provided by designer/architect.

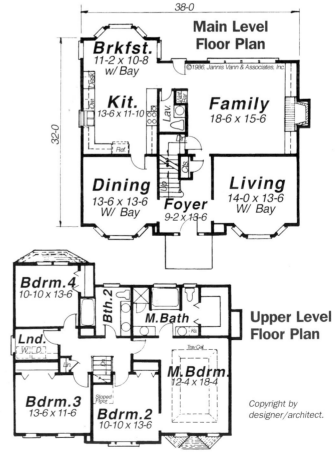

38-0

Main Level Floor Plan

Brkfst.
11-2 x 10-8
w/ Bay

©1986, Jannis Vann & Associates, Inc.

Kit.
13-6 x 11-10

Family
18-6 x 15-6

Lav.

Ref.

Dining
13-6 x 13-6
W/ Bay

Foyer
9-2 x 13-6

Living
14-0 x 13-6
W/ Bay

32-0

Bdrm.4
10-10 x 13-6

Bth.2

M.Bath

Lnd.
W D

M.Bdrm.
12-4 x 18-4

Bdrm.3
13-6 x 11-6

Sloped Floor

Bdrm.2
10-10 x 13-6

Upper Level Floor Plan

Copyright by designer/architect.

Main Level Floor Plan

Gathering
18x17

Nook
9-6x9

Kitchen

Utility

Pantry

Garage
27-8x23-4

Dining
11x12

Den
12-6x12

Dn

Dn

Covered Porch

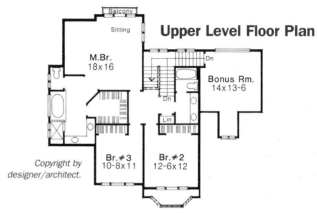

Upper Level Floor Plan

Balcony

Sitting

M.Br.
18x16

Dn

Bonus Rm.
14x13-6

Dn

Lin

Br.#3
10-8x11

Br.#2
12-6x12

Images provided by designer/architect.

Copyright by designer/architect.

Plan #231025

Dimensions: 66' W x 46' D

Levels: 2

Square Footage: 2,501

Main Level Sq. Ft.: 1,170

Upper Level Sq. Ft.: 1,331

Bedrooms: 3

Bathrooms: 2½

Foundation: Crawl space

Materials List Available: No

Price Category: E

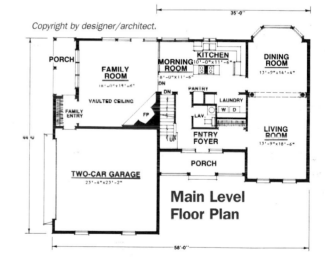

Copyright by designer/architect.

35'-0"

PORCH

FAMILY ROOM
18'-0"x19'-6"
VAULTED CEILING

MORNING ROOM
8'-0"x11'-6"

KITCHEN
10'-0"x11'-6"

DINING ROOM
13'-9"x14'-4"

FAMILY ENTRY

PANTRY

LAUNDRY
W D

FP

LAV.

ENTRY FOYER

LIVING ROOM
13'-9"x18'-6"

DN

UP

TWO-CAR GARAGE
23'-4"x23'-2"

PORCH

44'-0"

58'-0"

Main Level Floor Plan

Plan #291012

Dimensions: 58' W x 44' D

Levels: 2

Square Footage: 1,898

Main Level Sq. Ft.: 1,182

Upper Level Sq. Ft.: 716

Bedrooms: 4

Bathrooms: 2½

Foundation: Basement

Materials List Available: No

Price Category: D

Images provided by designer/architect.

Upper Level Floor Plan

BEDROOM
13'-0"x8'-10"

WIC

BEDROOM
12'-8"x11'-0"

LIN

BATH

DN

UPPER HALL

MASTER BATH

BEDROOM
12'-0"x11'-0"

WIC

MASTER BEDROOM
13'-9"x14'-2"

32'-0"

35'-0"

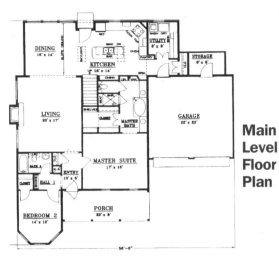

Main Level Floor Plan

Images provided by designer/architect.

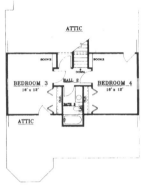

Upper Level Floor Plan

Copyright by designer/architect.

Plan #171005

Dimensions: 56' W x 58' D

Levels: 2

Square Footage: 2,276

Main Level Sq. Ft.: 1,748

Upper Level Sq. Ft.: 528

Bedrooms: 4

Bathrooms: 3

Foundation: Slab, crawl space

Materials List Available: Yes

Price Category: E

Main Level Floor Plan

Images provided by designer/architect.

Upper Level Floor Plan

Copyright by designer/architect.

Plan #321052

Dimensions: 57' W x 48'8" D

Levels: 2

Square Footage: 2,182

Main Level Sq. Ft.: 1,112

Upper Level Sq. Ft.: 1,070

Bedrooms: 3

Bathrooms: 3½

Foundation: Basement

Materials List Available: Yes

Price Category: D

Plan #151105

Dimensions: 60'6" W x 91'4" D
Levels: 1
Square Footage: 2,039
Bedrooms: 4
Bathrooms: 2
Foundation: Crawl space, slab, or optional basement
Materials List Available: Yes
Price Category: D

Images provided by designer/architect.

If you've always wanted a wraparound porch with columns, this could be your dream home.

Features:

- **Great Room:** Just off the foyer, this spacious room features a handsome fireplace where friends and family are sure to gather.

- **Dining Room:** Columns set off this dining room, and the large window area allows natural lighting during the day.

- **Kitchen:** Open to the dining room, this well-planned kitchen features a large central island with a sink and a dishwasher on one side and an eating bar on the other.

- **Breakfast Room:** You'll love the unusual shape of this room and its windows overlooking the rear porch. Access to the porch is from a hallway here.

- **Master Suite:** Enjoy two walk-in closets, plus a bath with a corner whirlpool tub, glass shower, linen closet, vanity, and compartmentalized toilet.

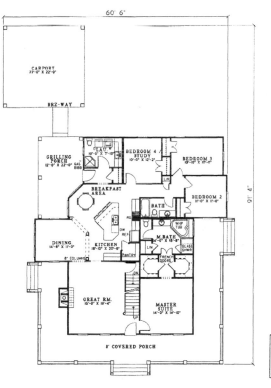

Bonus Area

Copyright by designer/architect.

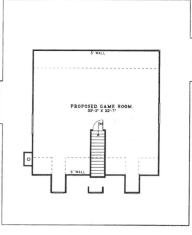

Photo and illustration provided by designer/architect.

Plan #191001

Dimensions: 62' W x 72' D

Levels: 1

Square Footage: 2,156

Bedrooms: 4

Bathrooms: 3

Foundation: Crawl space, slab, or basement

Materials List Available: No

Price Category: D

This lovely home has the best of old and new — a traditional appearance combined with fabulous comforts and conveniences.

Features:

- **Great Room:** A tray ceiling gives stature to this expansive room, and its many windows let natural light stream into it.

- **Kitchen:** When you're standing at the sink in this gorgeous kitchen, you'll have a good view of the patio. But if you turn around, you'll see the island cooktop, wall oven, walk-in pantry, and snack bar, all of which make this kitchen such a pleasure.

- **Master Suite:** Somewhat isolated for privacy, this area is ideal for an evening or weekend retreat. Relax in the gracious bedroom or luxuriate in the spa-style bath, with its corner whirlpool tub, large shower, two sinks, and access to the walk-in closet, which measures a full 8 ft. x 10 ft.

- **Mudroom:** No matter whether you live where mud season is as reliable as spring thaws or where rain is a seasonal event, you'll love having a spot to confine the muddy mess.

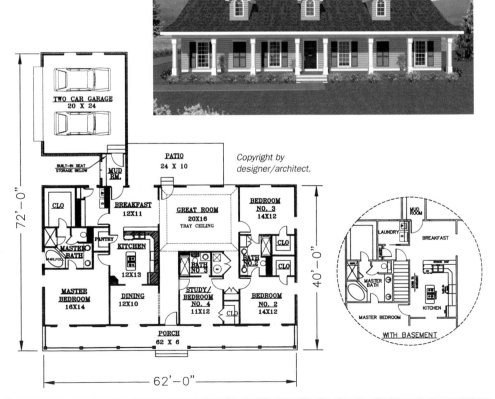

Copyright by designer/architect.

Photo provided by designer/architect.

Plan #121067

Dimensions: 56' W x 59'4" D
Levels: 2
Square Footage: 2,708
Main Level Sq. Ft.: 1,860
Upper Level Sq. Ft.: 848
Bedrooms: 4
Bathrooms: 3½
Foundation: Basement
Materials List Available: Yes
Price Category: F

You'll love this home because it is such a perfect setting for a family and still has room for guests.

Features:

- Family Room: Expect everyone to gather in this room, near the built-in entertainment centers that flank the lovely fireplace.

- Living Room: The other side of the see-through fireplace looks out into this living room, making it an equally welcoming spot in chilly weather.

- Kitchen: This room has a large center island, a corner pantry, and a built-in desk. It also features a breakfast area where friends and family will congregate all day long.

- Master Suite: Enjoy the oversized walk-in closet and bath with a bayed whirlpool tub, double vanity, and separate shower.

Main Level Floor Plan

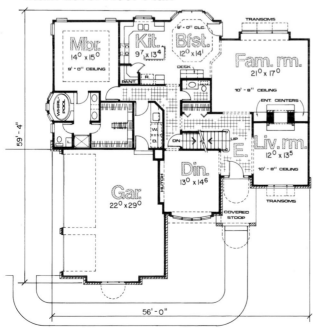

Upper Level Floor Plan

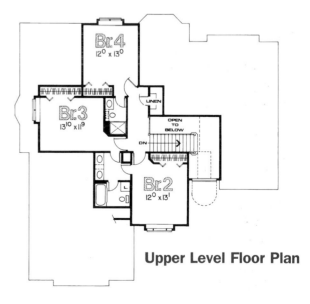

Copyright by designer/architect.

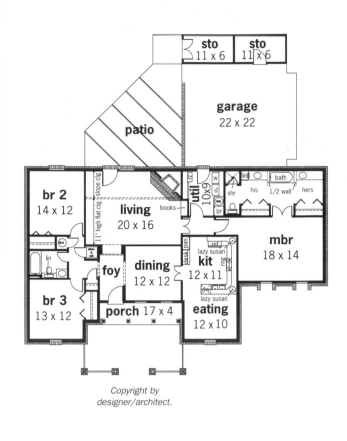

Plan #211039

Dimensions: 62' W x 64' D

Levels: 1

Square Footage: 1,868

Bedrooms: 3

Bathrooms: 2

Foundation: Slab

Materials List Available: Yes

Price Category: D

Images provided by designer/architect.

Copyright by designer/architect.

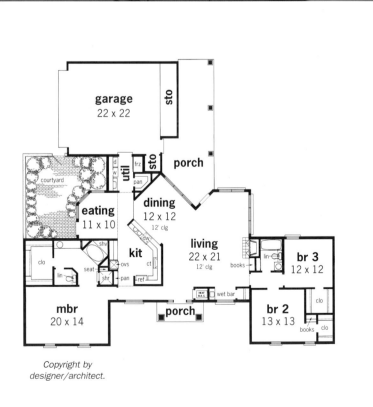

Plan #211049

Dimensions: 73' W x 66' D

Levels: 1

Square Footage: 2,000

Bedrooms: 3

Bathrooms: 2

Foundation: Slab

Materials List Available: Yes

Price Category: D

Images provided by designer/architect.

Copyright by designer/architect.

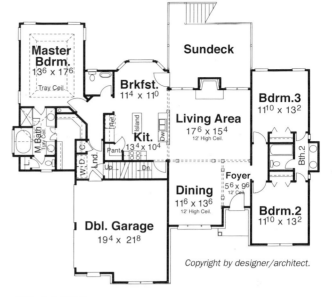

Images provided by designer/architect.

Copyright by designer/architect.

Plan #141007

Dimensions: 65' W x 56'5" D
Levels: 1
Square Footage: 1,854
Bedrooms: 3
Bathrooms: 2½
Foundation: Basement
Materials List Available: No
Price Category: D

SMARTtip

Painting Walls

Paint won't hide imperfections. Rather, it will make them stand out. So shine a bright light at a low angle across the surface to spot problem areas before painting.

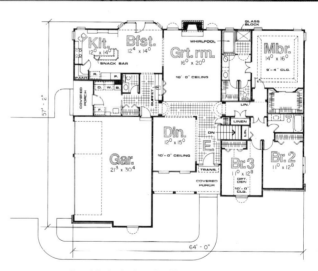

Copyright by designer/architect.

Images provided by designer/architect.

Plan #121057

Dimensions: 64' W x 57'2" D
Levels: 1
Square Footage: 2,311
Bedrooms: 3
Bathrooms: 2½
Foundation: Basement
Materials List Available: Yes
Price Category: E

SMARTtip

Installing Crown Molding

Test for the direction and location of ceiling joists with a stud sensor, by tapping with a hammer to hear the sound of hollow or solid areas or by tapping in test finishing nails.

Images provided by designer/architect.

Plan #261010

Dimensions: 61' W x 38'4" D
Levels: 2
Square Footage: 2,724
Main Level Sq. Ft.: 1,450
Upper Level Sq. Ft.: 1,274
Bedrooms: 3
Bathrooms: 2½
Foundation: Basement
Materials List Available: No
Price Category: F

The minute you see this lovely house with its corner turret, you'll know you've found the home of your dreams.

Features:

- Great Room: A vaulted ceiling and fireplace make this room a natural gathering spot.
- Office: Built-in shelves and a window seat are luxurious touches in this practical room.

- Kitchen: A work island and ample counter and cabinet space make this kitchen a cook's delight.
- Dinette: Two skylights give this rear-facing room extra light in every season of the year.
- Master Suite: Located on the first floor for privacy, this bedroom is endlessly versatile. French doors open to this room, and the master bath has twin sinks, a whirlpool tub, a walk-in shower, and a huge walk-in closet.

Optional Floor Plan for Master Suite

Main Level Floor Plan

Copyright by designer/architect.

Upper Level Floor Plan

Illustration provided by designer/architect.

Plan #141015

Dimensions: 46' W x 36'8" D
Levels: 2
Square Footage: 2,350
Main Level Sq. Ft.: 1,155
Upper Level Sq. Ft.: 1,195
Bedrooms: 4
Bathrooms: 2½
Foundation: Basement
Materials List Available: Yes
Price Category: E

This home offers classic Victorian details combined with modern amenities.

Features:

- Ceiling Height: 9 ft. unless otherwise noted.
- Porch: Enjoy summer breezes on this large wraparound porch, with its classic turret corner.
- Family Room: This room has a fireplace and two sets of French doors. One set of doors leads to the porch; the other leads to a rear sun deck.
- Living Room: This large room at the front of the house is designed for formal entertaining.
- Kitchen: This convenient kitchen features an island and a writing desk.
- Master Bedroom: Enjoy the cozy sitting area in the turret corner. The bedroom offers access to a second story balcony.
- Laundry: The second-floor laundry means you won't have to haul clothing up and down stairs.

Main Level Floor Plan

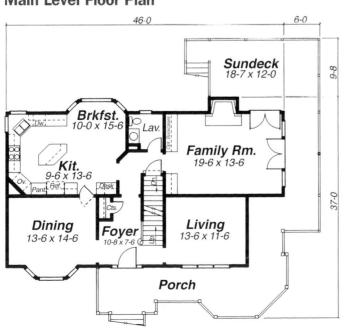

Upper Level Floor Plan

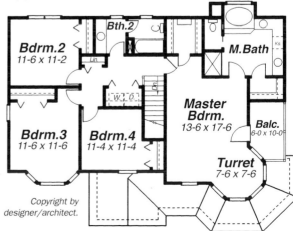

Copyright by designer/architect.

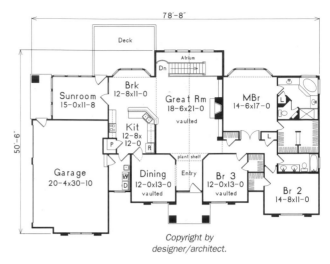

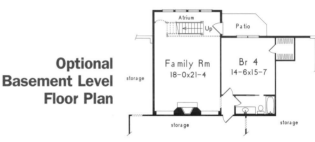

Plan #321037

Dimensions: 78'8" W x 50'6" D

Levels: 1

Square Footage: 2,397

Bedrooms: 3

Bathrooms: 2

Foundation: Basement

Materials List Available: Yes

Price Category: E

Images provided by designer/architect.

Copyright by designer/architect.

Optional Basement Level Floor Plan

Plan #151094

Dimensions: 66'4" W x 66'10" D

Levels: 1

Square Footage: 2,372

Bedrooms: 4

Bathrooms: 3

Foundation: Crawl space, slab (basement option for fee)

Materials List Available: Yes

Price Category: E

Images provided by designer/architect.

Copyright by designer/architect.

Optional Bonus Area Floor Plan

Plan #191010

Dimensions: 62' W x 40' D

Levels: 1

Square Footage: 2,189

Bedrooms: 3

Bathrooms: 2½

Foundation: Crawl space, slab

Materials List Available: No

Price Category: D

Images provided by designer/architect.

Copyright by designer/architect.

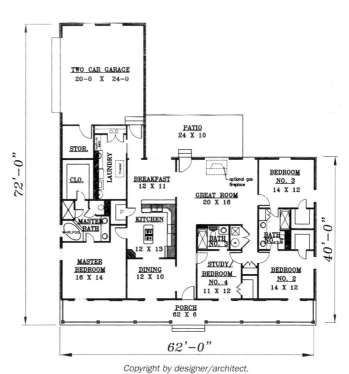

Plan #191008

Dimensions: 62' W x 72' D

Levels: 1

Square Footage: 2,188

Bedrooms: 4

Bathrooms: 3

Foundation: Crawl space or slab

Materials List Available: No

Price Category: D

Images provided by designer/architect.

Copyright by designer/architect.

Photo provided by designer/architect.

Plan #121050

Dimensions: 64' W x 50' D
Levels: 1
Square Footage: 1,996
Bedrooms: 2
Bathrooms: 2
Foundation: Basement
Materials List Available: Yes
Price Category: D

This compact design includes features usually reserved for larger homes and has styling that is typical of more-exclusive home designs.

Features:

- Entry: As you enter this home, you'll see the formal living and dining rooms—both with special ceiling detailing—on either side.

- Great Room: Located in the rear of the home for convenience, this great room is likely to be your favorite spot. The fireplace is framed by transom-topped windows, so you'll love curling up here, no matter what the weather or time of day.

- Kitchen: Ample counter and cabinet space make this kitchen a dream in which to work.

- Master Suite: A tray ceiling and lovely corner windows create an elegant feeling in the bedroom, and two walk-in closets make it easy to keep this space tidy and organized. The private bath has a skylight, corner whirlpool tub, and two separate vanities.

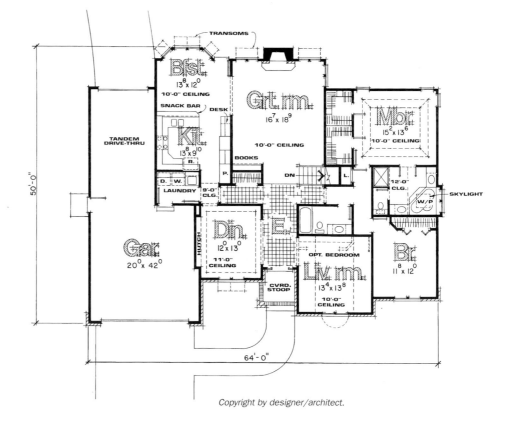

Copyright by designer/architect.

Plan #281001

Dimensions: 54' W x 47' D
Levels: 2
Square Footage: 2,423
Main Level Sq. Ft.: 1,388
Second Level Sq. Ft.: 1,035
Bedrooms: 3
Bathrooms: 2½
Foundation: Basement
Materials List Available: Yes
Price Category: E

This stately manor appears larger than it is and is filled with amenities for comfortable living.

Features:

- Ceiling Height: 8 ft. unless otherwise noted.
- Foyer: The grand entrance porch leads into this spacious two-story foyer, with an open staircase and architecturally interesting angles.

- Balcony: This second story has a balcony that overlooks the foyer.
- Living Room: This delightful living room seems even more spacious, thanks to its sloped vaulted ceiling.
- Dining Room: This elegant dining room shares the living room's sloped vaulted ceiling.
- Kitchen: This beautiful kitchen will be a real pleasure in which to cook. You'll love lingering over morning coffee in the breakfast nook, which is located on the sunny full-bayed wall.
- Family Room: Relax in this roomy family room, with its 9-ft. ceiling.

Photo and Illustration provided by designer/architect.

Main Level Floor Plan

Upper Level Floor Plan

Copyright by designer/architect.

Plan #171006

Dimensions: 68' W x 50' D
Levels: 1
Square Footage: 2,296
Bedrooms: 3
Bathrooms: 2½
Foundation: Slab, crawl space
Materials List Available: Yes
Price Category: E

Images provided by designer/architect.

This classic country farmhouse features a large, open rocking-chair front porch.

Features:

• Ceiling Height: 9 ft. unless otherwise noted.

• Great Room: This spacious great room is perfect for all types of entertaining.

SMARTtip

Window Shades

While decorative hems add interest to roller shades, they also increase the cost. If you're handy with a glue gun, choose one of the trims available at fabric and craft stores, and consider attaching it yourself. Give your shades fancy pulls for an inexpensive dash of pizzazz.

• Dining Room: This dining room is designed to accommodate formal dinner parties as well as less-formal family occasions. After dinner, step from the dining room onto the covered rear porch.

• Family Room: On cool evenings, enjoy the handsome fireplace in this family room. There's plenty of room for all kinds of family activities.

• Kitchen: This is truly a cook's kitchen with its cooktop range and U-shaped open traffic pattern. The snack bar will see lots of use for quick family meals.

• Master Suite: This master suite is separated from the other bedrooms for additional privacy. The large bedroom has a paddle fan and a roomy walk-in closet. The bathroom features his and her vanities, a deluxe bath, and a walk-in shower.

Copyright by designer/architect.

Plan #151117

Dimensions: 66' W x 55' D

Levels: 1

Square Footage: 1,957

Bedrooms: 3

Bathrooms: 3

Foundation: Crawl space, slab, or basement

Materials List Available: Yes

Price Category: D

You'll love this home if you have a family-centered lifestyle and enjoy an active social life.

Features:

- Foyer: A 10-ft. ceiling sets the tone for this home.

- Great Room: A 10-ft. boxed ceiling and fireplace are the highlights of this room, which also has a door leading to the rear covered porch.

- Dining Room: Columns mark the entry from the foyer to this lovely formal dining room.

- Study: Add the French doors from the foyer to transform bedroom 3, with its vaulted ceiling, into a quiet study.

- Kitchen: This large kitchen includes a pantry and shares an eating bar with the adjoining, bayed breakfast room.

- Master Suite: You'll love the access to the rear porch, as well as the bath with every amenity, in this suite.

Illustration provided by designer/architect.

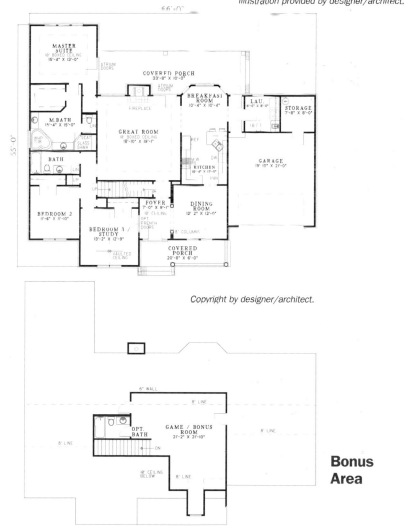

Copyright by designer/architect.

Bonus Area

Plan #231003

Dimensions: 74' W x 69' D

Levels: 1

Square Footage: 2,254

Bedrooms: 2

Bathrooms: 3

Foundation: Crawl space

Materials List Available: No

Price Category: A

Images provided by designer/architect.

Covered Patio

Patio

Great Room
28 x 19-6

Kitchen
19 x 12

Master Br.
15-6 x 16-6

Pan

Comp. Room
8 x 11

Foyer

Den
10 x 11

Util.

Porch

Garage
31-9 x 23-6

Guest Suite
14 x 13

Copyright by designer/architect.

Plan #191015

Dimensions: 74' W x 55' D

Levels: 1

Square Footage: 2,340

Bedrooms: 3

Bathrooms: 2½

Foundation: Crawl space or slab

Materials List Available: No

Price Category: E

Images provided by designer/architect.

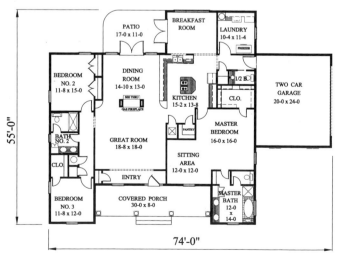

PATIO
17-0 x 11-0

BREAKFAST ROOM

LAUNDRY
10-4 x 11-4

BEDROOM NO. 2
11-8 x 15-0

DINING ROOM
14-10 x 13-0

KITCHEN
15-2 x 13-8

1/2 B

TWO CAR GARAGE
20-0 x 24-0

CLO.

55'-0"

BATH NO. 2

CLO

GREAT ROOM
18-8 x 18-0

PANTRY

MASTER BEDROOM
16-0 x 16-0

SITTING AREA
12-0 x 12-0

ENTRY

BEDROOM NO. 3
11-8 x 12-0

COVERED PORCH
30-0 x 8-0

MASTER BATH
12-0 x 14-0

74'-0"

Copyright by designer/architect.

Main Level Floor Plan

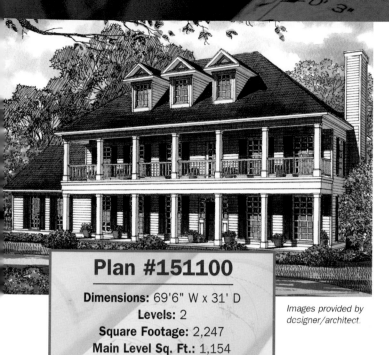

Plan #151100

Dimensions: 69'6" W x 31' D

Levels: 2

Square Footage: 2,247

Main Level Sq. Ft.: 1,154

Upper Level Sq. Ft.: 1,093

Bedrooms: 3

Bathrooms: 2½

Foundation: Crawl space, slab, or basement

Materials List Available: Yes

Price Category: E

Images provided by designer/architect.

Upper Level Floor Plan

Copyright by designer/architect.

Main Level Floor Plan

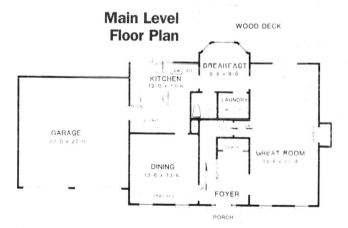

Copyright by designer/architect.

Plan #301006

Dimensions: 60' W x 32' D

Levels: 2

Square Footage: 2,162

Main Level Sq. Ft.: 1,098

Upper Level Sq. Ft.: 1,064

Bedrooms: 3

Bathrooms: 2½

Foundation: Crawl space, slab

Materials List Available: Yes

Price Category: D

Images provided by designer/architect.

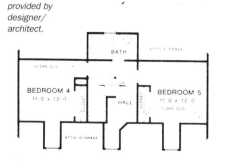

Optional Third Level

Upper Level Floor Plan

Plan #271025

Dimensions: 62' W x 57' D

Levels: 2

Square Footage: 2,223

Main Level Sq. Ft.: 1,689

Upper Level Sq. Ft.: 534

Bedrooms: 3

Bathrooms: 2½

Foundation: Basement

Materials List Available: Yes

Price Category: E

Photo provided by designer/architect.

This traditional home's unique design combines a dynamic, exciting exterior with a fantastic floor plan.

Features:

- **Living Room:** To the left of the column-lined, barrel-vaulted entry, this inviting space features a curved wall and corner windows.

- **Dining Room:** A tray ceiling enhances this formal meal room.

- **Kitchen:** This island-equipped kitchen includes a corner pantry and a built-in desk. Nearby, the sunny breakfast room opens onto a backyard deck via sliding glass doors.

- **Family Room:** A corner bank of windows provides a glassy backdrop for this room's handsome fireplace. Munchies may be served on the snack bar from the breakfast nook.

- **Master Suite:** This main-floor retreat is simply stunning, and includes a vaulted ceiling, access to a private courtyard, and of course, a sumptuous bath with every creature comfort.

Main Level Floor Plan

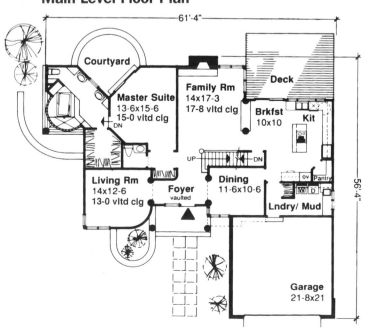

Upper Level Floor Plan

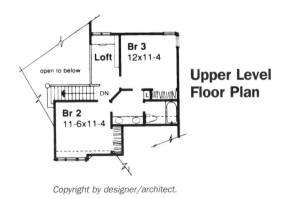

Copyright by designer/architect.

Photo provided by designer/architect.

Plan #271027

Dimensions: 61' W x 44' D
Levels: 2
Square Footage: 2,463
Main Level Sq. Ft.: 1,380
Upper Level Sq. Ft.: 1,083
Bedrooms: 4
Bathrooms: 2½
Foundation: Basement
Materials List Available: Yes
Price Category: D

This post-modern design uses half-round transom windows and a barrel-vaulted porch to lend elegance to its facade.

Features:

- Living Room: A vaulted ceiling and a striking fireplace enhance this formal gathering space.

- Dining Room: Introduced from the living room by square columns, this formal dining room is just steps from the kitchen.

- Kitchen: Thoroughly modern in its design, this walk-through kitchen includes an island cooktop and a large pantry. Nearby, a sunny, bayed breakfast area offers sliding-glass-door access to an angled backyard deck.

- Family Room: Columns provide an elegant preface to this fun gathering spot, which sports a vaulted ceiling and easy access to the deck.

- Master suite: A vaulted ceiling crowns this luxurious space, which includes a private bath and bright windows.

Main Level Floor Plan

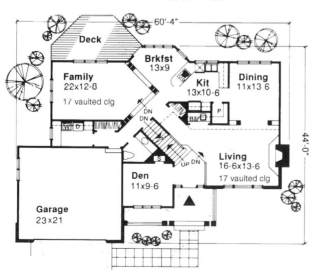

Upper Level Floor Plan

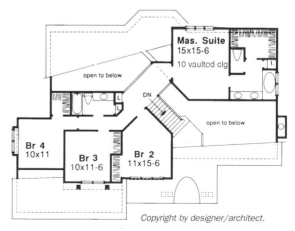

Copyright by designer/architect.

Plan #141017

Dimensions: 82' W x 49' D

Levels: 2

Square Footage: 2,480

Main Level Sq. Ft.: 1,581

Upper Level Sq. Ft.: 899

Bedrooms: 4

Bathrooms: 3½

Foundation: Basement, crawl space, or slab

Materials List Available: No

Price Category: E

Illustration provided by designer/architect.

Main Level Floor Plan

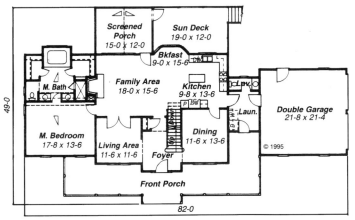

Copyright by designer/architect.

You'll enjoy cool summer breezes on the wraparound porch of this spacious home.

Features:

- Ceiling Height: 9 ft.

- Family Room: Through French doors leading from the living room you will enter the family domain. This large and open space features a handsome fireplace.

- Rear Porch: Accessible from the family room, this porch is screened in to create a comfortable, private warm-weather retreat.

- Master Suite: This luxurious suite is located on the first floor for added privacy. The master bath features separate walk-in closets and vanities.

- Kitchen: This open sunny kitchen has an island for food preparation.

- Laundry: This large laundry is conveniently located between the kitchen and the garage.

Upper Level Floor Plan

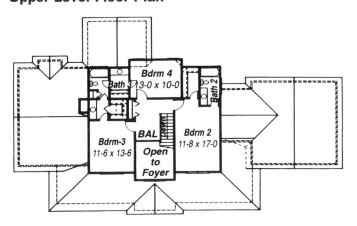

Plan #101005

Dimensions: 63' W x 57'2" D

Levels: 1

Square Footage: 1,992

Bedrooms: 3

Bathrooms: 2½

Foundation: Slab, crawl space, basement

Materials List Available: Yes

Price Category: D

Illustrations provided by designer/architect.

Rear View

This midsized ranch is accented with Palladian windows and inviting front porch.

Features:

- Ceiling Height: 9 ft. unless otherwise noted.

- Special Ceilings: Tray or vaulted ceilings adorn the living room, family room, dining room, and master suite.

- Kitchen: This bright and airy kitchen is designed to be a pleasure in which to work. It shares a big bay window with the contiguous breakfast room.

- Breakfast Room: The light streaming in from the bay window makes this the perfect place to linger with coffee and the Sunday paper.

- Master Suite: This exceptional suite has a sitting area and direct access to the deck, as well as a sitting area, full-featured bath, and spacious walk-in closet.

- Secondary Bedrooms: The other bedrooms each measure about 13 ft. x 11 ft. They have walk-in closets and share a "Jack-and-Jill" bath.

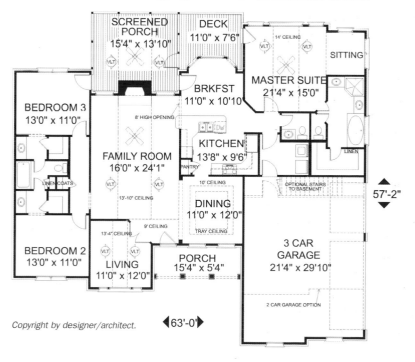

Copyright by designer/architect.

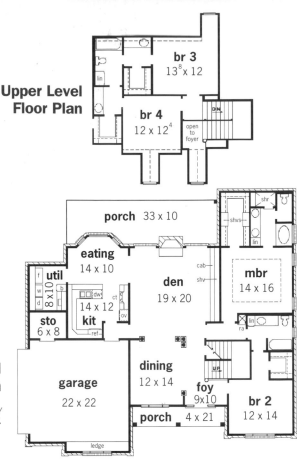

Plan #201103

Dimensions: 57'10" W x 56'10" D

Levels: 2

Square Footage: 2,490

Main Level Sq. Ft.: 1,911

Upper Level Sq. Ft.: 579

Bedrooms: 4

Bathrooms: 3

Foundation: Crawl space, slab, or basement

Materials List Available: Yes

Price Category: E

Images provided by designer/architect.

Upper Level Floor Plan

br 3
13⁸ x 12

br 4
12 x 12⁴

open to foyer

Main Level Floor Plan

Copyright by designer/architect.

porch 33 x 10

eating 14 x 10

util 8 x 10

den 19 x 20

mbr 14 x 16

kit 14 x 12

sto 6 x 8

garage 22 x 22

dining 12 x 14

foy 9x10

porch 4 x 21

br 2 12 x 14

ledge

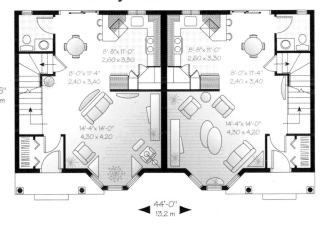

Plan #181140

Dimensions: 44' W x 26'6" D

Levels: 2

Square Footage: 2,172

Main Level Sq. Ft.: 1,086

Upper Level Sq. Ft.: 1,086

Bedrooms: 3 each unit

Bathrooms: 1½ each unit

Foundation: Basement

Materials List Available: Yes

Price Category: D

Images provided by designer/architect.

Two-Family Main Level Floor Plan

26'-6"
7,95 m

44'-0"
13,2 m

8'-8"x 11'-0"
2,60 x 3,30

8'-0"x 11'-4"
2,40 x 3,40

14'-4"x 14'-0"
4,30 x 4,20

Two-Family Upper Level Floor Plan

Copyright by designer/architect.

8'-8"x 10'-4"
2,60 x 3,10

9'-8"x 9'-0"
2,90 x 2,70

11'-0"x 12'-0"
3,30 x 3,60

11'-0"x 17'-8"
3,30 x 5,30

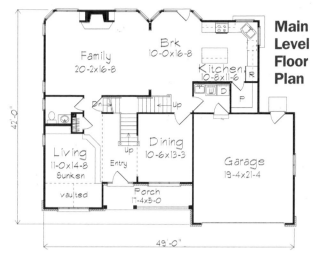

Main Level Floor Plan

Family
20-2x16-8

Brk
10-0x16-8

Kitchen
10-8x11-6

Living
11-0x14-8
Sunken

Dining
10-6x13-3

Garage
19-4x21-4

Entry

Porch
17-4x5-0
vaulted

42'-0"

49'-0"

Plan #321050

Dimensions: 49' W x 42' D

Levels: 2

Square Footage: 2,336

Main Level Sq. Ft.: 1,291

Upper Level Sq. Ft.: 1,045

Bedrooms: 4

Bathrooms: 2½

Foundation: Basement

Materials List Available: Yes

Price Category: E

Images provided by designer/architect.

Upper Level Floor Plan

Copyright by designer/architect.

Br 2
11-0x10-0

MBr
13-0x17-8
vaulted

Br 3
11-0x11-0

Br 4
10-6x11-0

open to below

vaulted

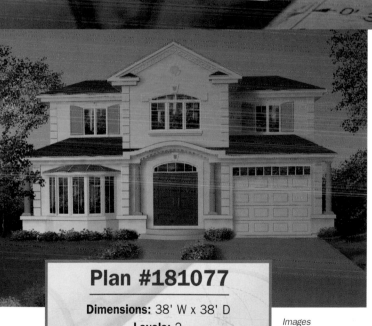

Plan #181077

Dimensions: 38' W x 38' D

Levels: 2

Square Footage: 2,119

Main Level Sq. Ft.: 1,087

Upper Level Sq. Ft.: 1,032

Bedrooms: 4

Bathrooms: 2½

Foundation: Full basement

Materials List Available: Yes

Price Category: D

Images provided by designer/ architect.

Main Level Floor Plan

38'-0"
11,4 m

38'-0"
11,4 m

Upper Level Floor Plan

Copyright by designer/architect.

Plan #261004

Dimensions: 82' W x 48'8" D

Levels: 2

Square Footage: 2,707

Main Level Sq. Ft.: 1,484

Upper Level Sq. Ft.: 1,223

Bedrooms: 3

Bathrooms: 2½

Foundation: Basement

Materials List Available: No

Price Category: F

Inside the classic Victorian exterior is a spacious home filled with contemporary amenities that the whole family is sure to love.

Features:

- **Porch:** This wraparound porch provides space for entertaining or sitting out to enjoy the evening.

- **Foyer:** Two stories high, the foyer opens to the formal dining room and front parlor.

- **Family Room:** French doors open from the parlor into this room, with its cozy fireplace.

- **Sunroom:** A cathedral ceiling adds drama to this versatile room.

- **Kitchen:** A pantry and a work island make this well-planned kitchen even more convenient.

- **Master Suite:** A tray ceiling and French doors to the bath give the bedroom elegance, while the sumptuous bath features a deluxe tub, walk-in shower, and split vanities.

Images provided by designer/architect.

Main Level Floor Plan

Copyright by designer/architect.

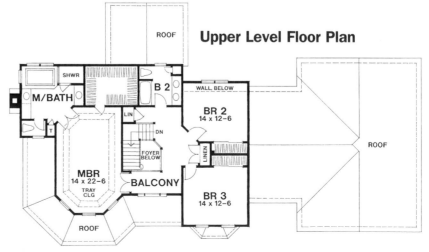

Upper Level Floor Plan

Plan #261007

Dimensions: 58' W x 44' D

Levels: 2

Square Footage: 2,635

Main Level Sq. Ft.: 1,435

Upper Level Sq. Ft.: 1,200

Bedrooms: 4

Bathrooms: 2½

Foundation: Basement

Materials List Available: No

Price Category: F

Images provided by designer/architect.

You'll love the dramatic roofline of this gracious home, which is as carefully designed inside as it is on the exterior.

Features:

- **Foyer:** This 2-story area opens to the formal dining and living rooms.

- **Living Room:** A pocket door between this room and the family room allows for plenty of space for large gatherings.

- **Dining Room:** Convenient to the kitchen, this room can be used for family meals as well as formal parties.

- **Family Room:** Enjoy the fireplace in this comfortable room.

- **Den:** You'll love the quiet and privacy here.

- **Master Suite:** This luxurious suite features a large walk-in closet and bath with two vanities, a corner whirlpool tub, and a separate shower.

Main Level Floor Plan

Copyright by designer/architect.

Upper Level Floor Plan

Main Level Floor Plan

Images provided by designer/architect.

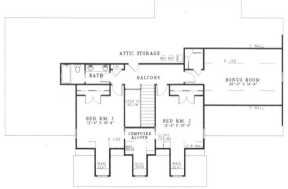

Upper Level Floor Plan

Copyright by designer/architect.

Plan #151015

Dimensions: 72'4" W x 48'4" D

Levels: 2

Square Footage: 2,789

Main Level Sq. Ft.: 1,977

Upper Level Sq. Ft.: 812

Bedrooms: 4

Bathrooms: 3

Foundation: Basement, crawl space, or slab

Materials List Available: Yes

Price Category: F

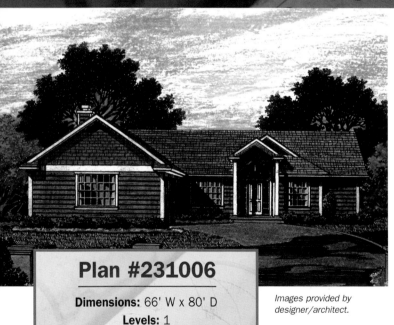

Plan #231006

Dimensions: 66' W x 80' D

Levels: 1

Square Footage: 1,961

Bedrooms: 3

Bathrooms: 2

Foundation: Crawl space

Materials List Available: No

Price Category: A

Images provided by designer/architect.

Copyright by designer/architect.

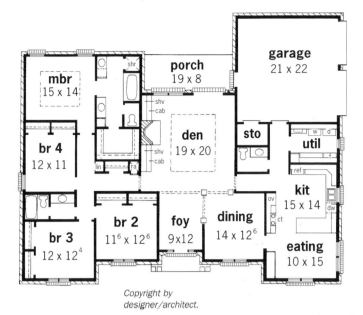

Images provided by designer/architect.

Plan #201061

Dimensions: 64'10" W x 54'10" D

Levels: 1

Square Footage: 2,387

Bedrooms: 4

Bathrooms: 2½

Foundation: Crawl space, slab, or basement

Materials List Available: Yes

Price Category: E

Copyright by designer/architect.

Floor plan labels (Plan #201061):
- mbr 15 x 14
- br 4 12 x 11
- br 3 12 x 12⁴
- br 2 11⁶ x 12⁶
- foy 9 x 12
- dining 14 x 12⁶
- porch 19 x 8
- den 19 x 20
- sto
- garage 21 x 22
- util
- kit 15 x 14
- eating 10 x 15

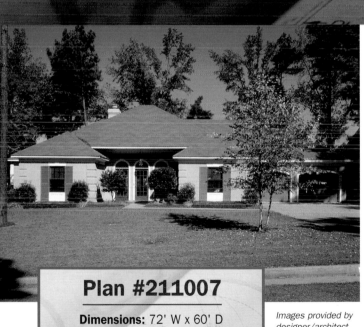

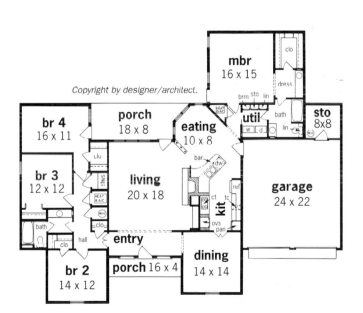

Copyright by designer/architect.

Floor plan labels (Plan #211007):
- mbr 16 x 15
- br 4 16 x 11
- br 3 12 x 12
- br 2 14 x 12
- porch 18 x 8
- living 20 x 18
- eating 10 x 8
- util
- sto 8x8
- garage 24 x 22
- kit
- dining 14 x 14
- entry
- porch 16 x 4

Plan #211007

Dimensions: 72' W x 60' D

Levels: 1

Square Footage: 2,252

Bedrooms: 4

Bathrooms: 2

Foundation: Slab

Materials List Available: Yes

Price Category: E

Images provided by designer/architect.

Plan #261008

Dimensions: 68' W x 64'6" D

Levels: 2

Square Footage: 2,226

Main Level Sq. Ft.: 1,689

Upper Level Sq. Ft.: 537

Bedrooms: 4

Bathrooms: 3

Foundation: Basement

Materials List Available: No

Price Category: E

Images provided by designer/architect.

You'll love the elements that transform this design into an amenity-filled home.

Features:

- Great Room: The upper-story balcony looking onto the foyer in the front and this great room in the rear adds elegance, while the high ceilings add to the spacious feeling.

- Sunroom: Adjoining the dining room and kitchen, this room is ideal for an indoor garden, extra dining area, or sitting space.

- Kitchen: This well-designed kitchen is open to the main living spaces and features a breakfast bar, walk-in pantry, and double sink in the corner.

- Master Suite: Privacy is assured in this suite. The double vanities, huge walk-in closet, whirlpool tub, and walk-in shower are luxurious touches.

- Garage: The angled design of this front entrance garage is as attractive as it is practical. You'll find space for two cars and a workshop here.

Main Level Floor Plan

Copyright by designer/architect.

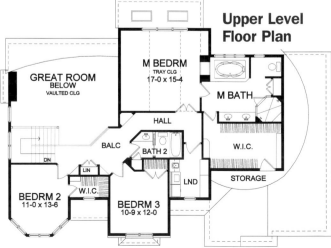

Upper Level Floor Plan

Plan #261005

Dimensions: 64' W x 31' D

Levels: 2

Square Footage: 2,419

Main Level Sq. Ft.: 1,228

Upper Level Sq. Ft.: 1,191

Bedrooms: 4

Bathrooms: 2½

Foundation: Basement

Materials List Available: No

Price Category: E

Images provided by designer/architect.

You'll love the spacious rooms and convenient layout of this lovely Colonial-style home.

Features:

- **Ceilings.** Ceilings are 9 ft. tall or higher, adding to the airy feeling inside this home.

- **Foyer:** This two-story foyer gives a warm welcome.

- **Family Room:** Everyone will gather in this well-positioned room, with its handsome fireplace and generous dimensions.

- **Living Room:** Both this room and the dining room are ideal for formal entertaining.

- **Kitchen:** A cook's dream, this kitchen has ample counter space, a large island, and a pantry.

- **Master Suite:** Enjoy the luxury of the walk-in closet, dual vanities, whirlpool tub, and shower here.

- **Additional Bedrooms:** Extensive closet space makes it easy to live in each of the bedrooms.

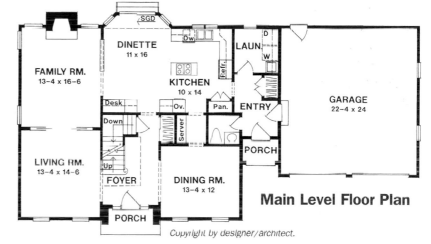

Main Level Floor Plan

Copyright by designer/architect.

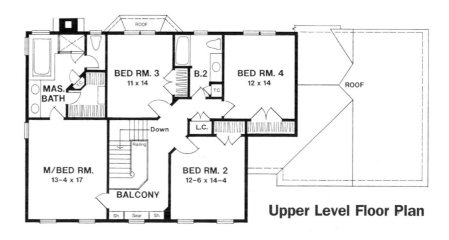

Upper Level Floor Plan

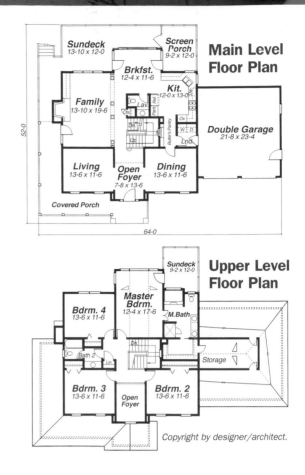

Main Level Floor Plan

Sundeck 13-10 x 12-0

Screen Porch 9-2 x 12-0

Brkfst. 12-4 x 11-6

Kit. 12-0 x 13-0

Family 13-10 x 19-6

Double Garage 21-8 x 23-4

Living 13-6 x 11-6

Open Foyer 7-8 x 13-6

Dining 13-6 x 11-6

Covered Porch

52-0

64-0

Images provided by designer/architect.

Upper Level Floor Plan

Sundeck 9-2 x 12-0

Master Bdrm. 12-4 x 17-6

M.Bath

Bdrm. 4 13-6 x 11-6

Bath 2

Storage

Bdrm. 3 13-6 x 11-6

Open Foyer

Bdrm. 2 13-6 x 11-6

Copyright by designer/architect.

Plan #141016

Dimensions: 64' W x 52' D

Levels: 2

Square Footage: 2,416

Main Level Sq. Ft.: 1,250

Upper Level Sq. Ft.: 1,166

Bedrooms: 4

Bathrooms: 2½

Foundation: Basement

Materials List Available: Yes

Price Category: E

Images provided by designer/architect.

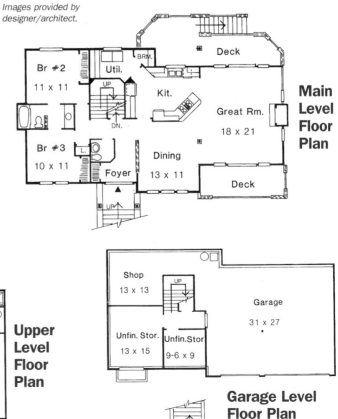

Main Level Floor Plan

Br #2 11 x 11

Util.

BRM.

Deck

Kit.

Great Rm. 18 x 21

Br #3 10 x 11

Dining 13 x 11

Foyer

Deck

UP

DN.

UP

Upper Level Floor Plan

DN.

M.Br 13 x 20-6

OPEN TO FOYER

Garage Level Floor Plan

Shop 13 x 13

UP

Garage 31 x 27

Unfin. Stor. 13 x 15

Unfin.Stor 9-6 x 9

UP

Copyright by designer/architect.

Plan #231020

Dimensions: 53' W x 35' D

Levels: 2

Square Footage: 2,166

Main Level Sq. Ft.: 1,538

Upper Level Sq. Ft.: 628

Bedrooms: 3

Bathrooms: 2½

Foundation: Slab, basement

Materials List Available: No

Price Category: D

Images provided by designer/architect.

Plan #211048

Dimensions: 66' W x 60'8" D

Levels: 1

Square Footage: 2,002

Bedrooms: 3

Bathrooms: 2

Foundation: Crawl space

Materials List Available: Yes

Price Category: D

Copyright by designer/architect.

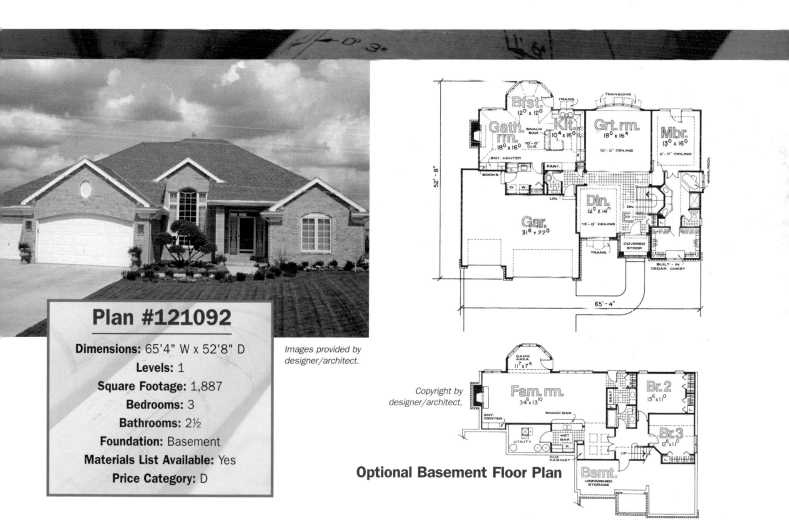

Plan #121092

Dimensions: 65'4" W x 52'8" D

Levels: 1

Square Footage: 1,887

Bedrooms: 3

Bathrooms: 2½

Foundation: Basement

Materials List Available: Yes

Price Category: D

Images provided by designer/architect.

Copyright by designer/architect.

Optional Basement Floor Plan

Plan #221015

Dimensions: 69'8" W x 46' D

Levels: 1

Square Footage: 1,926

Bedrooms: 3

Bathrooms: 2½

Foundation: Basement

Materials List Available: No

Price Category: D

Illustration provided by designer/architect.

You'll love the open plan in this lovely ranch and admire its many features, which are usually reserved for much larger homes.

Features:

- Ceiling Height: 8 ft.

- Great Room: A vaulted ceiling and tall windows surrounding the centrally located fireplace give distinction to this handsome room.

- Dining Room: Positioned just off the entry, this formal room makes a lovely spot for quiet dinner parties.

- Dining Nook: This nook sits between the kitchen and the great room. Central doors in the bayed area open to the backyard.

- Kitchen: An island will invite visitors while you cook in this well-planned kitchen, with its corner pantry and ample counter space.

- Master Suite: A tray ceiling, bay window, walk-in closet, and bath with whirlpool tub, dual-sink vanity, and standing shower pamper you here.

Rear Elevation

Copyright by designer/architect.

Images provided by designer/architect.

Plan #171004

Dimensions: 72' W x 52' D
Levels: 1
Square Footage: 2,256
Bedrooms: 3
Bathrooms: 2
Foundation: Slab, crawl space
Materials List Available: Yes
Price Category: E

This home greets you with a front porch featuring a high roofline and stucco columns.

Copyright by designer/architect.

Features:

- Ceiling Height: 9 ft. unless otherwise noted.
- Foyer: Step through the front porch into this impressive foyer, which opens to the formal dining room and the study.
- Dining Room: This dining room's 12-ft. ceiling enhances its sense of spaciousness, with plenty of room for large dinner parties.
- Family Room: With plenty of room for all kinds of family activities, this room also has a 12 ft. ceiling, a fireplace, and two paddle fans.
- Kitchen: This kitchen has all the counter space you'll need to prepare your favorite recipes. There's a pantry, desk, and angled snack bar.
- Master Bedroom: This master retreat is separate from the other bedrooms for added privacy. It has an elegant, high step-up ceiling and a paddle fan.
- Master Bath: This master bath features a large walk-in closet, deluxe corner bath, walk-in shower, and his and her vanities.

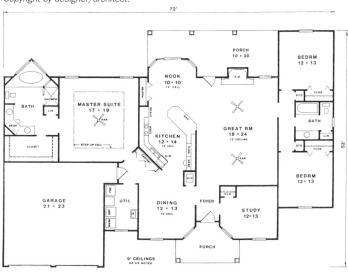

SMARTtip

Windows – Privacy

You can easily stencil a work of art onto a windowpane, perhaps only as a border around the edge. Choose or create a design that gives you as little or as much privacy and light control as you need. Use a ready-made stencil or a piece of openwork fabric such as lace, or mask a design onto the glass using tape and a razor knife. Then apply glass paint or frosted glass spray, referring to the instructions and guidelines that come with the product.

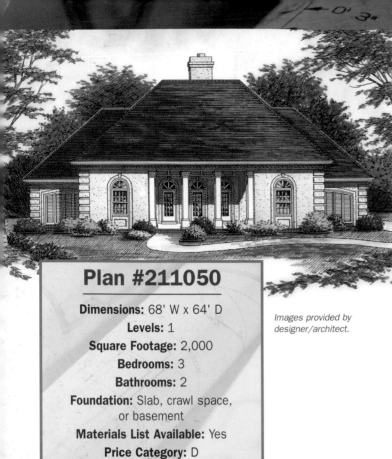

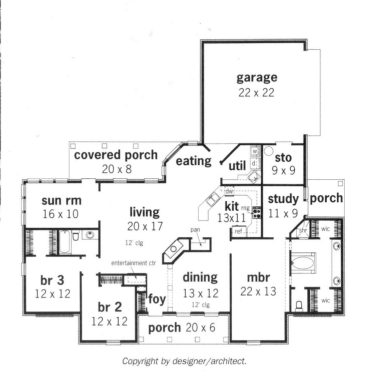

Plan #211050

Dimensions: 68' W x 64' D

Levels: 1

Square Footage: 2,000

Bedrooms: 3

Bathrooms: 2

Foundation: Slab, crawl space, or basement

Materials List Available: Yes

Price Category: D

Images provided by designer/architect.

Copyright by designer/architect.

Plan #151005

Dimensions: 58' W x 54'10" D

Levels: 1

Square Footage: 1,940

Bedrooms: 4

Bathrooms: 2

Foundation: Basement, crawl space, or slab

Materials List Available: Yes

Price Category: D

Images provided by designer/architect.

Copyright by designer/architect.

Plan #151014

Dimensions: 70'2" W x 51'4" D

Levels: 2

Square Footage: 2,698

Main Level Sq. Ft.: 1,813

Upper Level Sq. Ft.: 885

Bedrooms: 5

Bathrooms: 3

Foundation: Crawl space, slab, optional basement for fee

Price Category: D

Photo provided by designer/architect.

A comfortable front porch welcomes you into this home that features a balcony over the great room, a study, and a kitchen designed for gourmet cooks.

Features:

- Ceiling Height: 9 ft.

- Front Porch: Stately 12-in.-wide pillars form the entryway.

- Foyer: Open to upper story.

- Great Room: A fireplace, vaulted 9-ft. ceiling, and balcony from the second floor add character to this lovely room.

- Dining Room: Open to the kitchen for convenience.

- Kitchen: A large walk-in pantry, well-designed work areas, and eat-in bar make this room a treasure.

- Breakfast Room: Enjoy this spot that opens to both the kitchen and a large covered porch at the rear of the house.

- Study: This quiet room has French doors leading to the yard.

- Master Suite: This spacious area has cozy window seats as well as his and her walk-in closets. The master bathroom is fitted with a whirlpool tub, a glass shower, and his and her sinks.

Upper Level Floor Plan

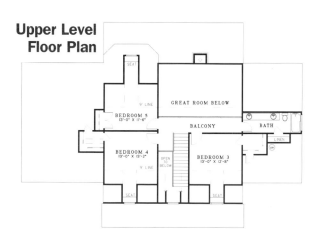

Main Level Floor Plan

Copyright by designer/architect.

Plan #121001

Dimensions: 56' W x 58' D

Levels: 1

Square Footage: 1,911

Bedrooms: 3

Bathrooms: 2

Foundation: Basement

Materials List Available: Yes

Price Category: D

Photo provided by designer/architect.

Detailed, soaring ceilings and top-notch amenities set this distinctive home apart.

Features:

- Ceiling Height: 8 ft. except as noted.

- Great Room: A soaring ceiling and six tall transom-topped windows make this a light and airy spot for entertaining.

- Formal Dining Room: The entry enjoys a pleasing view of this dining room's detailed 12-ft. ceiling and picture window.

- Great Room: At the back of the home, a see-through fireplace in this great room is joined by a built-in entertainment center.

- Hearth Room: This bayed room shares the see-through fireplace with the great room.

- Master Suite: Enjoy the stars and the sun in the private bath's whirlpool and separate shower. The bath features the same decorative ceiling as the dining room.

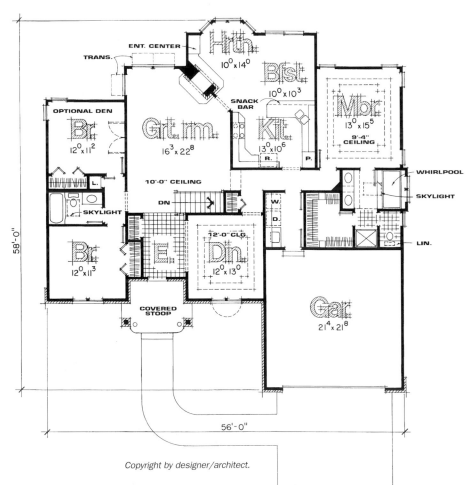

Copyright by designer/architect.

Plan #321051

Dimensions: 69'8" W x 46' D

Levels: 2

Square Footage: 2,624

Main Level Sq. Ft.: 1,774

Upper Level Sq. Ft.: 850

Bedrooms: 4

Bathrooms: 2½

Foundation: Basement

Materials List Available: Yes

Price Category: F

If you're looking for a home that deserves to be called "grand" and "elegant," you will love this spacious beauty.

Images provided by designer/architect.

Features:

- **Entryway:** Two stories high, this area sets the tone for the whole house.

- **Great Room:** The 18-ft. ceiling in this room gives a bright and airy feeling that the three magnificent Palladian windows surely enhance.

- **Dining Room:** A classic colonnade forms the entry to this lovely bayed room.

- **Kitchen:** Designed for gourmet cooks who love efficient work spaces, this kitchen will delight the whole family.

- **Master Suite:** Relax in the comfort of this luxurious suite at the end of the day. You'll find walk-in closets, a large bay window, and plant shelves in the bedroom, as well as a sunken tub in the bathroom.

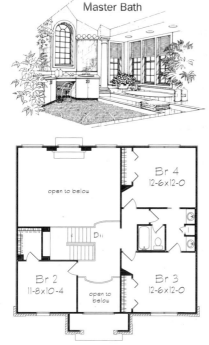

Master Bath

Main Level Floor Plan

Copyright by designer/architect.

Upper Level Floor Plan

Expandable Homes

N ew homes with expandable possibilities are the perfect solution for families that may still be growing but are ready to put down roots now. A plan that offers 1,500 to 2,500 sq. ft. of ready living space could be just right for your young family, especially if staying put is important to you—financially or otherwise. A house this size has much to offer with features that include welcoming gathering places—a great room or a family room and a spacious family kitchen with separate but flexible zones for different activities such as cooking, playing, or just hanging out. Plus, there are important private havens—a restful master suite for pampering the parents and bedrooms where the kids can be kids.

This comfortable home, above, has expandable areas upstairs.

A house that has the potential for expansion, left, is a practical choice for a growing family.

A nook under the stairs, below, is a cozy spot for a small desk.

But the best part of the house may be it's potential additional living space of 1,000 sq. ft. or more that you can use for anything. Add more bedrooms, a grandparents' suite, a home office, a gym, or more storage. Put together a "power laundry room" where you and the kids can do all the messy stuff together—cleaning, crafting, sewing—or just hang out while getting the chores done. Why move when you can have the space you need by expanding upstairs, and sometimes downstairs? If you like the property, the neighbors, and the schools, a house with room to grow may be your exact fit.

Photo provided by designer/architect.

Plan #311003

Dimensions: 70'10" W x 65'4" D
Levels: 2
Square Footage: 2,428
Main Level Sq. Ft.: 2,348
Upper Level Sq. Ft.: 80
Bedrooms: 3
Bathrooms: 2½
Foundation: Crawl space, slab
Materials List Available: Y
Price Category: E

If you admire the gracious colonnaded porch, curved brick steps, and stunning front windows, you'll fall in love with the interior of this home.

Features:

- **Great Room:** Enjoy the vaulted ceiling, balcony from the upper level, and fireplace with flanking windows that let you look out to the patio.

- **Dining Room:** Columns define this formal room, which is adjacent to the breakfast room.

- **Kitchen:** A bayed sink area and extensive curved bar provide visual interest in this well-designed kitchen, which every cook will love.

- **Breakfast Room:** Huge windows let the sun shine into this room, which is open to the kitchen.

- **Master Suite:** The sitting area is open to the rear porch for a special touch in this gorgeous suite. Two walk-in closets and a vaulted ceiling and double vanity in the bath will make you feel completely pampered.

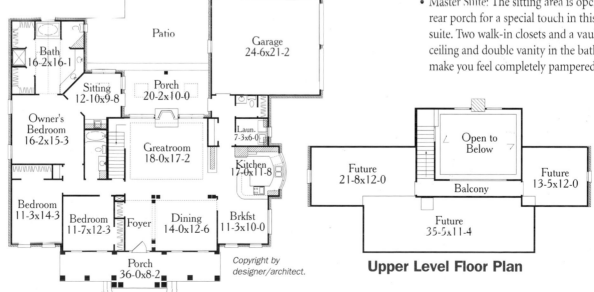

Main Level Floor Plan

Bath 16-2x16-1
Patio
Garage 24-6x21-2
Sitting 12-10x9-8
Porch 20-2x10-0
Owner's Bedroom 16-2x15-3
Greatroom 18-0x17-2
Laun. 7-3x6-0
Kitchen 17-0x11-8
Bedroom 11-3x14-3
Bedroom 11-7x12-3
Foyer
Dining 14-0x12-6
Brkfst 11-3x10-0
Porch 36-0x8-2

Copyright by designer/architect.

Upper Level Floor Plan

Open to Below
Future 21-8x12-0
Future 13-5x12-0
Balcony
Future 35-5x11-4

Upper Level Floor Plan

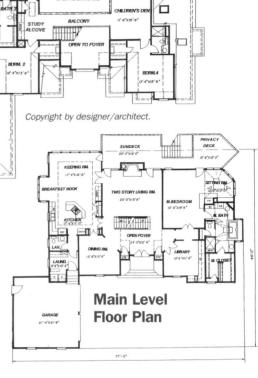

Copyright by designer/architect.

Plan #141034

Dimensions: 77' W x 66' D

Levels: 2

Square Footage: 3,588

Main Level Sq. Ft.: 2,329

Upper Level Sq. Ft.: 1,259

Bedrooms: 4

Bathrooms: 3 full, 2 half

Foundation: Basement

Materials List Available: Yes

Price Category: H

Images provided by designer/architect.

Main Level Floor Plan

Plan #251010

Dimensions: 53' W x 52' D

Levels: 2

Square Footage: 1,854

Main Level Sq. Ft.: 1,317

Upper Level Sq. Ft.: 537

Bedrooms: 3

Bathrooms: 2½

Foundation: Basement

Materials List Available: Yes

Price Category: D

Images provided by designer/architect.

Main Level Floor Plan

Upper Level Floor Plan

Copyright by designer/architect.

Plan #181034

Dimensions: 60' W x 44' D

Levels: 2

Square Footage: 2,687

Main Level Sq. Ft.: 1,297

Upper Level Sq. Ft.: 1,390

Bedrooms: 3

Bathrooms: 2½

Foundation: Full basement

Materials List Available: Yes

Price Category: F

Main Level Floor Plan

Images provided by designer/architect.

Upper Level Floor Plan

Copyright by designer/architect.

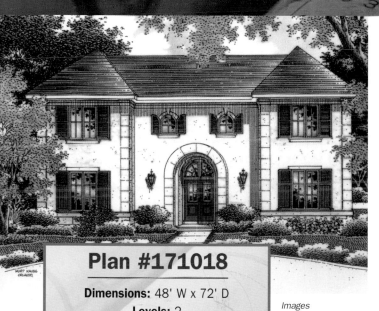

Plan #171018

Dimensions: 48' W x 72' D

Levels: 2

Square Footage: 2,599

Main Level Sq. Ft.: 1,967

Upper Level Sq. Ft.: 632

Bedrooms: 4

Bathrooms: 4

Foundation: Slab, crawl space

Materials List Available: Yes

Price Category: E

Images provided by designer/architect.

Upper Level Floor Plan

Main Level Floor Plan

Copyright by designer/architect.

Plan #161038

Dimensions: 58'6" W x 49' D

Levels: 2

Square Footage: 2,209

Main Level Sq. Ft.: 1,542

Upper Level Sq. Ft.: 667

Bedrooms: 3

Bathrooms: 2½

Foundation: Slab

Materials List Available: No

Price Category: E

Images provided by designer/architect.

Brick trim, sidelights, and a transom window at the entry are a few of the many features that convey the elegance and style of this exciting home.

Features:

- **Great Room:** This great room is truly the centerpiece of this elegant home. The ceiling at the rear wall is 14 ft. and slopes forward to a second floor study loft that overlooks the magnificent fireplace and entertainment alcove. The high ceiling continues through the foyer, showcasing a deluxe staircase.

- **Kitchen:** This modern kitchen is designed for efficient work patterns and serves both the formal dining room and breakfast area.

- **Master Suite:** The highlight of this master suite is a wonderful whirlpool tub. Also

included are two matching vanities and a large walk-in closet.

- **Bonus Room:** A bonus room above the garage completes this exciting home.

Rear Elevation

Main Level Floor Plan

Copyright by designer/architect.

Upper Level Floor Plan

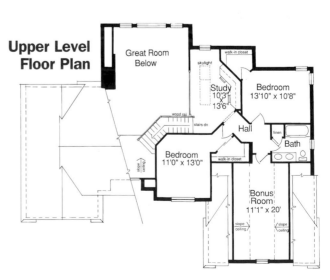

Illustration provided by designer/architect.

Plan #181101

Dimensions: 58' W x 43' D
Levels: 2
Square Footage: 1,936
Main Level Sq. Ft.: 1,044
Second Level Sq. Ft.: 892
Bedrooms: 3
Bathrooms: 2½
Foundation: Basement
Materials List Available: Yes
Price Category: D

This lovely Victorian-style home features a double columned porch and a two-story bay window.

Features:

- Ceiling Height: 8 ft.
- Home Office: Although Victorian in style, the interior of this home is designed for the 21st-century lifestyle as evidenced by this terrific home office. You'll have plenty of natural light by which to work, thanks to the multi-paned bay window.
- Kitchen: This large, sun-drenched kitchen boasts a breakfast area, a center island, double sinks, a pantry, and sliding-glass-door access

to the backyard, as well as access to the front porch.
- Living Room: This inviting front room is separated from the dining room by a stunning see-through fireplace.
- Dining Room: This dining room is conveniently located next to the kitchen.
- Master Suite: This bedroom features a walk-in closet. The stunning private bath includes dual vanities and a tub set into a bay window.

Main Level Floor Plan

Upper Level Floor Plan

Plan #131027

Dimensions: 62'4" W x 53'6" D
Levels: 2
Square Footage: 2,567
Main Level Sq. Ft.: 2,017
Upper Level Sq. Ft.: 550
Bedrooms: 4
Bathrooms: 3
Foundation: Crawl space, slab, or basement
Materials List Available: Yes
Price Category: F

Images provided by designer/architect.

The features of this home are so good that you may have trouble imagining all of them at once.

Features:

- **Great Room:** Imagine a stepped ceiling, corner fireplace, built-media center, and wall of windows with a glass door to the backyard—in one room.

- **Dining Room:** A stepped ceiling and server with a sink add to the elegance of this formal room.

- **Breakfast Room:** Eat at the bar this room shares with the island kitchen, and admire the 12-ft. cathedral ceiling and bayed group of

8- and 9-ft. windows. Or go through the sliding glass door to the covered side porch.

- **Master Suite:** The bedroom has a tray ceiling and cozy sitting area, and a whirlpool tub, shower, and walk-in closet are in the skylighted bath.

- **Optional Study:** The private bath in bedroom 2 makes it ideal for a study or home office.

- **Bonus Room:** Enjoy the extra 300 sq. ft.

Breakfast Nook

Rear View

Great Room

Main Level Floor Plan

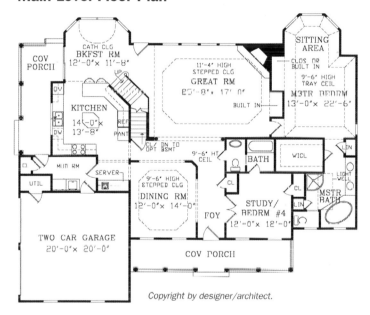

Copyright by designer/architect.

Upper Level Floor Plan

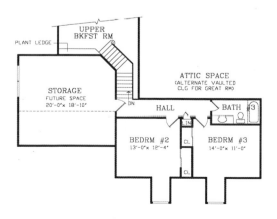

Painting Tips

As with any skill, there is a right and a wrong way to paint. There is a right way to hold a brush, a right way to maneuver a roller, a right way to spray a wall, etc. Follow these basic professional tips:

Brushing vs. Rolling. Some painters insist that only a brush-painted job looks right. However, most painters will "cut in" the edges with a brush, and then finish the main body of a wall or ceiling using a roller. Brushing alone can be time-consuming, and it is typically reserved for architectural woodwork.

Using the Right Brush. Use the largest brush with which you are comfortable. Professional painters seldom pick up anything smaller than a 4-inch brush. Most homeowners will achieve good results using a 4-inch brush for "cutting in" and for large surfaces, and an angled 2½- to 3-inch sash brush for trim around windows and doors. Be sure, also, to use brushes that are appropriate for the type of paint being applied. Oil-based paints require a natural bristle (also called "China bristles"), while water-based paints are applied with a synthetic bristle brush.

Handling a Brush. Many people grip a paintbrush as if they were shaking someone's hand. It is better to grip a brush more like a pencil, with the fingers and thumb wrapped around the metal ferrule. This grip provides the hand and wrist with a wider range of motion and therefore greater speed and precision. If your hand cramps, switch hands or switch temporarily to the handshake grip.

Wiping Rags. Before you begin painting, put a dust rag in your pocket. This is helpful for clearing away cobwebs and dust before painting. It is also handy for wiping off paint drips before they have a chance to dry.

Paint Hooks. When working on a ladder, use a good-quality paint hook to secure the paint bucket to your ladder. Avoid makeshift hooks made with wire or coat hangers. Paint hooks are inexpensive and available at virtually all paint and hardware stores.

Main Level Floor Plan

GREAT ROOM
18'-0" X 15'-6"
(VAULTED)

CL.
LIN
SHOWER
MASTER BATH
UTIL
D W
F
1/2 BATH
CL

DOUBLE GARAGE
20'-0" X 21'-0"

MASTER SUITE
13'-0" X 16'-0"
(VAULTED)

FOYER
UP
PANT
ISLAND
KIT
REF
D.W.

DINING
10'-0" X 12'-4"

EATING BAR

PORCH

BRK.
12'-0" X 11'-0"

38'-6"

62'-9"

**Main Level
Floor Plan**

*Illustration provided by
designer/architect.*

GREAT ROOM
BELOW

FLUE

BALCONY
DN

FUTURE PLAYROOM
20'-5" X 12'-0"

W.I.O.
BEDR'M-3
10'-0" X 12'-4"

BATH
LIN
CL

BEDR'M-2
12'-0" X 12'-0"

**Upper Level
Floor Plan**

*Copyright by
designer/architect.*

Plan #241009

Dimensions: 62'9" W x 38'6" D
Levels: 2
Square Footage: 1,974
Main Level Sq. Ft.: 1,480
Upper Level Sq. Ft.: 494
Bedrooms: 3
Bathrooms: 2½
Foundation: Slab
Materials List Available: No
Price Category: D

Plan #241013

Dimensions: 68' W x 46' D
Levels: 2
Square Footage: 2,779
Main Level Sq. Ft.: 1,918
Upper Level Sq. Ft.: 861
Bedrooms: 4
Bathrooms: 3½
Foundation: Slab
Materials List Available: No
Price Category: F

*Illustration provided by
designer/architect.*

Main Level Floor Plan

BRK
11'-0" X 13'-6"

SUNROOM
20'-7" X 12'-4"

UTIL
D W
F

F/P
REAR ENTRY
UP STOR
1/2 BATH

MASTER BATH
GLASS SHOWER
CL.
LIN

GREAT ROOM
19'-1" X 16'-1"

EATING BAR
KIT.
REF
D.W.
OVEN MICRO.

46'-0"

MASTER SUITE
15'-1" X 16'-0"

HALL
CL.
LANDING
DINING
10'-8" X 13'-0"

DOUBLE GARAGE
20'-1" X 21'-0"

STUDY
7'-8" X 9'-1"
DROP CEILING

UP
FOYER

PORCH

68'-0"

BEDROOM 2
11'-2" X 16'-6"

BEDROOM 3
12'-9" X 12'-0"

BATH-3

CL.
LANDING
DN

PLAYROOM
14'-0" X 15'-1"

SEAT

CL.
BATH 2
DN
LIN
BALCONY

FOYER BELOW

BEDROOM 4
11'-0" X 11'-3"

CL.

SHOWER
SEAT
LIN

BALCONY

**Upper Level
Floor Plan**

*Copyright by
designer/architect.*

Main Level Floor Plan

Illustrations provided by designer/architect.

Copyright by designer/architect.

Upper Level Floor Plan

Plan #291013

Dimensions: 72' W x 75' D

Levels: 2

Square Footage: 3,553

Main Level Sq. Ft.: 1,830

Upper Level Sq. Ft.: 1,723

Bedrooms: 4

Bathrooms: 2½

Foundation: Basement

Materials List Available: No

Price Category: H

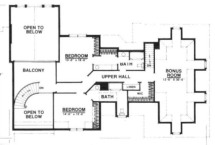

Main Level Floor Plan

Upper Level Floor Plan

Illustrations provided by designer/architect.

Copyright by designer/architect.

Plan #291014

Dimensions: 104' W x 60' D

Levels: 2

Square Footage: 4,372

Main Level Sq. Ft.: 3,182

Upper Level Sq. Ft.: 1,190

Bedrooms: 3

Bathrooms: 3 full, 2 half

Foundation: Basement

Materials List Available: No

Price Category: I

Plan #131034

Dimensions: 40' W x 32' D
Levels: 2 (Upper unfinished)
Square Footage: 1,040
Bedrooms: 5
Bathrooms: 2½
Foundation: Crawl space, slab, or basement
Materials List Available: Yes
Price Category: C

Illustration provided by designer/architect.

You'll love the versatility this expandable ranch-style home gives, with its unfinished, second story that you can transform into two bedrooms and a bath if you need the space.

Features:

- **Porch:** Decorate this country-style porch to accentuate the charm of this warm home.

- **Living Room:** This formal room features a wide, dramatic archway that opens to the kitchen and the dining room.

- **Kitchen:** The angled shape of this kitchen gives it character, while the convenient island and well-designed floor plan make cooking and cleaning tasks unusually efficient.

- **Bedrooms:** Use the design option in the blueprints of this home to substitute one of the bedrooms into an expansion of the master bedroom, which features an amenity-laden, private bathroom for total luxury.

Optional Main Level Floor Plan

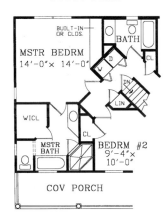

Main Level Floor Plan

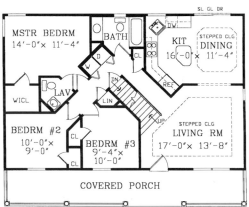

Kitchen

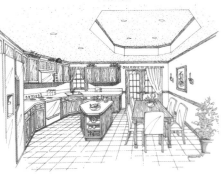

Upper Level Floor Plan

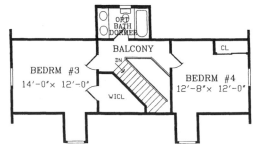

Copyright by designer/architect.

Plan #141014

Dimensions: 72' W x 38' D

Levels: 2

Square Footage: 2,091

Main Level Sq. Ft.: 1,362

Upper Level Sq. Ft.: 729

Bedrooms: 3

Bathrooms: 2½

Foundation: Basement

Materials List Available: Yes

Price Category: D

Illustration provided by designer/architect.

The wraparound front porch and front dormers evoke an old-fashioned country home.

Features:

- Ceiling Height: 8 ft. unless otherwise noted.

- Living Room: This spacious area has an open flow to the dining room, so you can graciously usher guests when it is time to eat.

- Dining Room: This elegant dining room has a bay that opens to the sun deck.

- Kitchen: This warm and inviting kitchen looks out to the front porch. Its bayed breakfast area is perfect for informal family meals.

- Master Suite: The bedroom enjoys a view through the front porch and features a master bath with all the amenities.

- Flexible Room: A room above the two-bay garage offers plenty of space that can be used for anything from a home office to a teen suite.

- Study Room: The two second-floor bedrooms share a study that is perfect for homework.

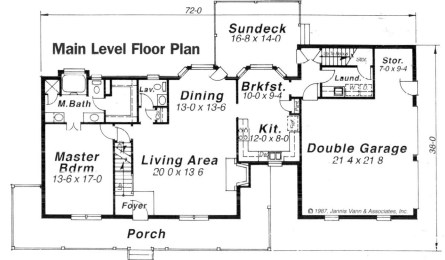

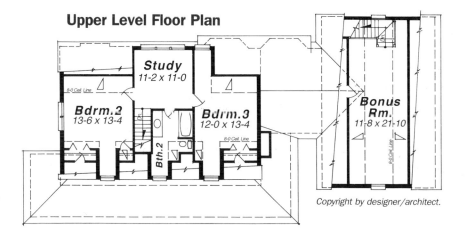

Copyright by designer/architect.

Images provided by designer/architect.

Plan #241008

Dimensions: 65' W x 56'8" D
Levels: 1
Square Footage: 2,526
Bedrooms: 4
Bathrooms: 3
Foundation: Slab
Materials List Available: No
Price Category: E

A covered back porch—with access from the master suite and the breakfast area—makes this traditional home ideal for siting near a golf course or with a backyard pool.

Features:

- **Great Room:** From the foyer, guests enter this spacious and comfortable great room, which features a handsome fireplace.

- **Kitchen:** This kitchen—the hub of this family-oriented home—is a joy in which to work, thanks to abundant counter space, a pantry, a convenient eating bar, and an adjoining breakfast area and sunroom.

- **Master Suite:** Enjoy the quiet comfort of this coffered-ceiling master suite, which features dual vanities and separate walk-in closets.

- **Additional Bedrooms:** Two secondary bedrooms, which share a full bath, are located at the opposite end of the house from the master suite. Bedroom 4—in front of the house—can be converted into a study.

Copyright by designer/architect.

SMARTtip

Traditional-Style Kitchen Cabinetry

You can modify stock kitchen cabinetry to enjoy fine furniture-quality details. Prefabricated trims may be purchased at local lumber mills and home centers. For example, crown molding, applied to the top of stock cabinetry and stained or painted to match the door style, may be all you need. Likewise, you can replace hardware with reproduction polished-brass door and drawer knobs or pulls for a finishing touch.

Plan #131050

Dimensions: 72'8" W x 47' D
Levels: 2
Square Footage: 2,874
Main Level Sq. Ft.: 2,146
Upper Level Sq. Ft.: 728
Bedrooms: 4
Bathrooms: 3
Foundation: Crawl space, slab, or basement
Materials List Available: Yes
Price Category: G

Illustrations provided by designer/architect.

A gazebo and long covered porch at the entry let you know that this is a spectacular design.

Features:

- **Foyer:** This vaulted foyer divides the formal living room and dining room, setting the stage for guests to feel welcome in your home.

- **Great Room:** This large room is defined by several columns; a corner fireplace and vaulted ceiling add to its drama.

- **Kitchen:** An island work space

separates this area from the bayed breakfast nook.

- **Master Suite:** You'll have privacy in this main-floor suite, which features two walk-in closets and a compartmented bath with a dual-sink vanity.

- **Upper Level:** The two large bedrooms share a bath and a dramatic balcony.

- **Bonus Room:** Walk down a few steps into this large bonus room over the 3-car garage.

Main Level Floor Plan

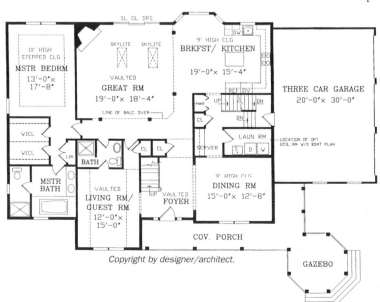

Copyright by designer/architect.

Upper Level Floor Plan

Rear Elevation

Illustration provided by designer/architect.

Main Level Floor Plan

HEARTH ROOM 20'-0" X 13'-0"
GREAT ROOM 15'-0" X 20'-0"
MASTER SUITE 14'-0" X 16'-0"
F/P
F/P
BRK
KIT
S
DW
GALLERY
W.I.C.
PANT
REF
R
CTS
UTIL
F
1/2 BATH
D W
CTS
MASTER BATH
SHOWER
LIN
DINING 13'-1" X 11'-0"
UP
FOYER
DOUBLE GARAGE 20'-0" X 20'-0"
PORCH
56'-3"
63'-9"

FUTURE PLAYROOM 15'-0" X 20'-6"
UP BALCONY
DN
BATH-2
LIN
CL
HALL
BEDR'M 2 10'-0" X 14'-9"
FOYER
CL
BEDR'M 3 12'-0' X 14'-0"

Upper Level Floor Plan

Copyright by designer/architect.

Plan #241012

Dimensions: 64' W x 56' D

Levels: 2

Square Footage: 2,743

Main Level Sq. Ft.: 2,153

Upper Level Sq. Ft.: 590

Bedrooms: 3

Bathrooms: 2½

Foundation: Slab

Materials List Available: No

Price Category: E

Plan #241014

Dimensions: 66'6" W x 55'6" D

Levels: 2

Square Footage: 3,046

Main Level Sq. Ft.: 2,292

Upper Level Sq. Ft.: 754

Bedrooms: 4

Bathrooms: 3

Foundation: Slab

Materials List Available: No

Price Category: G

Illustration provided by designer/architect.

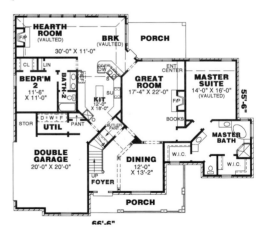

Main Level Floor Plan

HEARTH ROOM (VAULTED)
30'-0" X 11'-0"
F/P
BRK (VAULTED)
PORCH
CL
LIN
DW
S
ENT CENTER
BEDR'M 2 11'-6" X 11'-0"
BATH-2
KIT X 18'-0"
SU
GREAT ROOM 17'-4" X 22'-0"
F/P
MASTER SUITE 14'-0" X 16'-0" (VAULTED)
BOOKS
STOR
D W F
UTIL
PANT
BUTLER PANT
MASTER BATH
DOUBLE GARAGE 20'-0" X 20'-0"
UP
FOYER
DINING 12'-0" X 13'-2"
W.I.C.
W.I.C.
PORCH
55'-6"
66'-6"

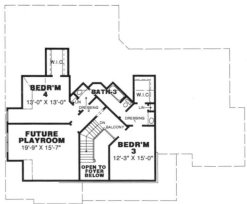

Upper Level Floor Plan

Copyright by designer/architect.

BEDR'M 4 13'-0" X 13'-0"
BATH-3
W.I.C.
DRESSING
DRESSING
LIN
DN
BALCONY
FUTURE PLAYROOM 19'-9" X 15'-7"
BEDR'M 3 12'-3" X 15'-0"
OPEN TO FOYER BELOW

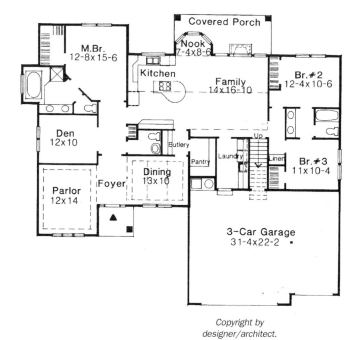

Images provided by designer/architect.

Copyright by designer/architect.

Plan #231001

Dimensions: 67'6" W x 58' D

Levels: 1

Square Footage: 2,177

Bedrooms: 3

Bathrooms: 2½

Foundation: Crawl space

Materials List Available: No

Price Category: D

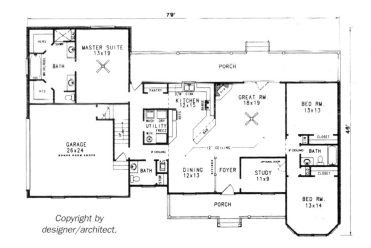

Images provided by designer/architect.

Copyright by designer/architect.

Plan #171015

Dimensions: 79' W x 46' D

Levels: 1

Square Footage: 2,089

Bedrooms: 3

Bathrooms: 2½

Foundation: Slab, crawl space

Materials List Available: Yes

Price Category: D

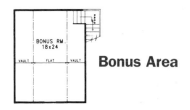

Bonus Area

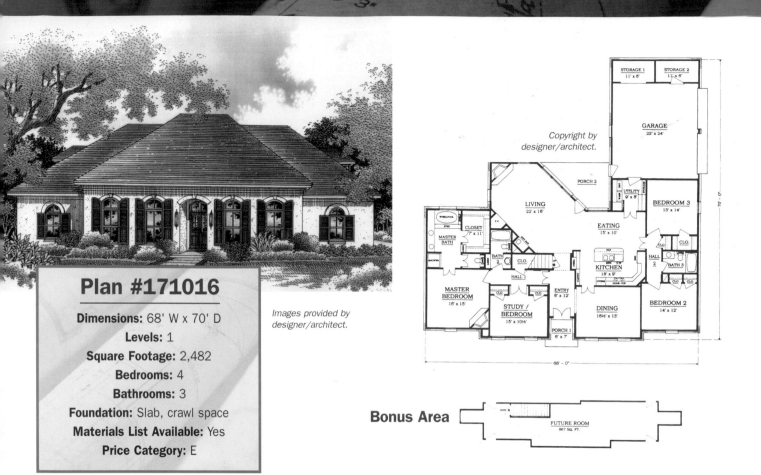

Images provided by designer/architect.

Plan #171016

Dimensions: 68' W x 70' D

Levels: 1

Square Footage: 2,482

Bedrooms: 4

Bathrooms: 3

Foundation: Slab, crawl space

Materials List Available: Yes

Price Category: E

Images provided by designer/architect.

Plan #231008

Dimensions: 60' W x 62' D

Levels: 1

Square Footage: 1,941

Bedrooms: 3

Bathrooms: 2½

Foundation: Crawl space

Materials List Available: No

Price Category: A

Plan #251012

Dimensions: 57'9" W x 62'10" D

Levels: 2

Square Footage: 2,009

Main Level Sq. Ft.: 1,520

Upper Level Sq. Ft.: 489

Bedrooms: 3

Bathrooms: 2½

Foundation: Basement

Materials List Available: Yes

Price Category: D

Images provided by designer/architect.

Main Level Floor Plan

Master 13/8 x 15 — Recessed Ceiling
Family Room 19/8 x 15 — 12' Ceiling
Porch 21/8 x 6/6 — Skylight
Breakfast 11 x 12 — 9' Ceiling
Kitchen 10 x 12 — 9' Ceiling
Foyer 8/5 x 6/6 — 12' Ceiling
Dining 11 x 13 — 9' Ceiling
Stoop
China Cab.
Desk
Stairs Up
Stairs Down
Utility
Storage 9/6 x 6/3
Garage 22 x 22

Upper Level Floor Plan

Skylight
Roof
Br. #2 11 x 12 — 9' Ceiling
Br. #3 11 x 10/7 — 8' Ceiling
Stairs Down
Ledge
Roof
Attic Storage
Opt. Bonus 12 x 21/5

Copyright by designer/architect.

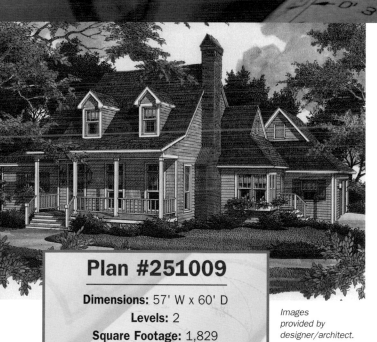

Plan #251009

Dimensions: 57' W x 60' D

Levels: 2

Square Footage: 1,829

Main Level Sq. Ft.: 1,339

Upper Level Sq. Ft.: 490

Bedrooms: 4

Bathrooms: 2½

Foundation: Basement

Materials List Available: No

Price Category: D

Images provided by designer/architect.

Main Level Floor Plan

57'
60'
GARAGE 21x21
DRIVE
DECK
DINING 11x12
KITCHEN 12x12
LAUNDRY
PORCH
MASTER 13x16
BREAKFAST 11x12
Open Above
FAMILY RM. 14x19
FOYER
PORCH 6x22

Upper Level Floor Plan

down
Br.#4 12x10
Br.#3 10x11/8
Desk
Br.#2 10/8x11/8
roof

Copyright by designer/architect.

Illustration provided by designer/architect.

Plan #181085

Dimensions: 56'4" W x 44' D

Levels: 2

Square Footage: 2,183

Main Level Sq. Ft.: 1,232

Second Level Sq. Ft.: 951

Bedrooms: 3

Bathrooms: 2½

Foundation: Basement

Materials List Available: Yes

Price Category: D

This country home features an inviting front porch and a layout designed for modern living.

Features:

- Ceiling Height: 8 ft.

- Solarium: Sunlight streams through the windows of this solarium at the front of the house.

- Living Room: Walk through French doors, and you will enter this inviting living room. Family and friends will be drawn to the corner fireplace.

- Formal Dining Room: Usher your guests directly from the living room into this formal dining room. The kitchen is located on the other side of the dining room for convenient service.

- Kitchen: This generously sized kitchen is a delight, it offers a center island, separate eat-in area, and access to the back deck.

- Bonus Room: This room just off the entry hall can become a family room, a bedroom, or an office.

- Master Suite: Curl up by the corner fireplace in this master retreat, with its walk-in closet and lavish bath with separate shower and tub.

Main Level Floor Plan

Upper Level Floor Plan

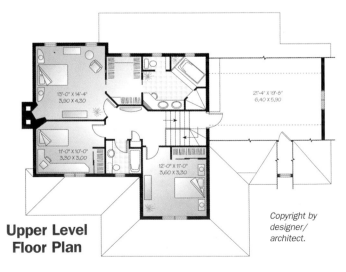

Copyright by designer/architect.

Plan #131036

Dimensions: 72' W x 69'10" D
Levels: 1
Square Footage: 2,585
Bedrooms: 4
Bathrooms: 3
Foundation: Crawl space, slab, or basement
Materials List Available: Yes
Price Category: F

Illustrations provided by designer/architect.

This sprawling brick home features living spaces for everyone in the family and makes a lovely setting for any sort of entertaining.

Features:

- Foyer: Pass through this foyer, which leads into either the living room or dining room.

- Living Room: An elegant 11-ft. stepped ceiling here and in the dining room helps to create the formality their lines suggest.

- Great Room: This room, with its 10-ft.-7-in.-high stepped ceiling, fireplace, and many built-ins, leads to the rear covered porch.

- Kitchen: This kitchen features an island, a pantry closet, and a wraparound snack bar that serves the breakfast room and gives a panoramic view of the great room.

- Master Suite: Enjoy a bayed sitting area, walk-in closet, and private bath with garden tub.

- Office: A private entrance and access to a full bath give versatility to this room.

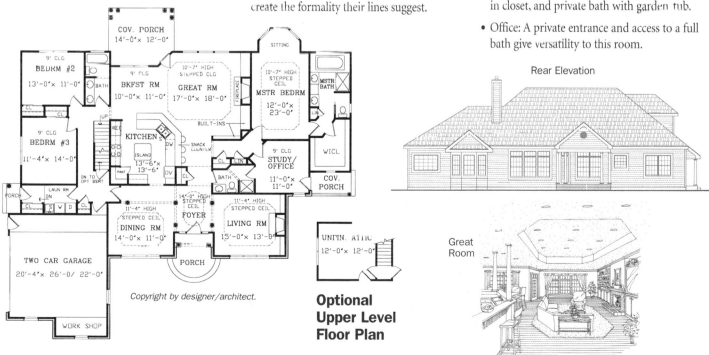

Rear Elevation

Great Room

Copyright by designer/architect.

Optional Upper Level Floor Plan

Plan #131035

Dimensions: 65'4" W x 45'10" D

Levels: 1

Square Footage: 1,892

Bedrooms: 3

Bathrooms: 2½

Foundation: Basement, crawl space, or slab

Materials List Available: Yes

Price Category: E

Images provided by designer/architect.

Rear Elevation

Bonus Area

Copyright by designer/architect.

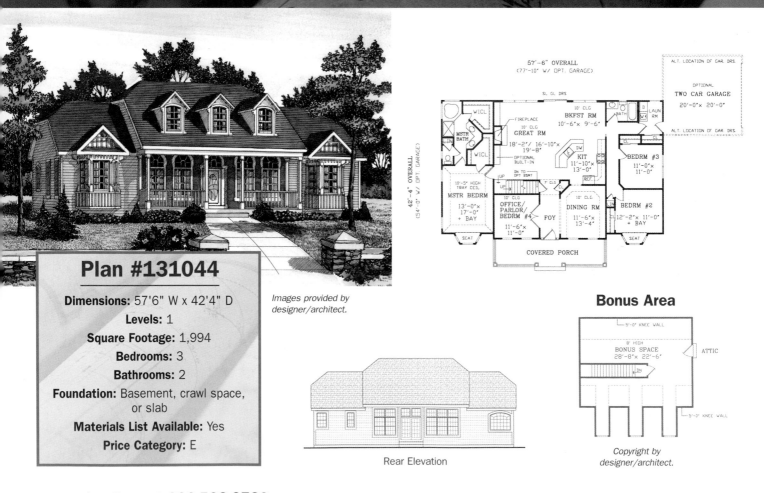

Plan #131044

Dimensions: 57'6" W x 42'4" D

Levels: 1

Square Footage: 1,994

Bedrooms: 3

Bathrooms: 2

Foundation: Basement, crawl space, or slab

Materials List Available: Yes

Price Category: E

Images provided by designer/architect.

Bonus Area

Rear Elevation

Copyright by designer/architect.

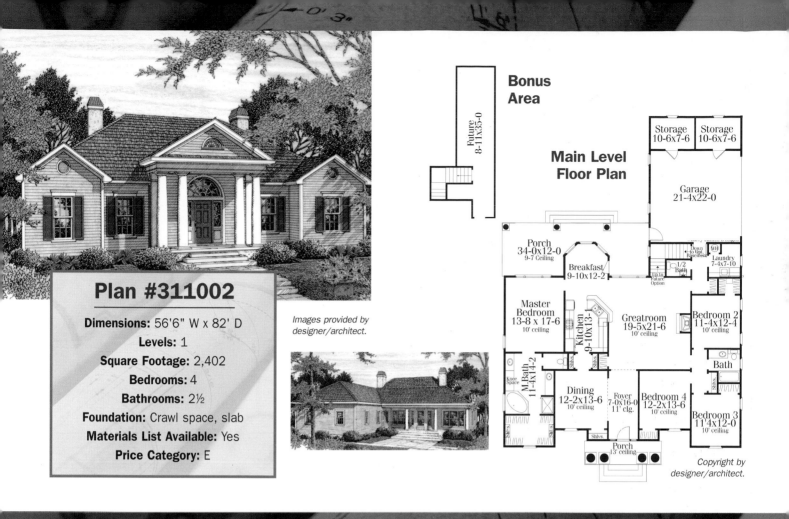

Bonus Area

Future 8-11x35-0

Main Level Floor Plan

Storage 10-6x7-6 | Storage 10-6x7-6

Garage 21-4x22-0

Porch 34-0x12-0 9-7 Ceiling

Breakfast/ 9-10x12-2

Laundry 7-4x7-10

1/2 Bath

Master Bedroom 13-8 x 17-6 10' ceiling

Kitchen 9-10x13-

Greatroom 19-5x21-6 10' ceiling

Bedroom 2 11-4x12-4 10' ceiling

Bath

M. Bath 11-4x14-2

Knee Space

Dining 12-2x13-6 10' ceiling

Foyer 7-0x16-0 11' clg.

Bedroom 4 12-2x13-6 10' ceiling

Bedroom 3 11'4x12-0 10' ceiling

Porch 13' ceiling

Copyright by designer/architect.

Plan #311002

Dimensions: 56'6" W x 82' D

Levels: 1

Square Footage: 2,402

Bedrooms: 4

Bathrooms: 2½

Foundation: Crawl space, slab

Materials List Available: Yes

Price Category: E

Images provided by designer/architect.

Patio

M. Br 15 x 17

Living 13-8 x 17

Nook

Kit.

Family 16 x 10

Patio

Foyer

Dining 11-4 x 13

Br #2 11 x 12-6

Br #3 12 x 11

Den 12-6 x 11

Porch

Util./Mud

Garage 33 x 29-4

Copyright by designer/architect.

Bonus Rm. 16-6 x 24-6

Optional Bonus Area

Plan #231009

Dimensions: 111'6" W x 77'1" D

Levels: 1

Square Footage: 2,765

Bedrooms: 3

Bathrooms: 2½

Foundation: Crawl space

Materials List Available: No

Price Category: A

Images provided by designer/architect.

Plan #271057

Dimensions: 67' W x 41' D

Levels: 2

Square Footage: 2,195

Main Level Sq. Ft.: 1,095

Upper Level Sq. Ft.: 1,100

Bedrooms: 3

Bathrooms: 2½

Foundation: Daylight basement

Materials List Available: No

Price Category: D

Images provided by designer/architect.

With its shingle and lap siding, tapered columns and inviting porch, this traditional home gives a gentle nod to Craftsman architecture.

Features:

• Study: Its proximity to the front door makes this cozy room the perfect choice for a home office.

• Great Room: Warmed by a crackling fireplace, this gathering spot looks out over the backyard through a trio of bumped-out windows.

• Kitchen: Ample counter space and a double-sink island (with a generous snack counter) enhance the spacious kitchen. A neighboring dinette provides access to the backyard.

• Owner's Suite: An elegant tray ceiling crowns the sleeping chamber. In the private bath, a whirlpool tub, separate shower, and dual-sink vanity pamper you.

• Bonus Room: A cavernous bonus room waits for you to transform it for any use your family desires.

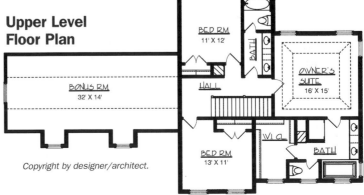

Main Level Floor Plan

Upper Level Floor Plan

Copyright by designer/architect.

Plan #241005

Dimensions: 53' W x 55'9" D
Levels: 1
Square Footage: 1,670
Bedrooms: 3
Bathrooms: 2
Foundation: Slab
Materials List Available: No
Price Category: C

This charming starter home, in split-bedroom format, combines big-house features in a compact design.

Features:

- **Great Room:** With easy access to the formal dining room, kitchen, and breakfast area, this great room features a cozy fireplace.

- **Kitchen:** This big kitchen, with easy access to a walk-in pantry, features an island for added work space and a lovely plant shelf that separates it from the great room.

- **Master Suite:** Separated for privacy, this master suite offers a roomy bath with whirlpool tub, dual vanities, a separate shower, and a large walk-in closet.

- **Additional Rooms:** Additional rooms include a laundry/utility room—with space for a washer, dryer, and freezer—a large area above the garage, well-suited for a media or game room, and two secondary bedrooms.

Images provided by designer/architect.

Copyright by designer/architect.

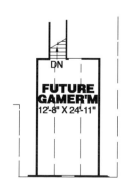

SMARTtip

Window Scarf

The best way to wrap a window scarf around a pole is as follows:

- Lay out the material on a large, clean surface. Gather the fabric at the top of each jabot, and use elastic to hold it together.

- Swing one jabot into place over the pole and, starting from there, wind the swag portion as many times as you need around the pole until you reach the elastic at the second jabot, which should have landed at the opposite pole end.

- Readjust wraps along the pole. Generally, wrapped swags just touch or slightly overlap.

- For a dramatic effect, stuff the wrapped swags with tissue paper or thin foam, depending on the translucence and weight of fabric.

- Release elastics at tops of jabots.

Main Level Floor Plan

SCREENED PORCH 14' x 5'

DINING 9' x 10'

KITCHEN

MASTER BATH 11' x 14'

WHIRLPOOL

MASTER SUITE 13' x 17'

PANTRY

GREAT ROOM 15' x 20'

1/2 BATH

UTILITY 9' x 6'

HERS 7' x 6'

HIS 6' x 6'

GARAGE 22' x 23'

PORCH 19' x 6'

47'-0"

Upper Level Floor Plan

BEDROOM # 2 12' x 13'

BATH 2 12' x 5'

BEDROOM # 3 11' x 13'

CLOSET

SITTING AREA 14' x 9'

CLOSET

OPEN TO BELOW

BONUS ROOM 16' x 30'

VAULT VAULT VAULT

Images provided by designer/architect.

Copyright by designer/architect.

Plan #171014

Dimensions: 47' W x 52' D

Levels: 2

Square Footage: 1,815

Main Level Sq. Ft.: 1,257

Upper Level Sq. Ft.: 558

Bedrooms: 3

Bathrooms: 2½

Foundation: Slab, crawl space

Materials List Available: Yes

Price Category: D

DECK

COV. PORCH

9' CLG DINING RM 11'-0"x 15'-4"

KITCHEN 9'-0"x 10'-0"

OPTIONAL TWO CAR GARAGE 20'-0"x 20'-0"

BEDRM #3 11'-4"x 10'-0"

BUILT-IN

UP

LAUN RM

W D PANT

CL LIN

BATH #2

FIREPLACE

10' CLG GREAT RM 20'-0"x 15'-4"

OPT BSMT ENTRY

UTIL

WICL

MSTR BATH

CL LIN

CL

CL

CL

TRAY CEIL

BEDRM #2 11'-4"x 12'-4"

COV. PORCH

UP

MSTR BEDRM 12'-0"x 16'-4"

Copyright by designer/architect.

Plan #131014

Dimensions: 48' W x 43'4" D

Levels: 1

Square Footage: 1,380

Bedrooms: 3

Bathrooms: 2

Foundation: Basement, crawl space, or slab

Materials List Available: Yes

Price Category: C

Images provided by designer/architect.

FUTURE EXPANSION 20'-0"x 15'-4"

DN

DN

Bonus Room

Rear Elevation

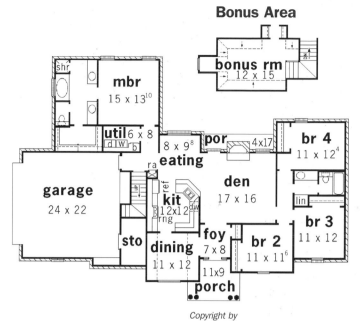

Bonus Area

bonus rm
12 x 15

shr

mbr
15 x 13¹⁰

util 6 x 8
d W b

8 x 9⁸

por
4x17

br 4
11 x 12⁴

garage
24 x 22

ra

eating

den
17 x 16

lin

ref

kit
12x12

dw

br 3
11 x 12

rng

sto

dining
11 x 12

foy
7 x 8

br 2
11 x 11⁶

11x9

porch

Images provided by designer/architect.

Copyright by designer/architect.

Plan #201089

Dimensions: 72'10" W x 54'5" D

Levels: 1

Square Footage: 1,873

Bedrooms: 4

Bathrooms: 2

Foundation: Crawl space, slab, or basement

Materials List Available: Yes

Price Category: D

Plan #141021

Dimensions: 71' W x 79' D

Levels: 1

Square Footage: 2,614

Bedrooms: 3

Bathrooms: 2½

Foundation: Basement

Materials List Available: Yes

Price Category: F

Images provided by designer/architect.

Family
17-4 x 20-6

Bdrm.3
13-8 x 11-6

Brkfst.
10-0 x 12-8

Sundeck
30-5 x 24-0

Kitchen
17-8 x 12-2

Dining
13-10 x 13-0
w/ Bay

Master
Bdrm.
13-4 x 19-6
w/ Bay

Bdrm.2
13-8 x 11-6

78-9

Foyer
6-0 x 15-8

Living/
Library
13-8 x 11-8

M. Bath

Double Garage
21-4 x 27-8

70-10

Copyright by designer/architect.

Living Room

Dining Room

Rear View

Plan #221023

Dimensions: 90'3" W x 65'8" D
Levels: 2
Square Footage: 3,511
Main Level Sq. Ft.: 1,931
Upper Level Sq. Ft.: 1,580
Bedrooms: 4
Bathrooms: 3½
Foundation: Basement
Materials List Available: No
Price Category: H

Images provided by designer/architect.

Features:

- Ceiling Height: 9 ft.
- Family Room: This large room is open to the kitchen and the dining nook, making it an ideal spot in which to entertain.
- Living Room: The high ceiling in this room contributes to its somewhat formal feeling, and the fireplace and built-in bookcase allow you to decorate for a classic atmosphere.
- Master Suite: The bedroom in this suite has a luxurious feeling, partially because of the double French doors that are flanked by niches for displaying small art pieces or collectables. The bathroom here is unusually large and features a walk-in closet.
- Upper Level: You'll find four bedrooms, three bathrooms, and a large bonus room to use as a study or play room on this floor.

The curb appeal of this traditional two-story home, with its brick-and-stucco facade, is well matched by the luxuriousness you'll find inside.

Main Level Floor Plan

FAM. RM.
22'4" X 17'0"

NK.
VAULT CEILING
11'0" X 10'0"

LIV.
10'-1 1/8" CEILING
14'4" X 18'6"

KIT.
18'8" X 13'6"

DEN
10'-1 1/8" CEILING
11'4" X 19'0"

BUTLER'S PANTRY

STOR.

3 CAR GAR.
22'0" X 43'4"

DIN.
13'0" X 15'0"

E.
2 STORY

90'-3"

65'-8"

Upper Level Floor Plan

BR. #3
11'4" X 14'0"

BR. #2
11'6" X 12'4"

MBR.
14'4" X 18'0"

ART NICHE

OPEN TO E.

BR. #4
CATHEDRAL CEILING
13'0" X 13'0"

BONUS RM.
11'4" X 33'8"

Copyright by designer/architect.

SMARTtip

Competing Interests- Fireplace, Media Center, and Windows

What should you do if the only place for the television is next to the fireplace? If the TV is small enough to keep on a cart that you can wheel away when the set is not in use, that's ideal. But with cable hookups, VCRs, DVDs, and large-screen TVs, that might be impractical. A cabinet that lets you store the all of this equipment behind closed doors may be the answer, especially if the storage unit is part of a large built-in paneled wall system that incorporates the fireplace into its overall design.

When large windows or glass doors share the wall with a fireplace, easy-to-adjust window treatments are essential: drapery panels on a traverse rod or suspended from rings on a pole, or shutters, shades, or blinds are options that can help with glare when viewing a TV during the daytime. But by all means, make certain your selection allows the sun shine in during the day when appropriate.

Also be aware that a pleasant window view by day just becomes a large dark hole at night. So in the evening, close the curtains while the fire sets the mood, whether you're entertaining or relaxing alone.

Rear Elevation

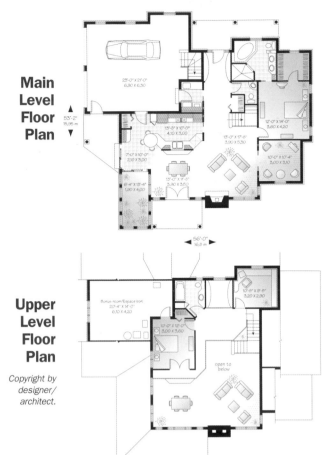

Main Level Floor Plan

Upper Level Floor Plan

Images provided by designer/architect.

Copyright by designer/architect.

Plan #181061

Dimensions: 56' W x 53'2" D

Levels: 2

Square Footage: 2,111

Main Level Sq. Ft.: 1,545

Upper Level Sq. Ft.: 566

Bedrooms: 2

Bathrooms: 2½

Foundation: Basement, crawl space

Materials List Available: Yes

Price Category: D

Main Level Floor Plan

Upper Level Floor Plan

Images provided by designer/architect.

Copyright by designer/architect.

Plan #261002

Dimensions: 83'8" W x 43' D

Levels: 2

Square Footage: 2,976

Main Level Sq. Ft.: 1,845

Upper Level Sq. Ft.: 1,131

Bedrooms: 4

Bathrooms: 2½

Foundation: Basement

Materials List Available: No

Price Category: F

Plan #181074

Dimensions: 42' W x 40' D

Levels: 2

Square Footage: 1,760

Main Level Sq. Ft.: 880

Upper Level Sq. Ft.: 880

Bedrooms: 3

Full Baths: 2½

Foundation: Full basement

Materials List Available: Yes

Price Category: C

Images provided by designer/architect.

Main Level Floor Plan

Upper Level Floor Plan

Copyright by designer/architect.

Plan #181102

Dimensions: 58' W x 58'4" D

Levels: 2

Square Footage: 2,265

Main Level Sq. Ft.: 1,371

Upper Level Sq. Ft.: 894

Bedrooms: 4

Bathrooms: 3½

Foundation: Full basement

Materials List Available: Yes

Price Category: E

Images provided by designer/architect.

Upper Level Floor Plan

Main Level Floor Plan

Copyright by designer/architect.

Plan #241007

Dimensions: 58'10" W x 59'1" D

Levels: 1

Square Footage: 2,036

Bedrooms: 3

Bathrooms: 2

Foundation: Slab

Materials List Available: No

Price Category: D

Illustration provided by designer/architect.

Enjoy summer breezes while relaxing on the large front porch of this charming country cottage.

Features:

- **Great Room:** Whether you enter from the front door or from the kitchen, you will feel welcome in this comfortable great room, which features a corner fireplace.

- **Kitchen:** This well-designed kitchen with extensive counter space offers a delightful eating bar, perfect for quick or informal meals.

- **Master Suite:** This luxurious master suite, located on the first floor for privacy, features his and her walk-in closets, separate vanities, a deluxe corner tub, a linen closet, and a walk-in shower.

- **Additional Bedrooms:** Two secondary bedrooms and an optional, large game room —well suited for a growing family—are located on the second floor.

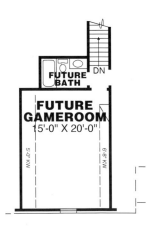

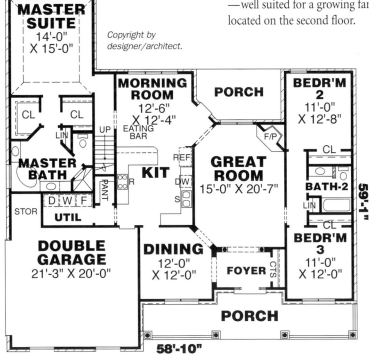

Copyright by designer/architect.

Plan #301007

Dimensions: 70'10" W x 54'6" D

Levels: 2

Square Footage: 2,398

Main Level Sq. Ft.: 1,812

Upper Level Sq. Ft.: 586

Bedrooms: 4

Bathrooms: 2½

Foundation: Crawl space or slab

Materials List Available: Yes

Price Category: E

Images provided by designer/architect.

Double bay windows add charm to this Georgian design

Features:

- Ceiling Height: 8 ft. unless otherwise noted.

- Foyer: This elegant foyer features a 2-story ceiling and is open to the formal dining room and the rear great room.

- Dining Room: This room has ample space for holidays and formal dinners.

- Family Room: This family room features a 2-story ceiling and a fireplace.

- Kitchen: This kitchen boasts a pantry, work island, and plenty of storage and counter space.

- Master Bedroom: This master bedroom includes his and her walk-in closets. The master bath has two separate vanities, a corner spa, and a walk-in shower.

Main Level Floor Plan

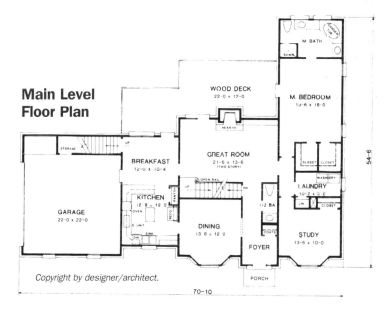

Copyright by designer/architect.

Upper Level Floor Plan

Main Level Floor Plan

Upper Level Floor Plan

Copyright by designer/architect.

Plan #251014

Dimensions: 54' W x 61' D

Levels: 2

Square Footage: 2,210

Main Level Sq. Ft.: 1,670

Upper Level Sq. Ft.: 540

Bedrooms: 3

Bathrooms: 2½

Foundation: Crawl space, basement

Materials List Available: Yes

Price Category: E

Images provided by designer/architect.

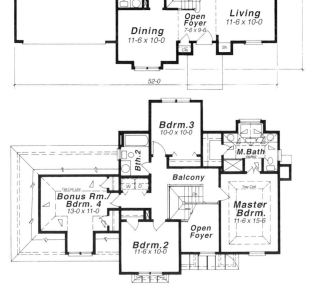

Main Level Floor Plan

Upper Level Floor Plan

Copyright by designer/architect.

Plan #141025

Dimensions: 52' W x 36' D

Levels: 2

Square Footage: 1,721

Main Level Sq. Ft.: 902

Upper Level Sq. Ft.: 819

Bedrooms: 4

Bathrooms: 2½

Foundation: Basement

Materials List Available: Yes

Price Category: C

Images provided by designer/architect.

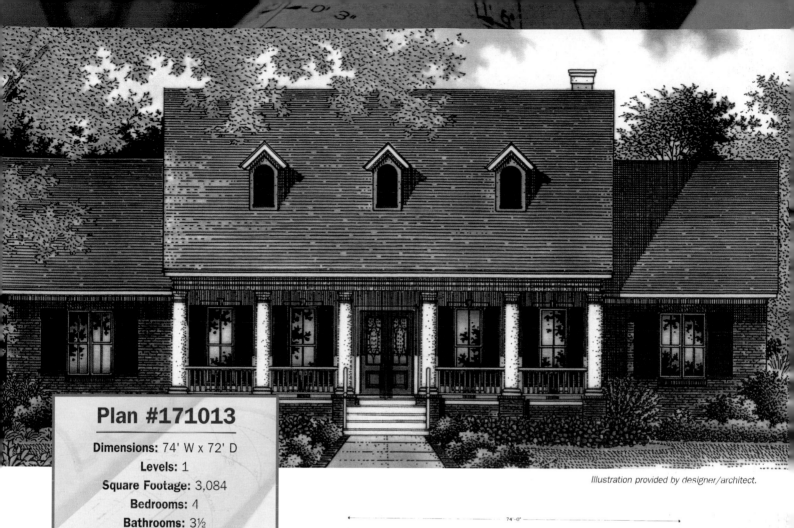

Plan #171013

Dimensions: 74' W x 72' D
Levels: 1
Square Footage: 3,084
Bedrooms: 4
Bathrooms: 3½
Foundation: Slab, crawl space
Materials List Available: Yes
Price Category: G

Illustration provided by designer/architect.

Impressive porch columns add to the country charm of this amenity-filled family home.

Features:

- Ceiling Height: 10 ft.

- Foyer: The sense of style continues from the front porch into this foyer, which opens to the formal dining room and the living room.

- Dining Room: Two handsome support columns accentuate the elegance of this dining room.

- Living Room: This living room features a cozy corner fireplace and plenty of room for the entire family to gather and relax.

- Kitchen: You'll be inspired to new culinary heights in this kitchen, which offers plenty of counter space, a snack bar, a built-in pantry, and a china closet.

- Master Suite: The bedroom of this master suite has a fireplace and overlooks a rear courtyard. The bath has two vanities a large walk-in closet, a deluxe tub, a walk-in shower, and a skylight.

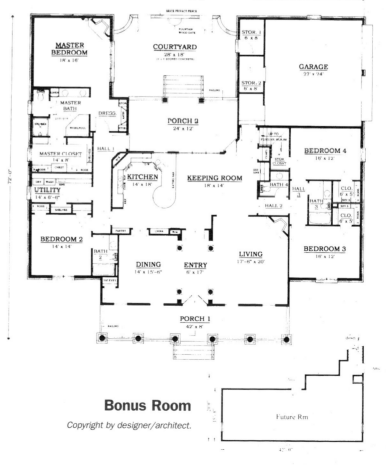

Bonus Room

Copyright by designer/architect.

Plan #201084

Dimensions: 66'10" W x 54'5" D

Levels: 1

Square Footage: 2,056

Bedrooms: 3

Bathrooms: 2

Foundation: Crawl space, slab, or basement

Materials List Available: Yes

Price Category: D

Illustration provided by designer/architect.

This classic family home features beautiful country styling with lots of curb appeal.

Features:

- Ceiling Height: 8 ft.
- Open Plan: When guests arrive, they'll enter a foyer that is open to the dining room and den. This open area makes the home seem especially spacious and offers the flexibility for all kinds of entertaining and family activities.
- Kitchen: You'll love preparing meals in this large, well-designed kitchen. There's plenty of counter space, and the breakfast bar is perfect impromptu family meals.
- Master Suite: This spacious and elegant master suite is separated from the other bedroom for maximum privacy.
- Bonus Room: This unfinished bonus room awaits the time to add another bedroom or a home office.
- Garage: This attached garage offers parking for two cars, plus plenty of storage space.

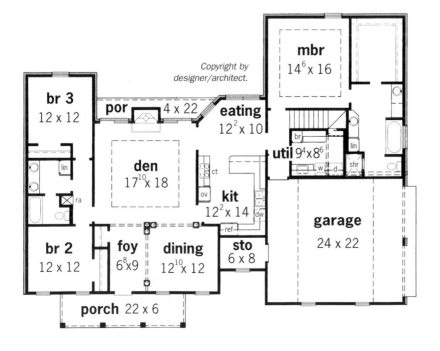

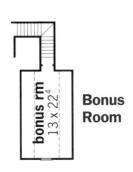

Bonus Room

Plan #311005

Dimensions: 87' W x 57'3" D

Levels: 1

Square Footage: 2,497

Bedrooms: 3

Bathrooms: 3½

Foundation: Crawl space, slab

Materials List Available: Yes

Price Category: E

Images provided by designer/architect.

You'll love this home, which mixes practical features with a gracious appearance.

Features:

- Great Room: A handsome fireplace and flanking windows that give a view of the back patio are the highlights of this gracious room.

- Kitchen: A curved bar defines the perimeter of this well-planned kitchen.

- Breakfast Room: Open to both the great room and the kitchen, this sunny spot leads to the rear porch, which in turn, leads to the patio beyond.

- Master Suite: Vaulted ceilings, a huge walk-in closet, and deluxe bath create luxury here.

- Bonus Room: Finish this 966-sq.-ft. area as a huge game room, or divide it into a game room, study, and sewing or craft room.

- Additional Bedrooms: Each bedroom has a private bath and good closet space.

Main Level Floor Plan

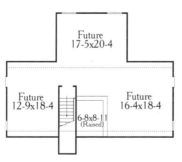

Bonus Area Floor Plan

Copyright by designer/architect.

SMARTtip

Front Porch

A front porch proclaims you to the outside world, so furnish it in a way that expresses what you want the world to know about you. Use the walls of your porch to hang interesting items such as sundials or old shutters. Set a mirror into an old window to reflect a portion of the garden.

Luxury Homes

A truly luxurious house is characterized by a sense of spaciousness while it is also sheltering. If you're ready to move up to a large house of 2,500 to 4,000 sq. ft. or more, you'll enjoy the opportunity of shaping space around the way your family lives, works, plays, and relaxes.

Dramatic architectural features such as high ceilings and tall windows are the grand backdrop for the special details that will personalize your home. In addition to formal living and dining rooms, other common areas include a family room and a large state-of-the-art kitchen with furniture-quality cabinetry, a beverage center, or special zones that can be configured for gourmet cooking, baking, hobbies, or crafts.

One popular amenity, a walk-in pantry, connects the kitchen to the dining room. This anteroom may be outfitted with cabinetry and a wet bar or it may be equipped with a desk and a computer to act as the home-management center. Other popular gathering areas for today's families are media rooms or home the-aters, game rooms or lofts, and music rooms. When it's time to rest and recharge for the next day, adults need a master suite with all of the accoutrements of a pampering personal retreat—a spacious bath with compartmentalized areas for dressing and grooming, toileting, bathing, and showering, and perhaps an adjacent den or small living room. In addition or in place of separate bedrooms, a suite of rooms, away from the parents, can be reserved for older kids.

A grand entrance, above, is accentuated by elegant appointments.

Classic architectural details grace the facade of this house, below.

A large plan, bottom, offers ample room for amenities.

Plan #121061

Dimensions: 56' W x 52' D
Levels: 2
Square Footage: 3,025
Main Level Sq. Ft.: 1,583
Upper Level Sq. Ft.: 1,442
Bedrooms: 4
Bathrooms: 3 ½
Foundation: Basement
Materials List Available: Yes
Price Category: G

Photo provided by designer/architect.

This large home with a contemporary feeling is ideal for the family looking for comfort and amenities.

Features:

• Entry: Stacked windows bring sunlight into this two-story entry, with its stylish curved staircase.

• Library: French doors off the entry lead to this room, with its built-in bookcases flanking a large, picturesque window.

• Family Room: Located in the rear of the home, this family room is sunken to set it apart. A spider-beamed ceiling gives it a contemporary feeling, and a bay window, wet bar, and pass-through fireplace add to this impression.

• Kitchen: The island in this kitchen makes working here a pleasure. The corner pantry joins a breakfast area and hearth room to this space.

Main Level Floor Plan

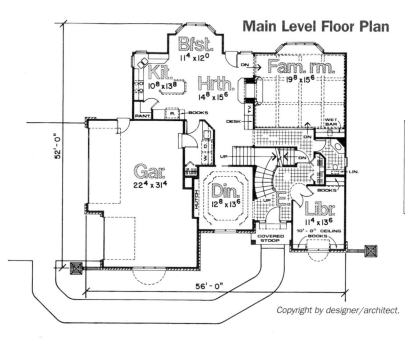

Copyright by designer/architect.

Upper Level Floor Plan

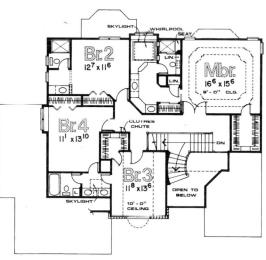

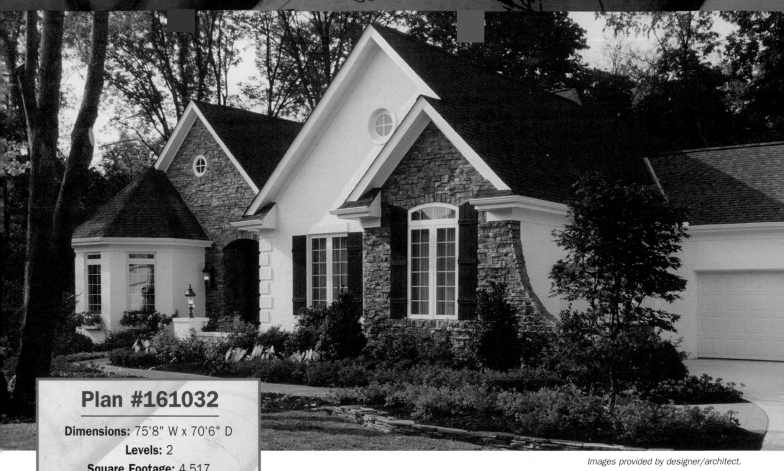

Plan #161032

Dimensions: 75'8" W x 70'6" D
Levels: 2
Square Footage: 4,517
Main Level Sq. Ft.: 2,562
Finished Lower Level Sq. Ft.: 1,955
Bedrooms: 3
Full Baths: 2
Half Baths: 3
Foundation: Slab
Materials List Available: Yes
Price Category: I

Images provided by designer/architect.

The brick-and-stone exterior, a recessed entry, and a tower containing a large library combine to convey the strength and character of this enchanting house.

Features:

- **Hearth Room:** Your family or guests will enjoy this large, comfortable hearth room, which has a gas fireplace and access to the rear deck, perfect for friendly gatherings.

- **Kitchen:** This spacious kitchen features a walk-in pantry and a center island.

- **Master Suite:** Designed for privacy, this master suite includes a sloped ceiling and opens to the rear deck. It also features a deluxe whirlpool bath, walk-in shower, separate his and her vanities, and a walk-in closet.

- **Lower Level:** This lower level includes a separate wine room, exercise room, sauna, two bedrooms, and enough space for a huge recreation room.

Rear View

SMARTtip

Art Underfoot

Make a simple geometric pattern with your flooring materials. Create a focal point in a courtyard or a small area of a patio by fashioning an intricate mosaic with tile, stone, or colored concrete. By combining elements and colors, a simple garden room floor becomes a wonderful work of art. Whether you commission a craftsman or do it yourself, you'll have a permanent art installation right in your own backyard.

Main Level
Floor Plan

Basement Level
Floor Plan

*Copyright by
designer/architect.*

Rear Elevation

Kitchen

Kitchen

Living Room

Plan #321036

Dimensions: 78'4" W x 68'6" D

Levels: 1, optional lower

Square Footage: 2,900

**Optional Basement Level
Sq. Ft.:** 1,018

Bedrooms: 4

Bathrooms: 2½

Foundation: Basement

Materials List Available: Yes

Price Category: F

Illustration provided by designer/architect.

This classic contemporary is wrapped in brick.

Features:

- **Great Room:** This grand-scale room offers a vaulted ceiling and Palladian windows flanking an 8-ft.-wide brick fireplace.

- **Kitchen:** This built-in-a-bay room features a picture window above the sink, a huge pantry, and a cooktop island. It opens to the large morning room.

- **Breakfast Area:** Open to the kitchen, this area features 12 ft. of cabinetry.

- **Master Bedroom:** This room features a coffered ceiling, and a walk-in closet gives you good storage space in this luxurious bedroom.

- **Garage:** This area can fit three cars with plenty of room to spare.

**Optional Basement Level
Floor Plan**

Plan #321004

Dimensions: 91'8" W x 62'4" D
Levels: 1
Square Footage: 2,808
Bedrooms: 3
Bathrooms: 2½
Foundation: Basement
Materials List Available: Yes
Price Category: F

Images provided by designer/architect.

You'll love the sophistication of this design, with its three porches and elegance at every turn.

Features:

- **Entry:** This impressive space welcomes guests into the living room on one side and the dining room on the other.

- **Living Room:** This spacious room will be a family favorite, especially in warm weather when you can use the adjoining porch as an outdoor extension of this area.

- **Dining Room:** Decorate this room to highlight its slightly formal feeling or to create a more casual ambiance for large family dinners.

- **Kitchen:** The family cooks will appreciate the thought that went into designing the convenient counter space and generous storage areas here.

- **Master Suite:** A vaulted ceiling, bath with a corner tub, double vanities, walk-in closet, and secluded screened porch make this area a joy.

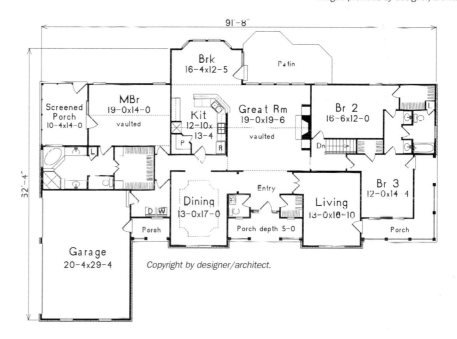

Copyright by designer/architect.

SMARTtip

Ornaments in a Garden

Placement is everything with ornaments in a garden. Some elements are best sitting by themselves. Others are better when they are part of a cohesive whole, perhaps placed in the greenery at a corner or flanking a structure.

Upper Level Floor Plan

Main Level Floor Plan

Images provided by designer/architect.

Copyright by designer/architect.

Plan #151121

Dimensions: 66'8" W x 60'4" D
Levels: 2
Square Footage: 3,108
Main Level Sq. Ft.: 2,107
Upper Level Sq. Ft.: 1,001
Bedrooms: 3
Bathrooms: 2½
Foundation: Crawl space, slab (basement option for fee)
Materials List Available: Yes
Price Category: G

Main Level Floor Plan

Upper Level Floor Plan

Images provided by designer/architect.

Copyright by designer/architect.

Plan #321054

Dimensions: 70'6" W x 55'6" D
Levels: 2
Square Footage: 2,828
Main Level Sq. Ft.: 2,006
Upper Level Sq. Ft.: 822
Bedrooms: 5
Bathrooms: 3½
Foundation: Basement
Materials List Available: Yes
Price Category: F

Plan #321031

Dimensions: 79'4" W x 59'6" D

Levels: 1

Square Footage: 3,200

Bedrooms: 3

Bathrooms: 2½

Foundation: Daylight basement

Materials List Available: Yes

Price Category: G

Illustration provided by designer/architect.

Copyright by designer/architect.

Optional Basement Level Floor Plan

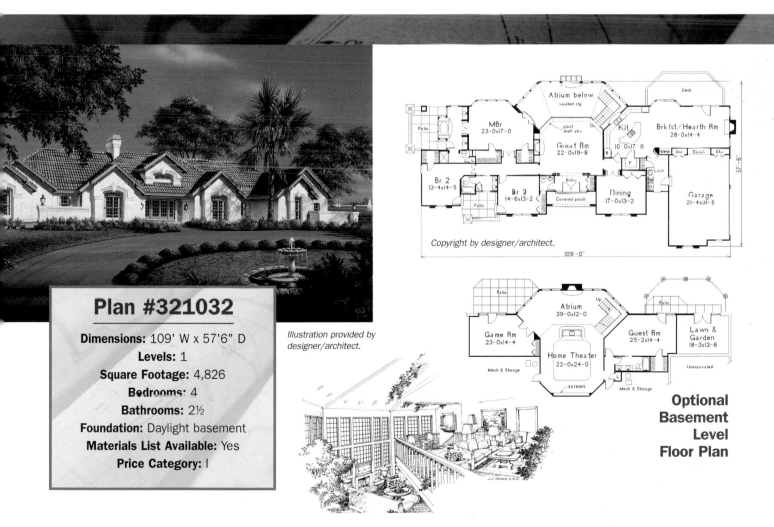

Plan #321032

Dimensions: 109' W x 57'6" D

Levels: 1

Square Footage: 4,826

Bedrooms: 4

Bathrooms: 2½

Foundation: Daylight basement

Materials List Available: Yes

Price Category: I

Illustration provided by designer/architect.

Copyright by designer/architect.

Optional Basement Level Floor Plan

Plan #121082

Dimensions: 68'8" W x 60' D

Levels: 2

Square Footage: 2,932

Main Level Sq. Ft.: 2,084

Upper Level Sq. Ft.: 848

Bedrooms: 4

Bathrooms: 3½

Foundation: Basement

Materials List Available: Yes

Price Category: F

Photo provided by designer/architect.

Enjoy the spacious covered veranda that gives this house so much added charm.

Features:

- Great Room: A volume ceiling enhances the spacious feeling in this room, making it a natural gathering spot for friends and family. Transom-topped windows look onto the veranda, and French doors open to it.

- Den: French doors from the entry lead to this room, with its unusual ceiling detail, gracious fireplace, and transom-topped windows.

- Hearth Room: Three skylights punctuate the cathedral ceiling in this room, giving it an extra measure of light and warmth.

- Kitchen: This kitchen is a delight, thanks to its generous working and storage space.

Main Level Floor Plan

Upper Level Floor Plan

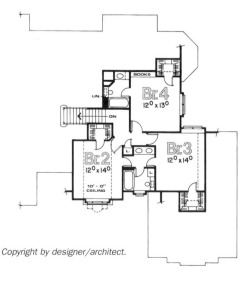

Copyright by designer/architect.

Plan #121062

Dimensions: 70' W x 62' D
Levels: 2
Square Footage: 3,448
Main Level Sq. Ft.: 2,375
Upper Level Sq. Ft.: 1,073
Bedrooms: 4
Bathrooms: 3½
Foundation: Basement
Materials List Available: Yes
Price Category: G

Photo provided by designer/architect.

You'll love this design if you're looking for a comfortable home with dimensions and details that create a sense of grandeur.

Features:

- Entry: A soaring ceiling, curved staircase, and balcony that overlooks a tall plant shelf combine to create your first impression of grandeur in this home.

- Great Room: A transom-topped bowed window highlights this room, with its 11-ft., beamed ceiling, built-in wet bar, and see-through fireplace.

- Kitchen: Designed for the gourmet cook, this kitchen has every amenity you could desire.

- Breakfast Room: Adjacent to the great room and the kitchen, this gazebo-shaped breakfast area lights both the kitchen and hearth room.

Main Level Floor Plan

Upper Level Floor Plan

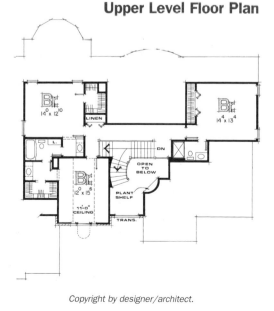

Copyright by designer/architect.

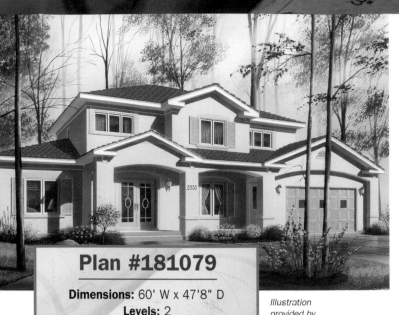

Main Level Floor Plan

Illustration provided by designer/architect.

Upper Level Floor Plan

Copyright by designer/architect.

Plan #181079

Dimensions: 60' W x 47'8" D

Levels: 2

Square Footage: 3,016

Main Level Sq. Ft.: 1,716

Upper Level Sq. Ft.: 1,300

Bedrooms: 6

Bathrooms: 4½

Foundation: Crawl space

Materials List Available: Yes

Price Category: G

Upper Level Floor Plan

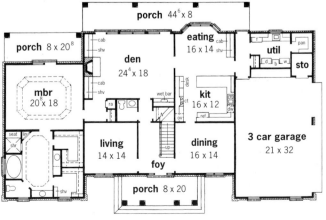

Plan #201126

Dimensions: 82'10" W x 54' D

Levels: 2

Square Footage: 3,813

Main Level Sq. Ft.: 2,553

Upper Level Sq. Ft.: 1,260

Bedrooms: 4

Bathrooms: 3½

Foundation: Crawl space, slab, or basement

Materials List Available: Yes

Price Category: H

Illustration provided by designer/architect.

Main Level Floor Plan

Copyright by designer/architect.

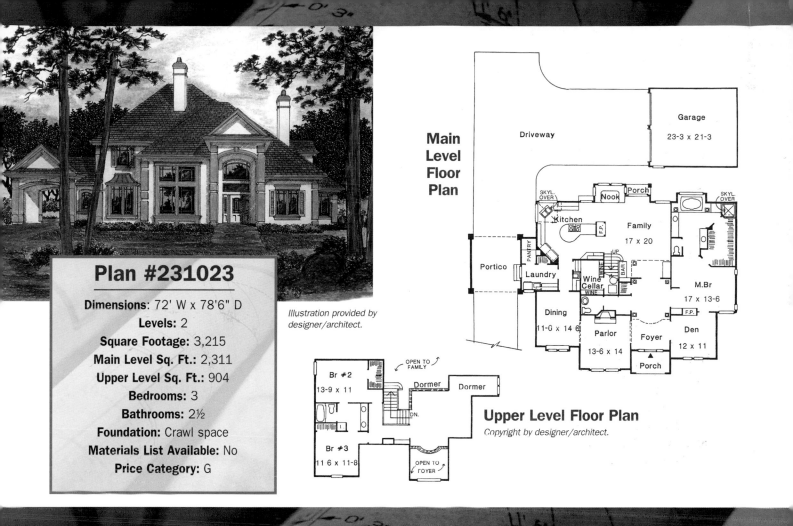

Plan #231023

Dimensions: 72' W x 78'6" D

Levels: 2

Square Footage: 3,215

Main Level Sq. Ft.: 2,311

Upper Level Sq. Ft.: 904

Bedrooms: 3

Bathrooms: 2½

Foundation: Crawl space

Materials List Available: No

Price Category: G

Main Level Floor Plan

Illustration provided by designer/architect.

Upper Level Floor Plan

Copyright by designer/architect.

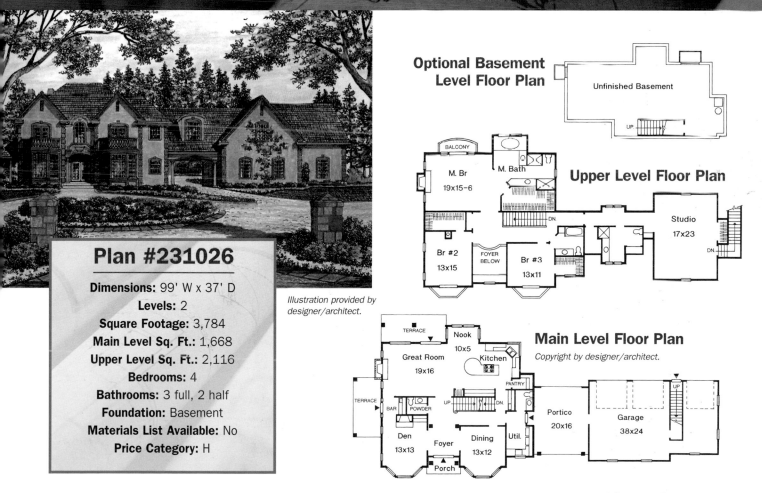

Plan #231026

Dimensions: 99' W x 37' D

Levels: 2

Square Footage: 3,784

Main Level Sq. Ft.: 1,668

Upper Level Sq. Ft.: 2,116

Bedrooms: 4

Bathrooms: 3 full, 2 half

Foundation: Basement

Materials List Available: No

Price Category: H

Optional Basement Level Floor Plan

Upper Level Floor Plan

Illustration provided by designer/architect.

Main Level Floor Plan

Copyright by designer/architect.

Plan #161029

Dimensions: 87' W x 82' D
Levels: 2
Square Footage: 4,470
Main Level Sq. Ft.: 3,300
Upper Level Sq. Ft.: 1,170
Bedrooms: 4
Bathrooms: 3 Full; 2 Half
Foundation: Slab
Materials List Available: Yes
Price Category: I

Images provided by designer/architect.

This gracious home is so impressive — inside and out — that it suits the most discriminating tastes.

Features:

- Foyer: A balcony overlooks this gracious area decorated by tall columns.
- Hearth Room: Visually open to the kitchen and the breakfast area, this room is ideal for any sort of gathering.

- Great Room: Colonial columns also form the entry here, and a magnificent window treatment that includes French doors leads to the terrace.
- Library: Built-in shelving adds practicality to this quiet retreat.
- Kitchen: Spread out on the oversized island with a cooktop and seating.
- Additional Bedrooms: Walk-in closets and private access to a bath define each bedroom.

Main Level Floor Plan

Copyright by designer/architect.

Upper Level Floor Plan

Rear View

Living Room

Living Room/Kitchen

Ideas for Entertaining

Whether an everyday family meal or a big party for 50, make it memorable and fun. With a world of options, it's easier than you think. Be imaginative with food and decoration. Although it is true that great hamburgers and hot dogs will taste good even if served on plain white paper plates, make the meal more fun by following a theme of some sort — color, occasion, or seasonal activity, for example. Be inventive with the basic elements as well as the extraneous touches, such as flowers and lighting. Here are some examples to get you started.

- For an all-American barbecue, set a picnic table with a patchwork quilt having red, white, and blue in it. Use similar colors for the napkins, and perhaps even bandannas. Include a star-studded centerpiece.

- Make a children-size dining set using an old door propped up on crates, and surround it with appropriate-size benches or chairs. Cover the table with brightly colored, easy-to-clean waxed or vinyl-covered fabric.

- If you're planning an elegant dinner party, move your dining room table outside and set it with your best linens, china, silver, and crystal. Add romantic lighting with candles in fabulous candelabras, and set a beautiful but small floral arrangement at each place setting.

- Design a centerpiece showcasing the flowers from your garden. Begin the arrangement with a base of purchased flowers, and fill in with some of your homegrown blooms. That way your flower beds will still be full of blossoms when the guests arrive.

- Base your party theme on the vegetables growing in your yard, and let them be the inspiration for the menu. When your zucchini plants are flowering, wow your family or guests by serving steamed squash blossoms. Or if the vegetables are starting to develop, lightly grill them with other young veggies — they have a much more delicate flavor than mature vegetables do.

- During berry season, host an elegant berry brunch. Serve mixed-berry crepes on your prettiest plates.

Media Rooms

A successor to the low-tech TV rooms of the 1950s and '60s, today's media room can offer a multimedia experience. It can be outfitted with everything from DVD and VHS players to sophisticated home-theater setups complete with speakers inconspicuously mounted into walls and ceilings.

However, creating a media room means more than hooking up electronics. You'll need proper housing for all of the components, such as a big-screen TV, as well as comfortable, attractive furnishings. You can go the custom route, or check out what's on the market. Cabinetry that's designed specifically for the equipment is readily available. So is movie-house-style row seating complete with cup holders and reclining chaises. You can also find floor-to-ceiling soundproofing systems that help hold and enhance the rich sound from digital equipment. It's your choice. It all depends on how much you want to spend.

A freestanding media cabinet, opposite, can be decorative and practical.

Semicustom kitchen cabinetry, above, can be outfitted and installed to suit your media-room needs.

Media-Wise Moves

No matter the size of your budget or the physical dimensions of your space, there are a full range of options that will make a media room look as good as it sounds.

Furniture

The focus here should be on functionality—enhancing your comfort and the entertainment experience. You can achieve both by furnishing the room with chairs, sectionals, and sofas that are upholstered in soft fabrics. Upholstery absorbs sound and can provide the comfort level you need when watching a two-hour movie. Add plush pillows to create an even cozier, more sound-friendly environment.

Leather furniture is always a fallback option. Although it does absorb sound better than hard materials, it can't compete with soft fabrics such as cotton, wool, and blended fabrics in terms of comfort or sound retention.

One smart option is a large upholstered storage ottoman, which can serve many purposes. It adds extra seating, serves as a coffee table, and provides a place for remote controls, DVDs, the television listings, and other media-room paraphernalia.

Cabinetry and Storage. Factor a lot of storage into your media-room plans. First, you need space for various components, such as a DVD player, VCR, receiver, CD player, and so forth. Next there's what will indeed be a growing collection of DVDs, videotapes, CDs, and remote controls. If you plan to order custom cabinetry for the space, buy your sound system and home-theater components first. Then have the cabinetmaker design the unit based on their specifications.

In terms of design, the cabinetry should accommodate components at eye level for easy operation. The topmost and lowest shelves can be reserved for lesser-used items. If you'll build the cabinet yourself, remember that there should be enough space around the components to "breathe;" built-in electronics need ventilation. Plus, you have to leave openings in the back to pull through any wires that have to be plugged into wall outlets.

In addition, be sure to include plenty of rollout drawers in the design to hold your library of favorite disks and tapes. Leave room for future purchases, too. Another option is to store tapes in a closet, a handsome trunk, or even a basket. Stockpiling tapes, CDs, and other clutter around the television screen can detract from the viewing experience.

When not in use, large TV monitors can look like big ugly boxes. Hide smaller televisions—27- or 32-inch—behind the handsome doors of a semicustom TV cabinet. Very large screens should probably be housed behind pocket, tambour, or concealed doors. Large cabinet doors that swing out into the room can obstruct traffic or even your view of the screen.

Walls, Floors, Ceilings, and Doors

Light-colored walls will reflect sunlight and artificial light and increase glare. Both can wash out the TV screen. For the same reason, mirrors and other shiny materials or glossy finishes in a media room don't make sense. Choose deep neutrals for walls, or even try a darker tone. Walls lined with corkboard, upholstered in fabric, or outfitted with high-tech sound-absorbing glass-

fiber panels covered in fashionable fabrics are all good options.

Acoustical ceiling tiles are a simple and effective solution to prevent sound from leaking into other areas. They come in a range of styles, one of which is bound to fit in with your decor.

One homeowner created a comfortable corner, above, for enjoying his collection of old recordings.

Stock cabinets, opposite, can be outfitted with optional features, such as drawers that neatly store CDs, DVDs, and VHS cassettes.

Carpeting is not only easy on the feet but also on the ear, preventing harsh echoes from bouncing around the room. Hard floor surfaces such as tile, stone, and marble can reflect and distort the sound coming from even the most expensive home-theater receiver and speakers. Cover the floor in a low-pile, low-maintenance Berber, sisal, or industrial carpet to keep sound true and pure.

Lighting

Indirect illumination that provides ambient light without on-screen glare is best for a media room. Lamps in a media room should have black or dark opaque lampshades that direct light up and down. Translucent shades radiate light in all directions. Rather than one or two bright-light sources, install several low-level lights. Dimmers will allow you to adjust lights for comfort. As a general rule, no light should be brighter than the TV screen. To avoid eyestrain and distraction, position light sources behind you and not between you and the screen.

If you want to create movie-house ambiance, install wall sconces like ones reminiscent of grand old theaters. Because you'll probably want to watch movies in a darkened room, make sure your plan includes aisle lighting, which you can plug into outlets. Wire them to one remote so you can dim them simultaneously.

Don't forget that you'll have to control natural light unless you plan to limit your home theater use to evenings. There are creative ways to reduce natural light as well. Shutters and blinds are easily adjustable window treatments. You can also check out the possibility of certain curtains that are made especially for home theaters.

Plugging into Your TV Options

Technology has clearly taken television to the next level. Even if you have an older standard model, you can improve the picture quality of broadcast viewing simply by adding cable, and even more by adding digital cable or digital satellite. But nothing beats DVD for watching movies.

HDTV, or high-definition television, has twice the picture clarity of standard TV, whether you're watching network or cable TV broadcasts or viewing a DVD. Ironically, most HDTVs don't contain high-definition tuners. So, although the picture may be better, you're not getting true HDTV unless you buy the tuning box, which is sold separately and costs around $700. Still, it's an improvement over the old versions.

Plasma and LCD TV Screens.

Thin TV is also a trend that is here to stay. Slimmed down flat-screen plasma TVs and LCD screens provide brilliant colors, better contrast and resolution, and a greater viewing angle. Because the screen is flat, there is no problem with glare. Having the lights on or off does not affect the picture. LCDs are smaller; screens range from 15 to 30 inches diagonally. Plasma TVs start at 32

Plump upholstered seating, opposite, arranged at the proper distance from the screen, lets you view TV and movies comfortably.

Ready-to-assemble furniture, above, is an affordable alternative to custom or semicustom cabinets.

inches and go up to big-screen size from there. Most of them accept HDTV signals, but they are usually not powerful enough to display all of the high resolution.

Rear Projection. The screen size of a rear-projection TV is large—40 to 82 inches—and can be viewed in natural light without sacrificing picture quality. In general, the picture is often inferior, unless it is an HDTV format. Another drawback: rear projection TVs must be watched at eye-level and straight-on for optimal viewing.

Front Projection. This system has a separate screen, which can either drop down from the ceiling or remain fixed on the wall, and a projector that is mounted at ceiling height across the room from the screen. It's akin to a movie-theater system. Front projection is expensive and requires a professional to install it. Although even minor light can wash out the picture, the image quality is unbeatable when the room is dark.

More Tips

If you're thinking of creating a home theater in your new house, here are a few pointers.

- Most home-theater designers recommend televisions screens that are at least 27 inches wide.
- Seating distance can add or subtract from the viewing quality. For optimal viewing,

there should be a distance between you and the TV that is 2 to 2½ times the width of the screen. That means placing sofa and chairs 54 to 68 inches from a 27-inch screen, for example. If your TV is a wide-screen high-definition model, place it a distance that is 1½ times the screen's diagonal width from your seating area.

- Five speakers will create a full-home theater sound. Place one speaker on each side of the TV screen, level with your ears when you are seated, and about 3 feet from the sidewalls. Place two speakers behind the sofa about 6 to 8 feet off the floor and at least as wide apart as the front speakers. Put the fifth speaker on top of the TV.
- Replace a collection of remote controls with a single universal model that can control everything from the DVD player to the lights (with a special receiver).

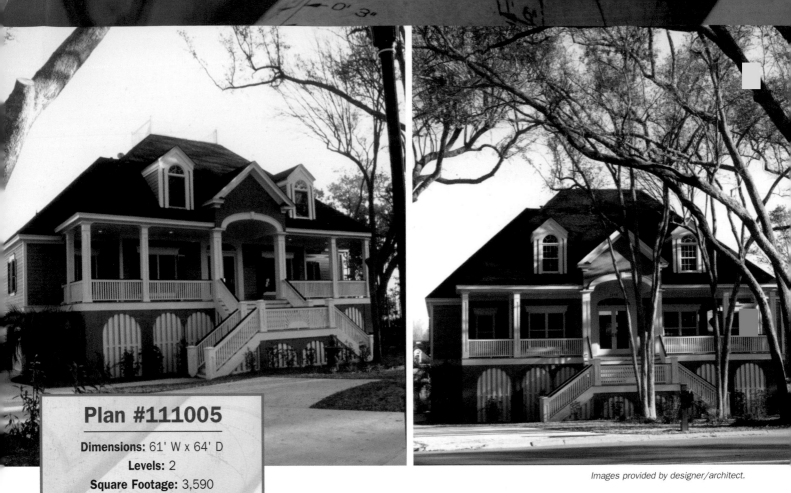

Images provided by designer/architect.

Plan #111005

Dimensions: 61' W x 64' D

Levels: 2

Square Footage: 3,590

Main Level Sq. Ft.: 2,390

Upper Level Sq. Ft.: 1,200

Bedrooms: 5

Bathrooms: 3

Foundation: Above ground basement

Materials List Available: No

Price Category: H

You'll love this historic, classic design, with its slightly Southern and very traditional feeling.

Features:

- Ceiling Height: 9 ft.

- Foyer: This gracious area opens to the formal dining room and, through French doors, to the quiet study.

- Living Room: A two-story ceiling emphasizes the spaciousness of this bright and airy room. A balcony from the upper level looks into the living room below.

- Multimedia Room: Positioned on the upper level for both quiet and the children's convenience, this room will be a gathering point for everyone.

- Kitchen: A working island and snack bar are practical touches. The adjoining breakfast area opens to the rear covered porch.

- Master Suite: French doors lead to the huge wooden deck, and the bath has two vanities, a walk-in closet, a corner tub, and a standing shower.

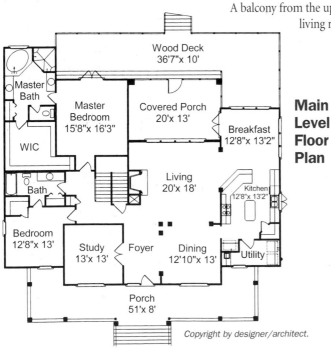

Main Level Floor Plan

Upper Level Floor Plan

Copyright by designer/architect.

Dining Room

Living Room

Living Room

SMARTtip

Window Trims

If conventional trims and braids don't excite you, look for untraditional or unusual elements for decorating your window treatments. Attach single beads, small shells, or crystal drops at regular intervals along the edge. Either glue them in place or, if they have holes, sew them on. A series of stars, leaves, or some other appropriate shape made of stiffened fabric and then glued or stitched on is another idea. Consider old or new buttons, jewelry, or metal chains. If your embroidery skills are good, use them to embellish the window treatment.

Plan #211111

Dimensions: 66' W x 74' D
Levels: 2
Square Footage: 3,035
Main Level Sq. Ft.: 2,008
Upper Level Sq. Ft.: 1,027
Bedrooms: 4
Bathrooms: 3½
Foundation: Crawl space
Materials List Available: Yes
Price Category: G

Kids can be kids without disturbing the adults, thanks to the rear stair in this large family house.

Features:

- Ceiling Height: 9 ft. unless otherwise noted.

- Formal Living Room: This large formal living room is connected to the formal dining room and to the family room by a pair of French doors, making this an ideal home for entertaining.

- Wet Bar: This wet bar is neatly placed between the kitchen and the family room, adding to the entertainment amenities.

- Deck: Step out of the family room onto a covered porch that leads to this spacious deck and a breezeway.

- Master Suite: This master suite is isolated for privacy. The master bath is flooded with natural light from sky windows in the sloped ceiling, and it has a dressing vanity with surrounding mirrors.

- Secondary Bedrooms: All secondary bedrooms have bath access and dual closets.

Illustration provided by designer/architect.

Copyright by designer/architect.

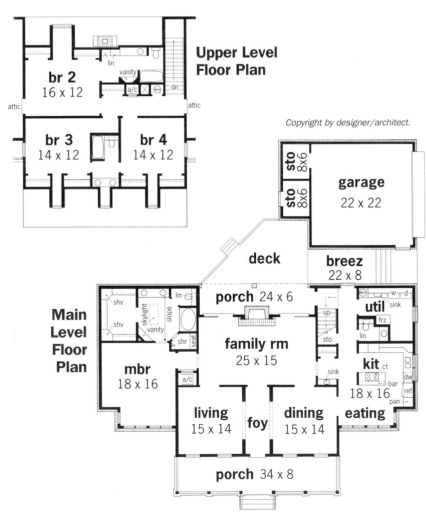

Plan #101019

Dimensions: 58'4" W x 55'2" D
Levels: 2
Square Footage: 2,954
Main Level Sq. Ft. 2093
Upper Level Sq. Ft. 861
Bedrooms: 4
Bathrooms: 3½
Foundation: Slab, crawl space, or basement
Materials List Available: No
Price Category: F

Illustration provided by designer/architect.

This luxurious home features a spectacular open floor plan and a brick exterior.

Features:

- Ceiling Height: 9 ft. unless otherwise noted.
- Foyer: This inviting two-story foyer, which vaults to 18 ft., will greet guests with an impressive "welcome."
- Dining Room: To the right of the foyer is this spacious dining room surrounded by decorative columns.

- Family Room: There's plenty of room for all kinds of family activities in this enormous room, with its soaring two-story ceiling.
- Master Suite: This sumptuous retreat boasts a tray ceiling. Optional pocket doors provide direct access to the study. The master bath features his and her vanities and a large walk-in closet.
- Breakfast Area: Perfect for informal family meals, this bayed breakfast area has real flair.
- Secondary Bedrooms: Upstairs are three large bedrooms with 8-ft. ceilings. One has a private bath.

Main Level Floor Plan

Upper Level Floor Plan

Copyright by designer/architect.

Plan #261009

Dimensions: 90' W x 46' D

Levels: 2

Square Footage: 4,048

Main Level Sq. Ft.: 2,388

Upper Level Sq. Ft.: 1,660

Bedrooms: 5

Bathrooms: 4½

Foundation: Basement

Materials List Available: No

Price Category: I

Images provided by designer/architect.

You'll love the elegant exterior of this classic Tudor manor and luxuriate in its amenity-filled, contemporary interior design.

Features:

- **Ceiling Heights:** High, volume ceilings give an airy feeling in the foyer, family room, and living room. All other rooms feature 9-ft. ceilings.

- **Family Room:** Gather around the fireplace here or in the living room in chilly weather.

- **Den:** Use this well-positioned first-floor room for a bedroom, guestroom, or home office.

- **Dining Room:** Everyone will love the pocket door here that leads to the kitchen.

- **Kitchen:** With a pantry and large work island, this kitchen is designed for efficiency and comfort.

- **Master Suite:** French doors open to the bedroom, and the private bath has double vanities, a corner whirlpool tub, and a walk-in shower.

Main Level Floor Plan

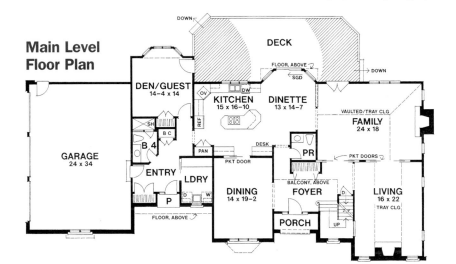

Copyright by designer/architect.

Upper Level Floor Plan

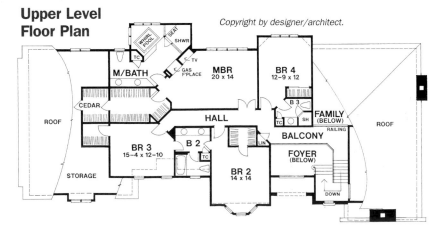

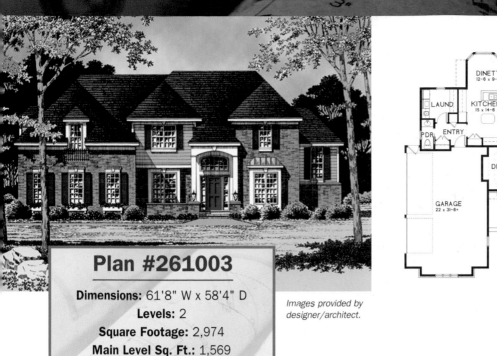

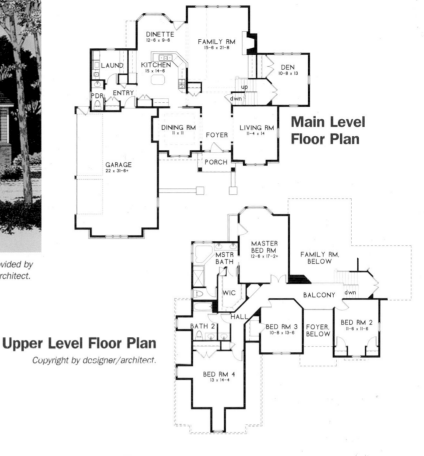

Plan #261003

Dimensions: 61'8" W x 58'4" D

Levels: 2

Square Footage: 2,974

Main Level Sq. Ft.: 1,569

Upper Level Sq. Ft.: 1,405

Bedrooms: 4

Bathrooms: 2½

Foundation: Basement

Materials List Available: No

Price Category: F

Images provided by designer/architect.

Main Level Floor Plan

Upper Level Floor Plan

Copyright by designer/architect.

Plan #261006

Dimensions: 73'10" W x 60' D

Levels: 2

Square Footage: 4,583

Main Level Sq. Ft.: 2,575

Upper Level Sq. Ft.: 2,008

Bedrooms: 4

Bathrooms: 3 full, 2 half

Foundation: Basement

Materials List Available: No

Price Category: I

Images provided by designer/architect.

Main Level Floor Plan

Upper Level Floor Plan

Copyright by designer/architect.

Plan #121071

Dimensions: 72'8" W x 51'4" D
Levels: 2
Square Footage: 2,957
Main Level Sq. Ft.: 2,063
Upper Level Sq. Ft.: 894
Bedrooms: 4
Bathrooms: 4½
Foundation: Basement
Materials List Available: Yes
Price Category: F

Photo provided by designer/architect.

You'll appreciate the mix of open public areas and private quarters that the layout of this home guarantees.

Features:

- Entry: From this entry, the formal living and dining rooms, as well as the great room, are all visible.

- Great Room: A soaring cathedral ceiling sets an elegant tone for this room, and the fireplace that's flanked with lovely transom-topped windows adds to it.

- Den: French doors from the great room lead to this den, where you'll find a generous bay window, a wet bar, and a decorative ceiling.

- Master Suite: On the main floor to give it needed privacy, this master suite will make you feel at home the first time you walk into it. The private bath has an angled ceiling and a whirlpool tub.

Main Level Floor Plan

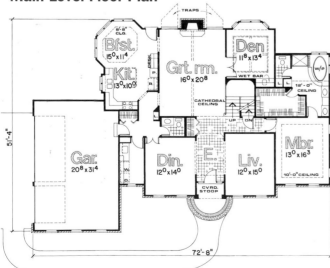

Upper Level Floor Plan

Copyright by designer/architect.

Plan #121069

Dimensions: 58' W x 59'4" D

Levels: 2

Square Footage: 2,914

Main Level Sq. Ft.: 1,583

Upper Level Sq. Ft.: 1,331

Bedrooms: 4

Bathrooms: 3½

Foundation: Basement

Materials List Available: Yes

Price Category: F

Photo provided by designer/architect.

You'll love this design if you're looking for a home to complement a site with a lovely rear view.

Features:

- **Great Room:** A trio of lovely windows looks out to the front entry of this home. The French doors in this room open to the breakfast area for everyone's convenience.

- **Kitchen:** Designed to suit a gourmet cook, this kitchen includes a roomy pantry and an island with a snack bar.

- **Breakfast Area:** The boxed window here is perfect for houseplants or a collection of culinary herbs. A door leads to the rear porch, where you'll love to dine in good weather.

- **Master Suite:** On the upper level, the bedroom features a cathedral ceiling, two walk-in closets, and a window seat. The bath also has a cathedral ceiling and includes dual lavatories, a large dressing area, and a sunlit whirlpool tub.

Main Level Floor Plan

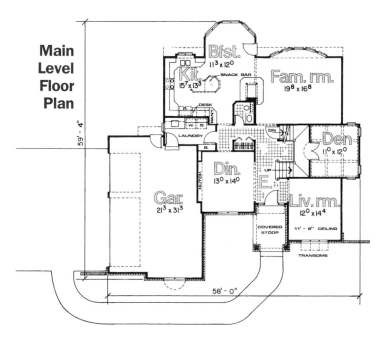

Upper Level Floor Plan

Copyright by designer/architect.

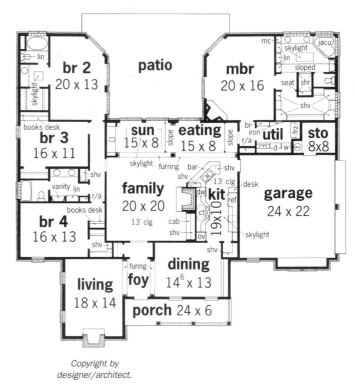

Illustration provided by designer/architect.

Plan #211065

Dimensions: 72' W x 70' D

Levels: 1

Square Footage: 3,158

Bedrooms: 4

Bathrooms: 3

Foundation: Crawl space

Materials List Available: Yes

Price Category: G

Copyright by designer/architect.

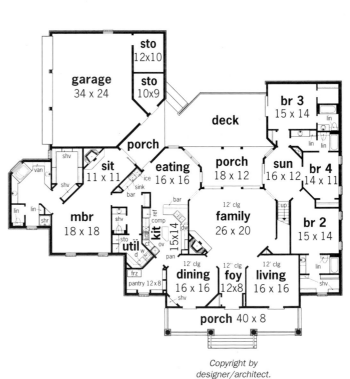

Illustration provided by designer/architect.

Plan #211067

Dimensions: 96' W x 90' D

Levels: 1

Square Footage: 4,038

Bedrooms: 4

Bathrooms: 4½

Foundation: Crawl space

Materials List Available: Yes

Price Category: I

Copyright by designer/architect.

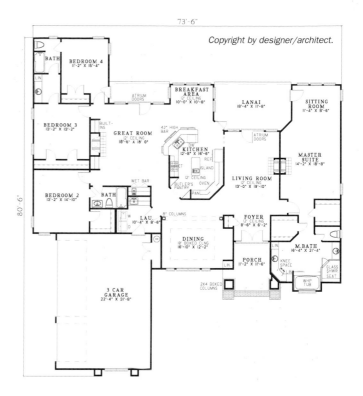

Copyright by designer/architect.

Illustration provided by designer/architect.

Plan #151057

Dimensions: 73'6" W x 80'6" D

Levels: 1

Square Footage: 2,951

Bedrooms: 4

Bathrooms: 3

Foundation: Crawl space, slab, or basement

Materials List Available: Yes

Price Category: F

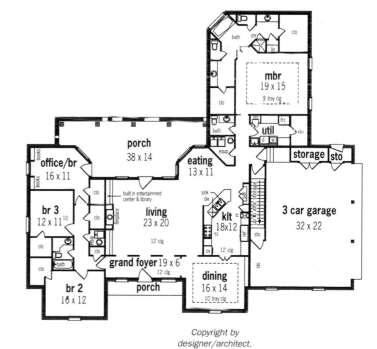

Illustration provided by designer/architect.

Plan #211064

Dimensions: 83' W x 78' D

Levels: 1

Square Footage: 2,936

Bedrooms: 4

Bathrooms: 2½

Foundation: Crawl space

Materials List Available: No

Price Category: F

Copyright by designer/architect.

Images provided by designer/architect.

Plan #211076

Dimensions: 95' W x 90' D
Levels: 2
Square Footage: 4,242
Main Level Sq. Ft.: 3,439
Upper Level Sq. Ft.: 803
Bedrooms: 4
Bathrooms: 4 full, 3 half
Foundation: Raised slab
Materials List Available: Yes
Price Category: I

Build this country manor home on a large lot with a breathtaking view to complement its beauty.

Features:

- Foyer: You'll love the two-story ceiling here.

- Living Room: A sunken floor, two-story ceiling, large fireplace, and generous balcony above combine to create an unusually beautiful room.

- Kitchen: Use the breakfast bar at any time of the day. The layout guarantees ample working space, and the pantry gives room for extra storage.

- Master Suite: A sunken floor, wood-burning fireplace, and 200-sq.-ft. sitting area work in concert to create a restful space.

- Bedrooms: The guest room is on the main floor, and bedrooms 2 and 3, both with built-in desks in special study areas, are on the upper level.

- Outdoor Grilling Area: Fitted with a bar, this area makes it a pleasure to host a large group.

Kitchen

Kitchen

Main Level Floor Plan

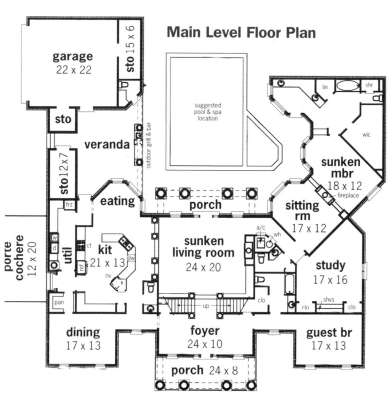

garage 22 x 22

sto 15 x 6

sto

veranda

outdoor grill & bar

sto 12x7

frz

eating

suggested pool & spa location

porch

a/c

wh

sunken living room 24 x 20

lin

shr

wic

sunken mbr 18 x 12

fireplace

sitting rm 17 x 12

study 17 x 16

porte cochere 12 x 20

w

d

ct

kit 21 x 13

dw

ref

ov

util

pan

up

clo

shvs

clo

clo

clo

dining 17 x 13

foyer 24 x 10

guest br 17 x 13

porch 24 x 8

Copyright by designer/architect.

Master Bathroom

Upper Level Floor Plan

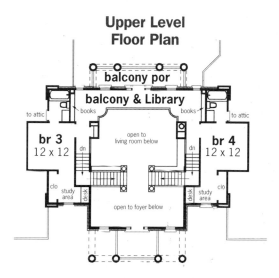

balcony por

balcony & Library

to attic

books

books

to attic

br 3 12 x 12

open to living room below

br 4 12 x 12

dn

dn

clo

study area

desk

open to foyer below

desk

study area

clo

Dining Room

Living Room

Plan #121065

Dimensions: 62' W x 55'4" D
Levels: 2
Square Footage: 3,407
Main Level Sq. Ft.: 1,719
Upper Level Sq. Ft.: 1,688
Bedrooms: 4
Bathrooms: 2½
Foundation: Basement
Materials List Available: Yes
Price Category: G

Photo provided by designer/architect.

If you love contemporary design, the unusual shapes of the rooms in this home will delight you.

Features:

• Entry: You'll see a balcony from the upper level that overlooks this entryway, as well as the lovely curved staircase to this floor.

• Great Room: This room is sunken to set it apart. A fireplace, wet bar, spider-beamed ceiling, and row of arched windows give it character.

• Dining Room: Columns define this lovely octagon room, where you'll love to entertain guests or create lavish family dinners.

• Master Suite: A multi-tiered ceiling adds a note of grace, while the fireplace and private library create a real retreat. The gracious bath features a gazebo ceiling and a skylight.

Main Level Floor Plan

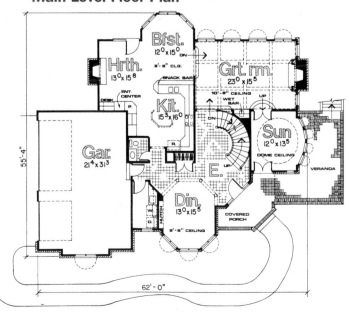

Upper Level Floor Plan

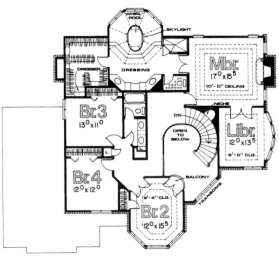

Copyright by designer/architect.

Plan #161030

Dimensions: 98'6" W x 61'5" D
Levels: 2
Square Footage: 4,562
Main Level Sq. Ft.: 3,364
Upper Level Sq. Ft.: 1,198
Bedrooms: 4
Bathrooms: 3½
Foundation: Slab
Materials List Available: Yes
Price Category: I

Images provided by designer/architect.

You'll be charmed by this impressive home, with its stone-and-brick exterior.

Features:

- **Great Room:** The two-story ceiling here adds even more dimension to this expansive space.

- **Hearth Room:** A tray ceiling and molding help to create a cozy feeling in this room, which is located so your guests will naturally gravitate to it.

- **Dining Room:** This formal room features columns at the entry and a butler's pantry for entertaining.

- **Master Suite:** A walk-in closet, platform whirlpool tub, and 2-person shower are only a few of the luxuries in the private bath, and tray ceilings and moldings give extra presence to the bedroom.

- **Upper Level:** A balcony offers a spectacular view of the great room and leads to three large bedrooms, each with a private bath.

Main Level Floor Plan

Upper Level Floor Plan

Copyright by designer/architect.

Plan #321034

Dimensions: 75'8" W x 52'6" D

Levels: 1

Square Footage: 3,508

Bedrooms: 4

Bathrooms: 3

Foundation: Daylight basement

Material List Available: Yes

Price Category: H

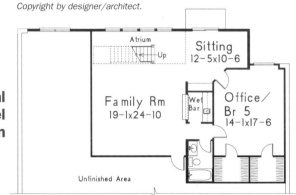

Images provided by designer/architect.

Copyright by designer/architect.

Optional Basement Level Floor Plan

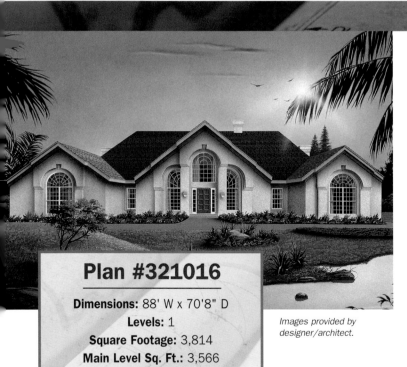

Plan #321016

Dimensions: 88' W x 70'8" D

Levels: 1

Square Footage: 3,814

Main Level Sq. Ft.: 3,566

Basement Level Sq. Ft.: 248

Bedrooms: 3

Bathrooms: 2½

Foundation: Daylight basement

Materials List Available: Yes

Price Category: H

Images provided by designer/architect.

Rear View

Copyright by designer/architect.

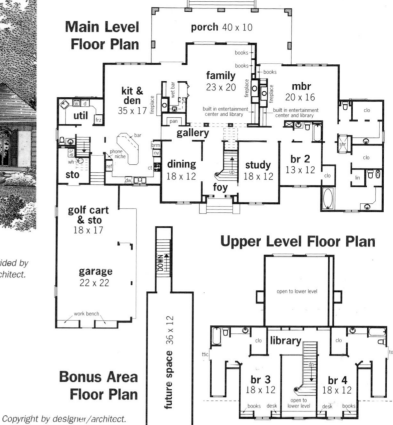

Main Level Floor Plan

porch 40 x 10

family 23 x 20

kit & den 35 x 17

mbr 20 x 16

util

wet bar

built in entertainment center and library

built in entertainment center and library

books
books
books

clo

gallery

bar

sto

phone niche

study 18 x 12

br 2 13 x 12

clo

clo

lin

dining 18 x 12

foy

up

ct

Upper Level Floor Plan

golf cart & sto 18 x 17

garage 22 x 22

work bench

DOWN

open to lower level

library

clo

clo

br 3 18 x 12

br 4 18 x 12

books desk

open to lower level

desk books

Bonus Area Floor Plan

future space 36 x 12

Images provided by designer/architect.

Copyright by designer/architect.

Plan #211125

Dimensions: 94' W x 92' D

Levels: 2

Square Footage: 4,440

Main Level Sq. Ft.: 3,465

Upper Level Sq. Ft.: 975

Bedrooms: 4

Bathrooms: 5½

Foundation: Crawl space

Materials List Available: Yes

Price Category: I

Main Level Floor Plan

Deck 25'8"x 9'

Den 13'8"x 12'9"

Porch 25'8"x 0'

Breakfast 10'6"x 10'

Living 25'4"x 18'

Kitchen 13'8"x 15'

Porch

Dining 13'8"x 12'

Porch

Master Bedroom 20'x 18'

Master Bath

WIC

WIC

Utility

Bath

Bedroom 15'8"x 11'

Porch

Bedroom 13'8"x 12'

Upper Level Floor Plan

Bath

Bedroom 15'8"x 11'

Images provided by designer/architect.

Copyright by designer/architect.

Plan #111012

Dimensions: 43' W x 77' D

Levels: 2

Square Footage: 3,366

Main Level Sq. Ft.: 1,742

Upper Level Sq. Ft.: 1,624

Bedrooms: 4

Bathrooms: 3

Foundation: Basement

Materials List Available: No

Price Category: G

Plan #121063

Dimensions: 84' W x 52' D
Levels: 2
Square Footage: 3,473
Main Level Sq. Ft.: 2,500
Upper Level Sq. Ft.: 973
Bedrooms: 4
Bathrooms: 3½
Foundation: Basement
Materials List Available: Yes
Price Category: G

Photo provided by designer/architect.

Enjoy the many amenities in this well-designed and gracious home.

Features:

- Entry: A large sparkling window and a tapering split staircase distinguish this lovely entryway.

- Great Room: This spacious great room will be the heart of your new home. It has a 14-ft. spider-beamed window that serves to highlight its built-in bookcase, built-in entertainment center, raised hearth fireplace,

wet bar, and lovely arched windows topped with transoms.

- Kitchen: Anyone who walks into this kitchen will realize that it's designed for both convenience and efficiency.

- Master Suite: The tiered ceiling in the bedroom gives an elegant touch, and the bay window adds to it. The two large walk-in closets and the spacious bath, with columns setting off the whirlpool tub and two vanities, complete this dream of a suite.

Main Level Floor Plan

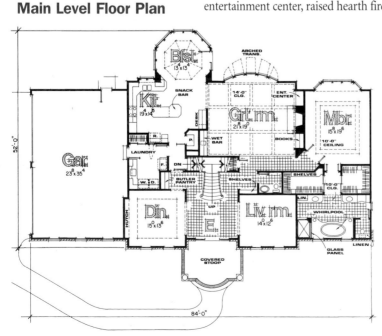

Upper Level Floor Plan

Copyright by designer/architect.

Plan #161028

Dimensions: 84'6" W x 69'4" D

Levels: 1

Square Footage: 3,570

Optional Finished Basement Sq. Ft.: 2,367

Bedrooms: 3

Bathrooms: 3½

Foundation: Basement

Materials List Available: Yes

Price Category: H

Images provided by designer/architect.

From the gabled stone-and-brick exterior to the wide-open view from the foyer, this home will meet your greatest expectations.

Features:

• Great Room/Dining Room: Columns and 13-ft. ceilings add exquisite detailing to the dining room and great room.

• Kitchen: The gourmet-equipped kitchen with an island and a snack bar merges with the cozy breakfast and hearth rooms.

• Master Bedroom: The luxurious master bed room pampers with a separate sitting room with a fireplace and a dressing room boasting a whirlpool tub and two vanities.

• Additional: Two bedrooms upstairs include a private bath and walk-in closet. The optional finished basement solves all your recreational needs: bar, media room, billiards room, exercise room, game room, as well as an office and fourth bedroom.

Rear Elevation

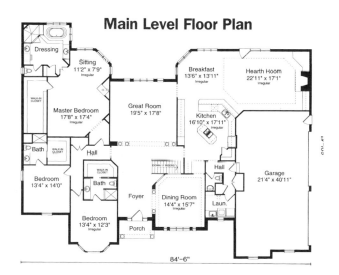

Main Level Floor Plan

Basement Level Floor Plan

Copyright by designer/architect.

Plan #261001

Dimensions: 77'8" W x 49' D

Levels: 2

Square Footage: 3,746

Main Level Sq. Ft.: 1,965

Upper Level Sq. Ft.: 1,781

Bedrooms: 4

Bathrooms: 3½

Foundation: Basement

Materials List Available: No

Price Category: H

If contemporary designs appeal to you, you're sure to love this stunning home.

Features:

- Foyer: A volume ceiling here announces the spaciousness of this gracious home.

- Great Room: Also with a volume ceiling, this great room features a fireplace where you can create a cozy sitting area.

- Kitchen: Designed for the pleasure of the family cooks, this room features a large pantry, ample counter and cabinet space, and a dining bar.

- Dinette: Serve the family in style, or host casual, informal dinners for friends in this dinette with its gracious volume ceiling.

- Master Suite: A fireplace makes this suite a welcome retreat on cool nights, but even in warm weather you'll love its spaciousness and the walk-in closet. The bath features dual vanities, a whirlpool tub, and a separate shower.

Images provided by designer/architect.

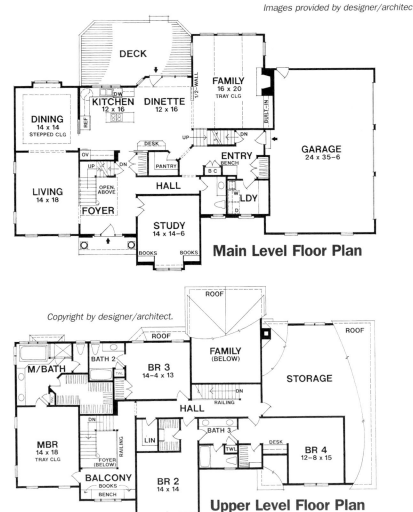

Main Level Floor Plan

Copyright by designer/architect.

Upper Level Floor Plan

Illustration provided by designer/architect.

Plan #221025

Dimensions: 69'8" W x 72' D

Levels: 2

Square Footage: 3,009

Main Level Sq. Ft.: 2,039

Upper Level Sq. Ft.: 970

Bedrooms: 4

Bathrooms: 2½

Foundation: Basement

Materials List Available: No

Price Category: G

Designed to resemble a country home in France, this two-story beauty will delight you with its good looks and luxurious amenities.

Features:

- **Great Room:** You'll look into this great room as soon as you enter the two-story foyer. A fireplace flanked by built-in bookcases and large windows looking out to the deck highlight this room.

- **Dining Room:** This formal room is located just off the entry for the convenience of your guests.

- **Kitchen:** A huge central island and large pantry make this kitchen a delight for any cook. The large nook looks onto the deck and opens to the lovely three-season porch.

- **Master Suite:** You'll love this suite, with its charming bay shape, great windows, walk-in closet, luxurious bath, and door to the deck.

- **Upper Level:** Everyone will love the two bedrooms, large bath, and huge game.

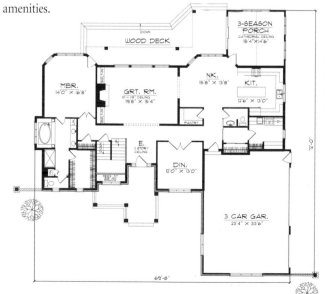

Main Level Floor Plan

Upper Level Floor Plan

Copyright by designer/architect.

Plan #121076

Dimensions: 64' W x 60'8" D

Levels: 2

Square Footage: 3,067

Main Level Sq. Ft.: 2,169

Upper Level Sq. Ft.: 898

Bedrooms: 4

Bathrooms: 3½

Foundation: Basement

Materials List Available: Yes

Price Category: G

Photo provided by designer/architect.

You'll love the combination of formal features and casual, family-friendly areas in this spacious home with an elegant exterior.

Features:

- **Entry:** The elegant windows in this two-story area are complemented by the unusual staircase.
- **Family Room:** This family room features an 11-ft. ceiling, wet bar, fireplace, and trio of windows that look out to the covered porch.
- **Living Room:** Columns set off both this room and the dining room. Decorate to accentuate their formality, or make them blend into a more casual atmosphere.
- **Master Suite:** Columns in this suite highlight a bayed sitting room where you'll be happy to relax at the end of the day or on weekend mornings.
- **Bedrooms:** Bedroom 2 has a private bath, making it an ideal guest room, and you'll find private vanities in bedrooms 3 and 4.

Main Level Floor Plan

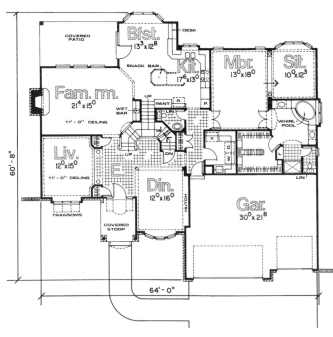

Upper Level Floor Plan

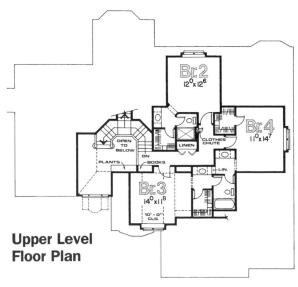

Copyright by designer/architect.

Plan #121072

Dimensions: 64' W x 53'4" D
Levels: 2
Square Footage: 3,031
Main Level Sq. Ft.: 1,640
Upper Level Sq. Ft.: 1,391
Bedrooms: 4
Bathrooms: 3½
Foundation: Basement
Materials List Available: Yes
Price Category: G

Photo provided by designer/architect.

If you're looking for a home with well-designed rooms and interesting architectural innovations, this could be your heart's desire.

Features:

- **Foyer:** This foyer has an impressive two-story ceiling and is lit by the arched transom and sidelights at the entryway.

- **Living Room:** Just off the foyer, this room has a 12-ft. angled ceiling. Decorate to emphasize the arched window here.

- **Den:** French doors open to the den, where a spider-beamed ceiling sets an elegant tone.

- **Kitchen:** This well-designed kitchen is sure to be the delight of every cook in the family.

- **Master Suite:** French doors open into this suite, with built-in dressers tucked into a huge closet and a bath with a whirlpool tub and two vanities.

- **Upper Level:** You'll love the view from the balcony into the foyer below.

Main Level Floor Plan

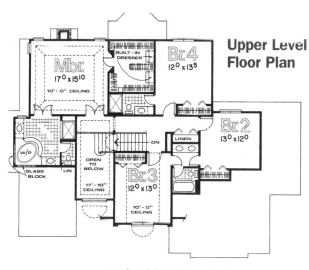

Upper Level Floor Plan

Copyright by designer/architect.

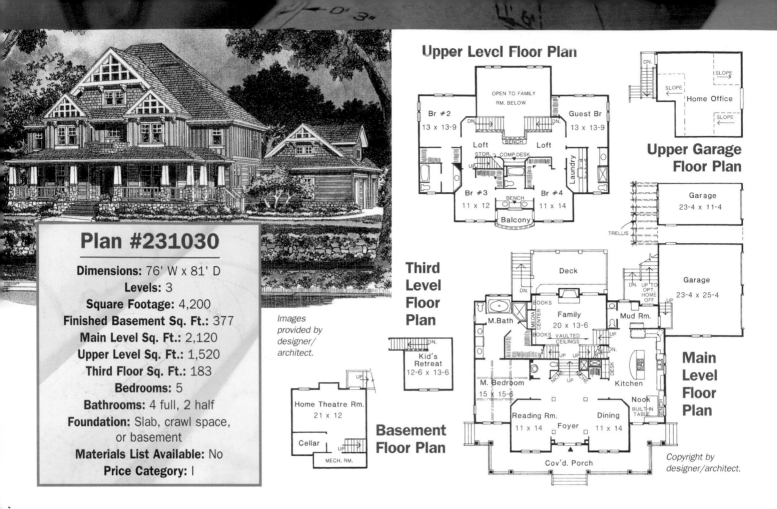

Plan #231030

Dimensions: 76' W x 81' D

Levels: 3

Square Footage: 4,200

Finished Basement Sq. Ft.: 377

Main Level Sq. Ft.: 2,120

Upper Level Sq. Ft.: 1,520

Third Floor Sq. Ft.: 183

Bedrooms: 5

Bathrooms: 4 full, 2 half

Foundation: Slab, crawl space, or basement

Materials List Available: No

Price Category: I

Images provided by designer/architect.

Upper Level Floor Plan

OPEN TO FAMILY RM. BELOW

Br #2 13 x 13-9 — Guest Br 13 x 13-9

Loft — Loft

STOR. — COMP.DESK

Br #3 11 x 12 — Br #4 11 x 14

Laundry

Balcony

BENCH

Upper Garage Floor Plan

DN.

SLOPE — Home Office — SLOPE

Garage 23-4 x 11-4

TRELLIS

Garage 23-4 x 25-4

UP TO OPT. HOME OFF.

Third Level Floor Plan

Kid's Retreat 12-6 x 13-6

Basement Floor Plan

Home Theatre Rm. 21 x 12

Cellar

MECH. RM.

Main Level Floor Plan

Deck

M.Bath

Family 20 x 13-6

VAULTED CEILINGS

BOOKS — MEDIA CENTER — BOOKS

Mud Rm.

M. Bedroom 15 x 15-6

NICHE — NICHE

DESK

Kitchen

Reading Rm. 11 x 14 — Foyer — Dining 11 x 14

Nook

BUILT-IN TABLE

BENCH

Cov'd. Porch

Copyright by designer/architect.

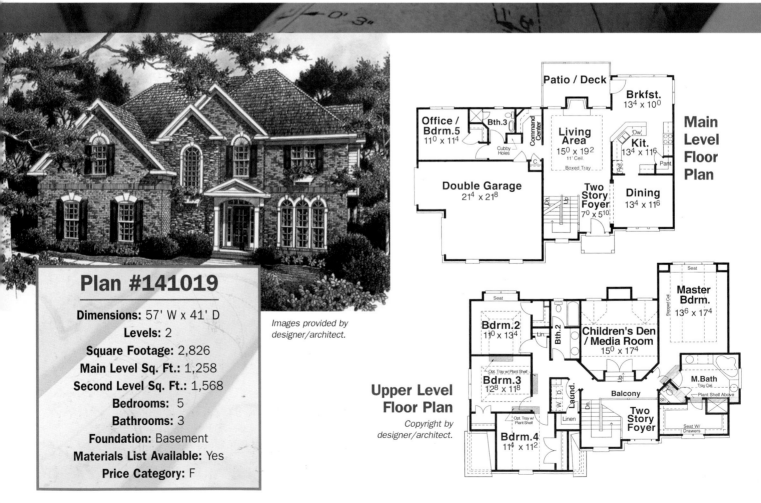

Plan #141019

Dimensions: 57' W x 41' D

Levels: 2

Square Footage: 2,826

Main Level Sq. Ft.: 1,258

Second Level Sq. Ft.: 1,568

Bedrooms: 5

Bathrooms: 3

Foundation: Basement

Materials List Available: Yes

Price Category: F

Images provided by designer/architect.

Main Level Floor Plan

Patio / Deck

Office / Bdrm.5 11⁰ x 11⁴

Bth.3

Command Center

Living Area 15⁰ x 19² 11' Ceil. Boxed Tray

Brkfst. 13⁴ x 10⁰

Kit. 13⁴ x 11⁶

Cubby Holes

Double Garage 21⁴ x 21⁸

Two Story Foyer 7⁰ x 5¹⁰

Dining 13⁴ x 11⁶

Upper Level Floor Plan

Copyright by designer/architect.

Master Bdrm. 13⁶ x 17⁴

Bdrm.2 11⁰ x 13⁴

Bth.2

Children's Den / Media Room 15⁰ x 17⁴

Bdrm.3 12⁸ x 11⁸

Opt. Tray w/ Plant Shelf

W/D

Laund.

Linen

Balcony

M.Bath

Bdrm.4 11⁴ x 11²

Two Story Foyer

Seat W/ Drawers

Plan #271095

Dimensions: 70' W x 74'4" D
Levels: 2
Square Footage: 3,220
Main Level Sq. Ft.: 2,040
Upper Level Sq. Ft.: 1,180
Bedrooms: 3
Bathrooms: 3½
Foundation: Crawl space, slab
Materials List Available: No
Price Category: G

Images provided by designer/architect.

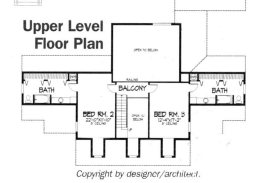

Main Level Floor Plan

Upper Level Floor Plan

Copyright by designer/architect.

Plan #321011

Dimensions: 83' W x 50'4" D
Levels: 1
Square Footage: 2,874
Bedrooms: 4
Bathrooms: 2½
Foundation: Basement
Materials List Available: Yes
Price Category: F

Images provided by designer/architect.

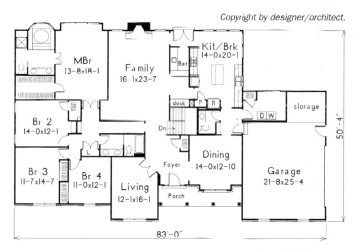

Copyright by designer/architect.

SMARTtip

Drilling for Kitchen Plumbing

Drill holes for plumbing and waste lines before installing the cabinets. It is easier to work when the cabinets are out in the middle of the floor, and there is no danger of knocking them out of alignment when creating the holes if they are not screwed to the wall studs or one another yet.

Plan #221022

Dimensions: 79' W x 55' D

Levels: 2

Square Footage: 3,382

Main Level Sq. Ft.: 2,376

Upper Level Sq. Ft.: 1,006

Bedrooms: 4

Bathrooms: 3½

Foundation: Basement

Materials List Available: No

Price Category: G

Images provided by designer/architect.

- **Master Suite:** Located on the main floor for privacy, this area includes a walk-in closet and a deluxe full bathroom.

- **Upper Level:** Look into the great room and entryway as you climb the stairs to the three large bedrooms and a full bath on this floor.

The traditional-looking facade of stone, brick, and siding opens into a home you'll love for its spaciousness, comfort, and great natural lighting.

Features:

- **Ceiling Height:** 9 ft.

- **Great Room:** The two-story ceiling here emphasizes the dimensions of this large room, and the huge windows make it bright and cheery.

- **Sunroom:** Use this area as a den or an indoor conservatory, where you can relax in the midst of health-promoting and beautiful plants.

- **Kitchen:** This well-planned kitchen features a snacking island and opens into a generous dining nook where everyone will gather.

Main Level Floor Plan

SMARTtip

Clearing the Canvas-
Arranging Furniture

If you are having trouble creating a pleasing arrangement of furniture in a room, it can help to remove all of the contents and start from scratch. This is a good idea if you have trouble picturing things on paper or if you aren't going to buy a lot of new furniture and just need a fresh start. If at all possible, strip the room down completely, removing all of the furnishings, including window treatments, rugs, wall art, and accessories. This way you can observe the true architectural nature of the space without distractions that influence your perceptions. For example, minus the trappings of curtains, you can see that two windows may be slightly different sizes or installed too close to a corner. Other things you may notice might be odd corners, uneven walls, radiators or heating registers that are conspicuously located, or any other quirky features that are unique to your home.

Don't be in a rush to start filling up the room again. Live with it empty for a few days so that you can really get a sense of the space. Then slowly begin to bring things back inside, starting with the largest objects. You'll know immediately when you've crossed the line with something that doesn't belong. But you have to be willing to pull back and pare down.

**Upper Level
Floor Plan**

OPEN TO
FAM.RM.

BR. #4
11'8" × 12'4"

BR. #2
13'4" × 12'8"

OPEN TO
E.

BR. #3
11'8" × 12'6"

LINEN

Rear
Elevation

Copyright by designer/architect.

Illustration provided by designer/architect.

Plan #141020

Dimensions: 58' W x 40'4" D
Levels: 2
Square Footage: 3,140
Main Level Sq. Ft.: 1,553
Upper Level Sq. Ft.: 1,587
Bedrooms: 5
Bathrooms: 4½
Foundation: Basement
Materials List Available: No
Price Category: G

This stately and spacious traditional home will add elegance to any neighborhood.

Features:

- Ceiling height: 9 ft. unless otherwise noted.
- Foyer: The angled staircase rises to this two-story entry and then overlooks the family room from a Juliet-style balcony. The stairs also break to allow direct access to the kitchen.
- Kitchen: This is a dream kitchen, with its oversize work island and walk-in pantry. The kitchen overlooks the breakfast room and family room.
- Master Suite: This luxurious retreat occupies its own side of the house for added privacy. It has its own sitting area and dual closets leading to the master bath.
- Guestroom: Your overnight guests will enjoy the privacy of this first floor bedroom.
- Bedrooms: All the upstairs bedrooms feature their own walk-in closets.

Main Level Floor Plan

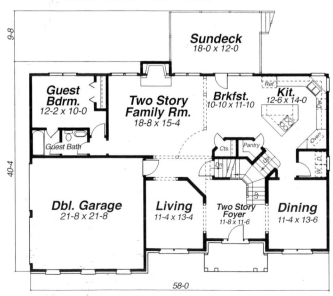

Upper Level Floor Plan

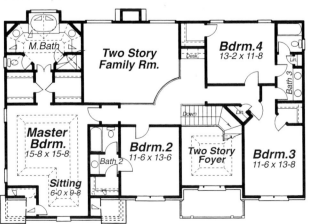

Copyright by designer/architect.

Plan #161018

Dimensions: 74'4" W x 69'11" D
Levels: 2
Square Footage: 2,816
+ 325 Sq. Ft. bonus room
Main Level Sq. Ft.: 2,231
Upper Level Sq. Ft.: 624
Bedrooms: 3
Bathrooms: 3 full, 2 half
Foundation: Basement
Materials List Available: No
Price Category: F

Images provided by designer/architect.

If you love classic European designs, look closely at this home with its multiple gables and countless conveniences and luxuries.

Features:

- Foyer: Open to the great room, the 2-story foyer offers a view all the way to the rear windows.

- Great Room: A fireplace makes this room cozy in any kind of weather.

- Kitchen: This large room features an island with a sink, and an angled wall with French doors to the back yard.

- Dining Room: The furniture alcove and raised ceiling make this room both formal and practical.

- Master Suite: You'll love the quiet in the bedroom and the luxuries—a whirlpool tub, separate shower, and double vanities—in the bath.

- Basement: The door from the basement to the side yard adds convenience to outdoor work.

Rear View

Main Level Floor Plan

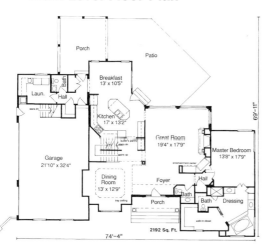

Upper Level Floor Plan

Copyright by designer/architect.

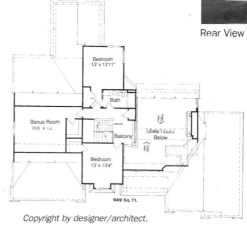

Foyer/Dining Room

Plan #321063

Dimensions: 87'8" W x 46'10" D

Levels: 2

Square Footage: 3,222

Main Level Sq. Ft.: 2,276

Upper Level Sq. Ft.: 946

Bedrooms: 4

Bathrooms: 3½

Foundation: Basement

Materials List Available: Yes

Price Category: G

Images provided by designer/architect.

This home will thrill any family looking for an elegant setting and plenty of space for entertaining as well as family time.

Features:

- **Foyer:** With a two-story ceiling and a central staircase to the upper level, this foyer also leads to the dining and living rooms.

- **Great Room:** This two-story room has a large fireplace and arched openings to the second floor. A door leads to the rear terrace, where it's easy to host parties for friends and family.

- **Kitchen:** This room will delight all the cooks in the family with its ample work and storage space and attached breakfast booth.

- **Master Suite:** This elegant suite includes a separate reading room with bookshelves and a fireplace as well as a luxury bath.

- **Additional Bedrooms:** Each bedroom has a walk-in closet. Bedroom 4 has a private bath.

Main Level Floor Plan

Upper Level Floor Plan

Copyright by designer/architect.

Plan #161045

Dimensions: 57' W x 49'8" D

Levels: 2

Square Footage: 2,288

Main Level Sq. Ft.: 1,532

Upper Level Sq. Ft.: 545

Bedrooms: 4

Bathrooms: 2½

Foundation: Slab

Materials List Available: Yes

Price Category: E

Images provided by designer/architect.

Multiple gables, arched windows, and the stone accents that adorn the exterior of this lovely two-story home create a dramatic first impression.

Features:

- **Great Room:** With multiple windows to light your way, grand openings, varied ceiling treatments, and angled walls let you flow from room to room. Enjoy the warmth of a gas fireplace in both this great room and the dining area.

- **Master Suite:** Experience the luxurious atmosphere of this master suite, with its coffered ceiling and deluxe bath.

- **Additional Bedrooms:** Angled stairs lead to a balcony with writing desk and to two additional bedrooms.

- **Porch:** Exit two sets of French doors to the rear yard and a covered porch, perfect for relaxing in comfortable weather.

Main Level Floor Plan

Copyright by designer/architect.

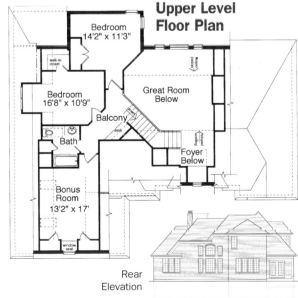

Upper Level Floor Plan

Rear Elevation

Photo provided by designer/architect.

Plan #121081

Dimensions: 76'8" W x 68' D
Levels: 2
Square Footage: 3,623
Main Level Sq. Ft.: 2,603
Upper Level Sq. Ft.: 1,020
Bedrooms: 4
Bathrooms: 4½
Foundation: Basement
Materials List Available: Yes
Price Category: G

You'll love this impressive home if you're looking for perfect spot for entertaining as well as a home for comfortable family living.

Features:

- Entry: Walk into this grand two-story entryway through double doors, and be greeted by the sight of a graceful curved staircase.
- Great Room: This two-story room features stacked windows, a fireplace flanked by an entertainment center, a bookcase, and a wet bar.
- Dining Room: A corner column adds formality to this room, which is just off the entryway for the convenience of your guests.
- Hearth Room: Connected to the great room by a lovely set of French doors, this room features another fireplace as well as a convenient pantry.

Main Level Floor Plan

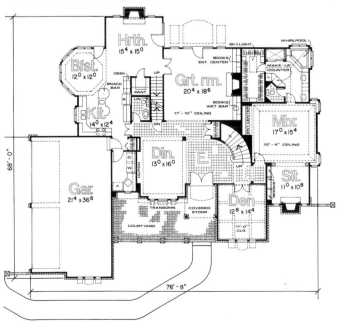

Upper Level Floor Plan

Copyright by designer/architect.

Plan #211077

Dimensions: 94' W x 68' D

Levels: 2

Square Footage: 5,560

Main Level Sq. Ft.: 4,208

Upper Level Sq. Ft.: 1,352

Bedrooms: 4

Bathrooms: 4 full, 2 half

Foundation: Slab, or crawl space

Materials List Available: No

Price Category: I

This palatial home has a two-story veranda and offers room and amenities for a large family.

Features:

- Ceiling Height: 10 ft.

- Library: Teach your children the importance of quiet reflection in this library, which boasts a full wall of built-in bookshelves.

- Master Suite: Escape the pressures of a busy day in this truly royal master suite. Curl up in front of your own fireplace. Or take a long, soothing soak in the private bath, with his and her sinks and closets.

- Kitchen: This room offers many modern comforts and amenities, and free-flowing traffic patterns.

Photo provided by designer/architect.

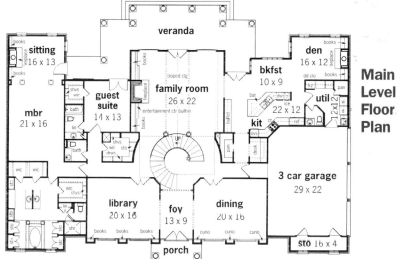

Main Level Floor Plan

Copyright by designer/architect.

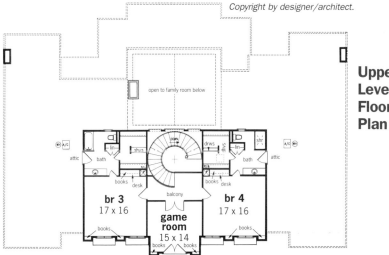

Upper Level Floor Plan

Empty-Nester Homes

If the kids are out on their own, you may be thinking about whether the family home still suits your lifestyle. Chances are there are things about your existing house that you don't need, while other features you'd like to have are missing. Although size isn't always an issue with empty nesters, amenities are. If you're like most others in this group, you don't want a house that will take up a lot of your time maintaining it. It's time to splurge on yourself for a change with items such as a gourmet kitchen and a well-appointed master bedroom and bath. Plus, you may be thinking about the future. According to the National Home Builders Association, more than half of the master suites built for empty-nester homes are located on the first floor, and more than 60 percent of them incorporate safety features such as grab bars and extra space allowances for doorways and for maneuvering around the room in a wheelchair or walker if the need arises. Thoughtful stylish design will be evident in the kitchen, too, where you'll find good-looking low-maintenance materials and easily accessible appliances and storage that won't require a lot of reaching and bending.

The kids may be gone, but they're not forgotten. Extra bedrooms and living space upstairs awaits them and the grandkids, or friends and relatives from out of town. These rooms also make great getaways for reading or meditation, hobby studios, home theaters, or home offices.

Low-maintenance materials, top, cut down on time-consuming chores.

An extra room can serve as a study or a home office, above.

Additional rooms upstairs, accommodate guests in this house, left.

Plan #221001

Dimensions: 87' W x 60' D
Levels: 1
Square Footage: 2,600
Bedrooms: 2
Bathrooms: 2½
Foundation: Basement
Materials List Available: No
Price Category: F

Photos provided by designer/architect.

You'll love this traditional ranch for its unusual spaciousness and many comfortable amenities.

Features:

- **Great Room:** As you enter the home, you'll have a clear view all the way to the backyard through the many windows in this huge room. Built-ins here provide a practical touch, and the fireplace makes this room cozy when the weather's cool.

- **Kitchen:** This large kitchen has been thoughtfully designed to make cooking a pleasure. It flows into a lovely dining nook, so it's also a great place to entertain.

- **Master Suite:** Relaxing will come naturally in this lovely suite, with its two walk-in closets, private sitting area, and large, sumptuous bathroom that features a Jacuzzi tub.

- **Additional Bedrooms:** Located on the opposite side of the house from the master

Copyright by designer/architect.

Rear Elevation

suite, these bedrooms are both convenient to a full bath. You can use one room as a den if you wish.

Kitchen

Plan #231011

Dimensions: 50' W x 46' D

Levels: 1

Square Footage: 2,716

Finished Basement Sq. Ft.: 1,300

Main Level Sq. Ft.: 1,416

Bedrooms: 3

Bathrooms: 2½

Foundation: Daylight basement

Materials List Available: No

Price Category: F

Images provided by designer/architect.

Copyright by designer/architect.

This craftsman-style ranch home radiates a feeling of solidity and comfort, giving it great curb appeal.

Features:

- **Living Room:** This sunken room invites friends and family to relax around either the cozy fireplace or the windows to enjoy the view.

- **Den:** Just off the foyer, this room can also make an ideal home office.

- **Dining Room:** Host a dinner party or serve family meals in this room, which adjoins both the living room and the kitchen.

- **Kitchen:** With a cooktop work area and a breakfast nook, this well-planned kitchen is designed for efficiency.

- **Master Suite:** Located on the first floor, this suite is split from the other two bedrooms for privacy. The bath includes double vanities, a deluxe tub, a walk-in closet, and a walk-in shower.

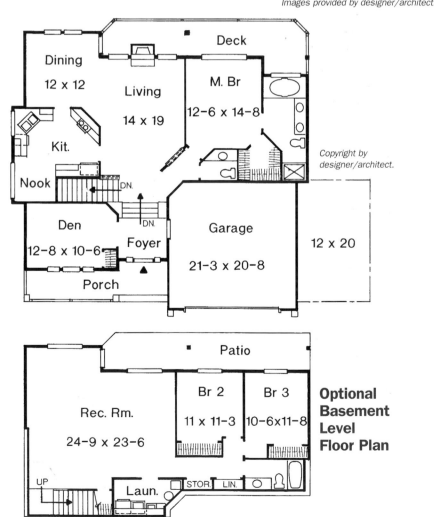

Optional Basement Level Floor Plan

Plan #321007

Dimensions: 76' W x 55'2" D

Levels: 1

Square Footage: 2,695

Bedrooms: 3

Bathrooms: 2½

Foundation: Basement

Materials List Available: Yes

Price Category: F

Images provided by designer/architect.

You'll love the way this spacious ranch reminds you of a French country home.

Features:

- **Foyer:** Come into this lovely home's foyer, and be greeted with a view of the gracious staircase and the great room just beyond.

- **Great Room:** Settle down by the cozy fireplace in cool weather, and reach for a book on the built-in shelves that surround it.

- **Kitchen:** Designed for efficient work patterns, this large kitchen is open to the great room.

- **Breakfast Room:** Just off the kitchen, this sunny room will be a family favorite all through the day.

- **Master Suite:** A bay window, walk-in closet, and shower built for two are highlights of this area.

- **Additional Bedrooms:** These large bedrooms both have walk-in closets and share a Jack-and-Jill bath for total convenience.

SMARTtip

Decorative Poles

Drapery poles are supported by the brackets fastened to the window frame or wall. The brackets that are provided with the poles generally coordinate and blend in with the pole finish. Brackets can be simple but also decorative. If you opt for a spectacular, attention-grabbing bracket, consider choosing less showy finials for the ends of the pole.

Plan #151002

Dimensions: 67' W x 66' D

Levels: 1

Square Footage: 2,444

Bedrooms: 3

Bathrooms: 2½

Foundation: Basement, crawl space, or slab

Materials List Available: Yes

Price Category: C

Images provided by designer/architect.

Copyright by designer/architect.

Plan #121088

Dimensions: 56'8" W x 48' D

Levels: 2

Square Footage: 2,340

Main Level Sq. Ft.: 1,701

Upper Level Sq. Ft.: 639

Bedrooms: 4

Bathrooms: 2½

Foundation: Basement

Materials List Available: Yes

Price Category: E

Images provided by designer/architect.

Main Level Floor Plan

Upper Level Floor Plan

Copyright by designer/architect.

Images provided by
designer/architect.

Plan #121053

Dimensions: 66' W x 68' D
Levels: 1
Square Footage: 2,456
Bedrooms: 3
Bathrooms: 2½
Foundation: Basement
Materials List Available: Yes
Price Category: E

SMARTtip

Installing Plastic Molding

Foam trim is best cut with a backsaw. Power miter
saws with fine-toothed blades also work. Larger-
toothed blades tend to tear the foam unevenly.

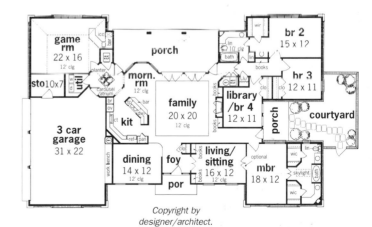

Images provided by
designer/architect.

Plan #211011

Dimensions: 84' W x 54' D
Levels: 1
Square Footage: 2,791
Bedrooms: 3 or 4
Bathrooms: 2
Foundation: Slab or crawl space
Materials List Available: Yes
Price Category: F

Plan #251013

Dimensions: 58' W x 44' D
Levels: 2
Square Footage: 2,073
Main Level Sq. Ft.: 1,441
Upper Level Sq. Ft.: 632
Bedrooms: 4
Bathrooms: 2½
Foundation: Basement
Materials List Available: Yes
Price Category: D

Images provided by designer/architect.

Main Level Floor Plan

Upper Level Floor Plan

Copyright by designer/architect.

Plan #301003

Dimensions: 84' W x 55'8" D
Levels: 1
Square Footage: 2,485
Bedrooms: 3
Bathrooms: 2½
Foundation: Crawl space, basement
Materials List Available: Yes
Price Category: E

Images provided by designer/architect.

Copyright by designer/architect.

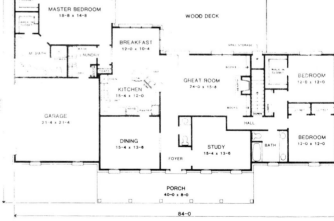

SMARTtip

Making Mitered Returns

Cut the small return piece from a substantial board that you can hold safely and securely against the saw fence.

Rear View

Plan #321017

Dimensions: 77' W x 36'8" D

Levels: 1

Square Footage: 2,531

Bedrooms: 1-4

Bathrooms: 1-2½

Foundation: Daylight basement

Materials List Available: Yes

Price Category: E

Illustration provided by designer/architect.

Optional Basement Level Floor Plan

Copyright by designer/architect.

Plan #321018

Dimensions: 88'4" W x 48'4" D

Levels: 1

Square Footage: 2,523

Bedrooms: 3

Bathrooms: 2

Foundation: Basement

Materials List Available: Yes

Price Category: E

Illustration provided by designer/architect.

Copyright by designer/architect.

SMARTtip®

Tiebacks

You don't have to limit yourself to tiebacks made from matching or contrasting fabric. Achieve creative custom looks by making tiebacks from unexpected items. Some materials to consider are old cotton bandannas or silk scarves, strings of beads, lengths of leather, or old belts and chains.

Plan #161020

Dimensions: 60' W" x 50'4" D

Levels: 2

Square Footage: 2,082; 2,349 with bonus space

Main Level Sq. Ft.: 1,524

Upper Level Sq. Ft.: 558

Bedrooms: 3

Bathrooms: 2

Foundation: Basement

Materials List Available: Yes

Price Category: D

Images provided by designer/architect.

You'll love the textured exterior finish and interesting roofline of this charming home.

Features:

- **Great Room:** Here you can enjoy the cozy fireplace, 12-ft. ceilings, and stylish French doors.

- **Dining Room:** A grand entry prepares you for the sloped ceiling that gives charm to this room.

- **Kitchen:** Natural light floods both the well-designed kitchen and adjacent breakfast room.

- **Master Suite:** Located on the first floor, this area boasts a whirlpool tub, a double-bowl vanity, and a large walk-in closet.

- **Upper Level:** Split stairs lead to a balcony over the foyer, a computer/study area, and two additional bedrooms.

- **Bonus Room:** Use this 267-sq.-ft. area over the garage for storage or a fourth bedroom.

Main Level Floor Plan

Upper Level Floor Plan

Copyright by designer/architect.

Plan #121070

Dimensions: 50' W x 58' D
Levels: 2
Square Footage: 2,139
Main Level Sq. Ft.: 1,506
Upper Level Sq. Ft.: 633
Bedrooms: 4
Bathrooms: 2½
Foundation: Basement
Materials List Available: Yes
Price Category: D

Photo provided by designer/architect.

You'll love this design if you're looking for a bright, airy home where you can easily entertain.

Features:

- **Entry:** A volume ceiling sets the tone for this home when you first walk in.

- **Great Room:** With a volume ceiling extending from the entry, this great room has an open feeling. Transom-topped windows contribute

natural light during the day.

- **Dining Room:** Because it is joined to the great room through a cased opening, this dining room can serve as an extension of the great room.

- **Kitchen:** An island with a snack bar, desk, and pantry make this kitchen a treat, and a door from the breakfast area leads to a private covered patio where dining will be a pleasure.

Main Level Floor Plan

Upper Level Floor Plan

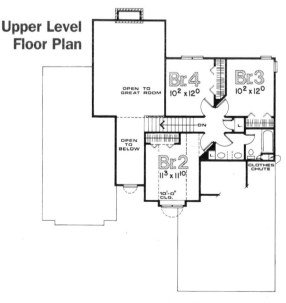

Copyright by designer/architect.

Images provided by designer/architect.

Plan #201062

Dimensions: 70'10" W x 59'5" D

Levels: 1

Square Footage: 2,551

Bedrooms: 4

Bathrooms: 2½

Foundation: Crawl space, slab, or basement

Materials List Available: Yes

Price Category: E

This home offers sophisticated Louisiana styling, plus all the space and amenities you need.

Features:

- Ceiling Height: 9 ft. unless otherwise noted.

- Great Room: Family and friends will be drawn to this great room, with its raised ceiling.

- Kitchen: This large, well-designed kitchen will bring out the gourmet cook in you. It has plenty of storage and counter space.

- Formal Living Room: This room is perfectly suited to entertaining guests.

- Formal Dining Room: Host elegant dinner parties in this lovely room.

- Master Bedroom: This private retreat features a raised ceiling.

- Master Bath: Enjoy the large walk-in closet, deluxe tub, walk-in shower, his and her vanities, and skylight in this truly plush master bathroom.

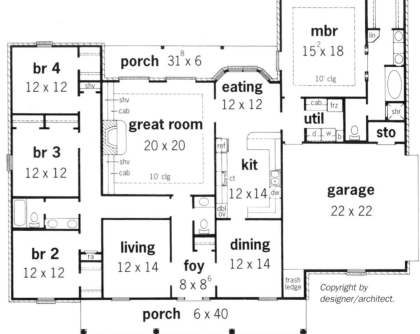

Copyright by designer/architect.

SMARTtip

Practical Role of a Window

Always consider the way a window opens and closes before choosing a window treatment. Double-hung windows pose the fewest problems. However, casement windows and French doors that swing into a room require a design that will not obstruct their paths of operation.

Plan #241010

Dimensions: 56' W x 44'5" D

Levels: 2

Square Footage: 2,044

Main Level Sq. Ft.: 1,203

Upper Level Sq. Ft.: 841

Bedrooms: 3

Bathrooms: 2½

Foundation: Slab

Materials List Available: No

Price Category: D

Illustration provided by designer/architect.

You will be immediately drawn by the warmth and charm of this award-winning Victorian design, which features an inviting front porch with corner gazebo.

Features:

- **Great Room:** Friends and family will gravitate to this comfortable great room and its cozy fireplace, well suited for holiday entertaining.

- **Kitchen:** This wonderful kitchen, which features a large pantry and cooktop island with eating bar, will become a natural gathering place for conversation and informal dining.

- **Master Suite:** Separated for privacy, this first-floor master suite features his and her walk-in closets, separate vanities, a deluxe corner tub, and a walk in shower.

- **Additional Rooms:** Two secondary bedrooms and a large playroom—perfect for a growing family—are located on the second floor.

Main Level Floor Plan

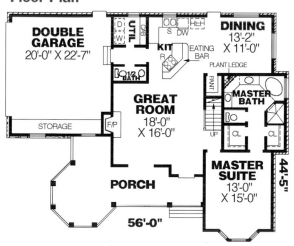

Upper Level Floor Plan

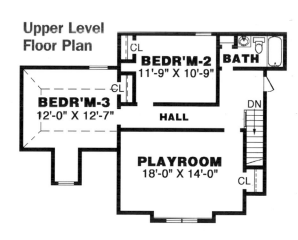

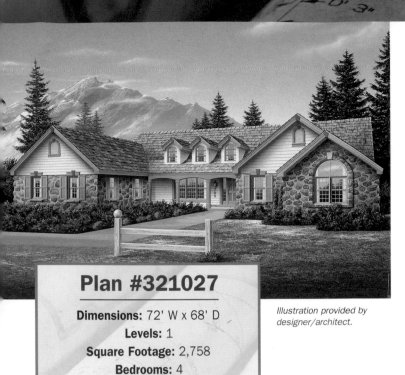

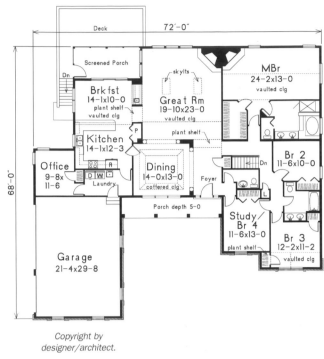

Plan #321027

Dimensions: 72' W x 68' D

Levels: 1

Square Footage: 2,758

Bedrooms: 4

Bathrooms: 2½

Foundation: Basement

Materials List Available: Yes

Price Category: F

Illustration provided by designer/architect.

Copyright by designer/architect.

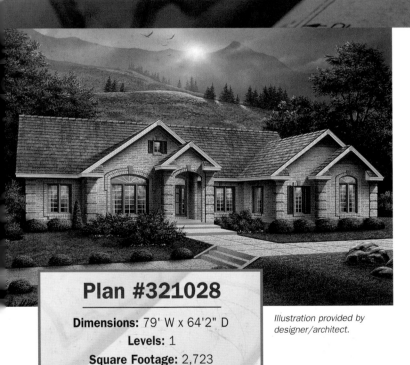

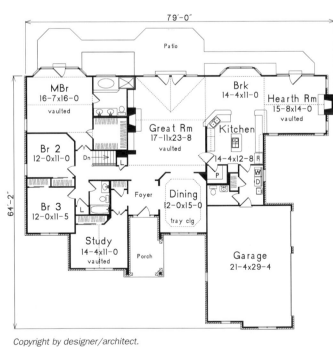

Plan #321028

Dimensions: 79' W x 64'2" D

Levels: 1

Square Footage: 2,723

Bedrooms: 3

Bathrooms: 2½

Foundation: Basement

Materials List Available: Yes

Price Category: F

Illustration provided by designer/architect.

Copyright by designer/architect.

Copyright by designer/architect.

Images provided by designer/architect.

Plan #151144

Dimensions: 66'4" W x 64' D

Levels: 1

Square Footage: 2,624

Bedrooms: 4

Bathrooms: 3

Foundation: Crawl space, slab (basement option for fee)

Materials List Available: Yes

Price Category: F

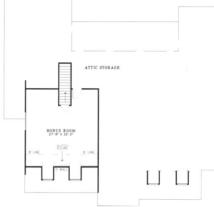

Optional Bonus Area Floor Plan

Plan #291004

Dimensions: 77'4" W x 54'4" D

Levels: 1

Square Footage: 2,529

Bedrooms: 3

Bathrooms: 2½

Foundation: Basement

Materials List Available: No

Price Category: E

Rear View

Images provided by designer/architect.

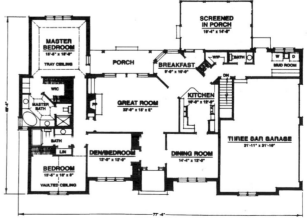

Copyright by designer/architect.

Plan #121073

Dimensions: 70' W x 52' D

Levels: 2

Square Footage: 2,579

Main Level Sq. Ft.: 1,933

Upper Level Sq. Ft.: 646

Bedrooms: 4

Bathrooms: 2½

Foundation: Basement

Materials List Available: Yes

Price Category: E

Photo provided by designer/architect.

Luxury will surround you in this home with contemporary styling and up-to-date amenities at every turn.

Features:

• **Great Room:** This large room shares both a see-through fireplace and a wet bar with the adjacent hearth room. Transom-topped windows add both light and architectural interest to this room.

• **Den:** Transom-topped windows add visual interest to this private area.

• **Kitchen:** A center island and corner pantry add convenience to this well-planned kitchen, and a lovely ceiling treatment adds beauty to the bayed breakfast area.

• **Master Suite:** A built-in bookcase adds to the ambiance of this luxury-filled area, where you're sure to find a retreat at the end of the day.

Main Level Floor Plan

Upper Level Floor Plan

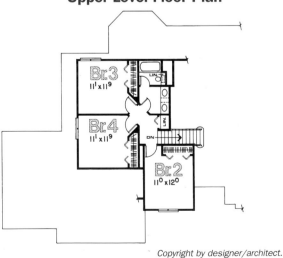

Copyright by designer/architect.

Plan #121074

Dimensions: 68'8" W x 47'8" D
Levels: 2
Square Footage: 2,486
Main Level Sq. Ft.: 1,829
Upper Level Sq. Ft.: 657
Bedrooms: 4
Bathrooms: 2½
Foundation: Basement
Materials List Available: Yes
Price Category: E

Photo provided by designer/architect.

Enjoy the natural light that streams through the many lovely windows in this well-designed home.

Features:

- Living Room: This room is sure to be your family's headquarters, thanks to the lovely 15-ft. ceiling, stacked windows, central location, and cozy fireplace.

- Dining Room: A boxed ceiling adds formality to this well-positioned room.

- Kitchen: The island cooktop in this kitchen is so large that it includes a snack bar area. A pantry gives ample storage space, and a built-in desk—where you can set up a computer station or a record-keeping area—adds efficiency.

- Master Suite: For the sake of privacy, this master suite is located on the opposite side of the home from the other living areas. You'll love the roomy bedroom and luxuriate in the private bath with its many amenities.

Main Level Floor Plan

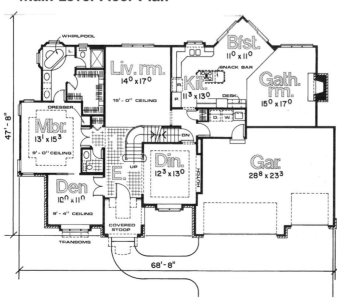

Upper Level Floor Plan

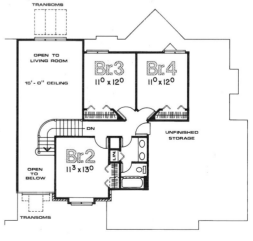

Copyright by designer/architect.

Copyright by
designer/architect.

*Images provided by
designer/architect.*

**Optional
Bonus Area
Floor Plan**

Plan #151125

Dimensions: 67'6" W x 73'10" D

Levels: 1

Square Footage: 2,606

Bedrooms: 3

Bathrooms: 2½

Foundation: Crawl space, slab,
or basement

Materials List Available: Yes

Price Category: F

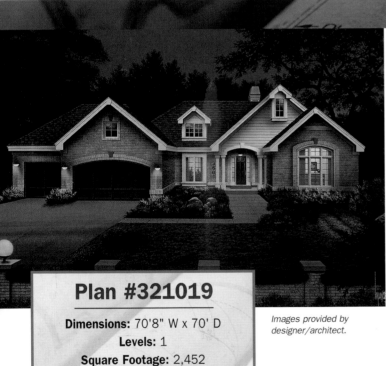

Plan #321019

Dimensions: 70'8" W x 70' D

Levels: 1

Square Footage: 2,452

Bedrooms: 4

Bathrooms: 2½

Foundation: Basement

Materials List Available: Yes

Price Category: E

*Images provided by
designer/architect.*

Copyright by
designer/architect.

Plan #151108

Dimensions: 84'6" W x 58'6" D

Levels: 1

Square Footage: 2,742

Bedrooms: 4

Bathrooms: 2½

Foundation: Crawl space, slab, or basement

Materials List Available: Yes

Price Category: F

Images provided by designer/architect.

Copyright by designer/architect.

Optional Bonus Space Floor Plan

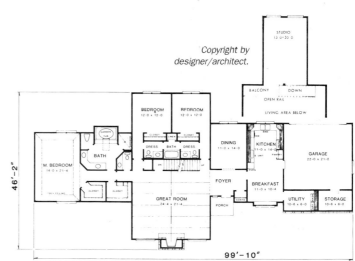

Plan #301001

Dimensions: 99'10" W x 46'2" D

Levels: 1

Square Footage: 2,720

Bedrooms: 3

Bathrooms: 2½

Foundation: Crawl space, slab

Materials List Available: Yes

Price Category: F

Images provided by designer/architect.

Copyright by designer/architect.

Plan #161040

Dimensions: 63'4" W x 48' D
Levels: 2
Square Footage: 2,403
Main Level Sq. Ft.: 1,710
Upper Level Sq. Ft.: 695
Bedrooms: 4
Bathrooms: 3½
Foundation: Slab
Materials List Available: Yes
Price Category: E

Designed with attention to detail, this elegant home will please the most discriminating taste.

Images provided by designer/architect.

Features:

- **Great Room:** The high ceiling in this room accentuates the fireplace and the rear wall of windows. A fashionable balcony overlooks the great room.

- **Dining Room:** This lovely formal dining room is introduced by columns and accented by a boxed window.

- **Kitchen:** This wonderful kitchen includes a snack bar, island, and large pantry positioned to serve the breakfast and dining rooms with equal ease.

- **Master Suite:** This master suite features a dressing room, private sitting area with 11-ft.

ceiling, whirlpool tub, double-bowl vanity, and large walk-in closet.

- **Additional Bedrooms:** Three additional bedrooms complete this spectacular home.

Rear Elevation

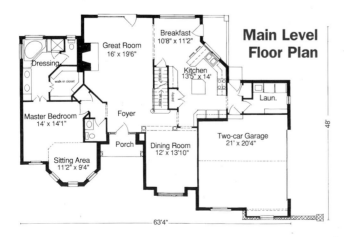

Main Level Floor Plan

Upper Level Floor Plan

Copyright by designer/architect.

Plan #321005

Dimensions: 69' W x 53'8" D

Levels: 1

Square Footage: 2,483

Bedrooms: 4

Bathrooms: 2

Foundation: Basement

Materials List Available: Yes

Price Category: E

You'll love the grand feeling of this home, which combines with the very practical features that make living in it a pleasure.

Features:

- **Porch:** The open brick arches and Palladian door set the tone for this magnificent home.

- **Great Room:** An alcove for the entertainment center and vaulted ceiling show the care that went into designing this room.

- **Dining Room:** A tray ceiling sets off the formality of this large room.

- **Kitchen:** The layout in this room is designed to make your work patterns more efficient and to save you steps and time.

- **Study:** This quiet room can be a wonderful refuge, or you can use it for a fourth bedroom if you wish.

- **Master Suite:** Made for relaxing at the end of the day, this suite will pamper you with luxuries.

Images provided by designer/architect.

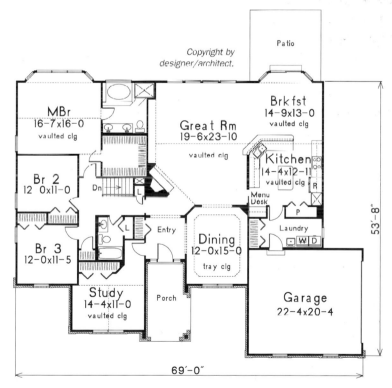

Copyright by designer/architect.

SMARTtip

Art in Pools

The tiled walls and floor of a pool make great canvases for art, so incorporate a serious or whimsical design. Also, make the stairs wide and shallow to form a wading area for kids.

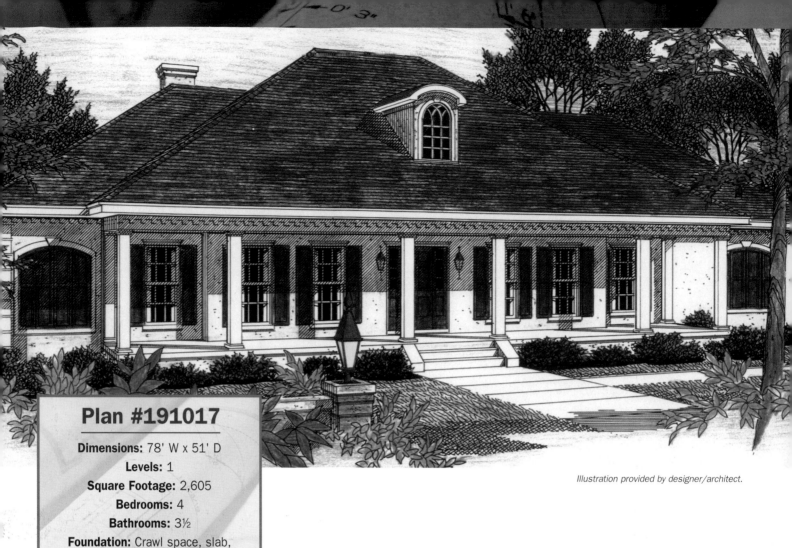

Illustration provided by designer/architect.

Plan #191017

Dimensions: 78' W x 51' D

Levels: 1

Square Footage: 2,605

Bedrooms: 4

Bathrooms: 3½

Foundation: Crawl space, slab, or basement

Materials List Available: No

Price Category: F

You'll love the elegance of this gorgeous home, which includes every amenity you can imagine.

Features:

- **Great Room:** An archway from the foyer welcomes you to this expansive room, with its recessed ceiling, gas fireplace, custom cabinets, and French doors leading to the covered rear porch.

- **Kitchen:** This large room includes a pantry, stove on an island, angled sink, snack bar, and built-in desk close to the hall stairs.

- **Laundry Room:** You'll find a sink, storage closets, and wall-to-wall cabinets above the washer/dryer and freezer area in this practical spot.

- **Master Suite:** A wall of windows greets you in the bedroom, and built-in cabinets add storage space. The huge walk-in closet is close to the dressing area. The luxurious bath has a skylight over the dual sinks and is located so that one person can sleep while the other uses it.

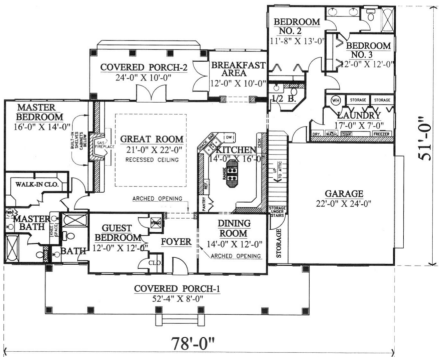

Copyright by designer/architect.

Plan #201067

Dimensions: 68'10" W x 67'4" D

Levels: 1

Square Footage: 2,735

Bedrooms: 4

Bathrooms: 3

Foundation: Crawl space, slab, or basement

Materials List Available: Yes

Price Category: F

Images provided by designer/architect.

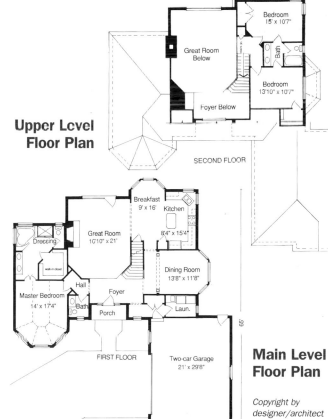

mbr 15 x 21⁴ raised clg

porch 8 x 30⁸

br 4 14 x 12

sto 8⁶ x 8

util 8⁶ x 9²

eating 13 x 11

den 18 x 24 raised clg

br 3 14 x 12

garage 21 x 22

kit 12⁸ x 13

foy 8 x 9⁶

dining 14 x 12

porch

br 2 14² x 12

ledge

Copyright by designer/architect.

Plan #161042

Dimensions: 59'4" W x 65' D

Levels: 2

Square Footage: 2,198

Main Level Sq. Ft.: 1,706

Upper Level Sq. Ft.: 492

Bedrooms: 3

Bathrooms: 2½

Foundation: Slab

Materials List Available: Yes

Price Category: D

Images provided by designer/architect.

Upper Level Floor Plan

Bedroom 15' x 10'7"

Great Room Below

Bath

Bedroom 13'10" x 10'7"

Foyer Below

SECOND FLOOR

Breakfast 9' x 16'

Kitchen 8'4" x 15'4"

Great Room 16'10" x 21'

Dining Room 13'8" x 11'8"

Dressing

Master Bedroom 14' x 17'4"

Hall

Bath

Foyer

Laun.

walk-in closet

Porch

FIRST FLOOR

Two-car Garage 21' x 29'8"

Main Level Floor Plan

Copyright by designer/architect

59'4"

Plan #121068

Dimensions: 54' W x 49'10" D

Levels: 2

Square Footage: 2,391

Main Level Sq. Ft.: 1,697

Upper Level Sq. Ft.: 694

Bedrooms: 4

Bathrooms: 2½

Foundation: Basement

Materials List Available: Yes

Price Category: E

Photo provided by designer/architect.

This home allows you a great deal of latitude in the way you choose to finish it, so you can truly make it "your own."

Features:

• Living Room: Located just off the entryway, this living room is easy to convert to a stylish den. Add French doors for privacy, and relish the style that the 12-ft. angled ceiling and picturesque arched window provide.

• Great Room: The highlight of this room is the two-sided fireplace that easily adds as much design interest as warmth to this area. The three transom-topped windows here fill the room with light.

• Kitchen: A center island, walk-in pantry, and built-in desk combine to create this wonderful kitchen, and the attached gazebo breakfast area adds the finishing touch.

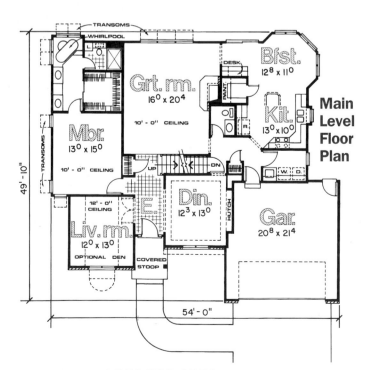

Main Level Floor Plan

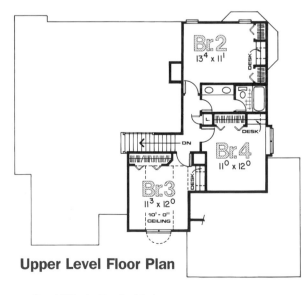

Upper Level Floor Plan

Copyright by designer/architect.

Plan #161016

Dimensions: 59'4" W x 58'8" D
Levels: 2
Square Footage: 2,101
Main Level Sq. Ft.: 1,626
Upper Level Sq. Ft.: 475
Bedrooms: 3
Bathrooms: 2½
Foundation: Basement
Materials List Available: Yes
Price Category: D

Images provided by designer/architect

Features:

- **Great Room:** Made for relaxing and entertaining, the great room is sunken to set it off from the rest of the house. A balcony from the second floor looks down into this spacious area, making it easy to keep track of the kids while they are playing.

- **Kitchen:** Convenience marks this well laid-out kitchen where you'll love to cook for guests and for family.

- **Master Bedroom:** A vaulted ceiling complements the unusual octagonal shape of the master bedroom. Located on the first floor, this room allows some privacy from the second floor bedrooms. It is also ideal for anyone who no longer wishes to climb stairs to reach a bedroom.

Rear Elevation

You'll love the exciting roofline that sets this elegant home apart from its neighbors as well as the embellished, solid look that declares how well-designed it is—from the inside to the exterior.

Main Level Floor Plan

Deck
Breakfast 9-2 x 16
Sunken Great Room 16-10 x 21
Kitchen 8 x 13-4
Bath
Walk-in closet
Dining Room 16 x 11-8
Foyer
Master Bedroom 14 x 17-4
Slope ceiling
Bath
Hall
Laundry
Two-car Garage 21 x 20-8
58'-8"
59'-4"

Copyright by designer/architect.

Upper Level Floor Plan

Bedroom 15x 10-8
Great Room Below
Bath
Bedroom 14x 10-6
Foyer Below

Vacation and Second Homes

A sense of status definitely comes with owning a new vacation house. But besides impressing your friends, you're making a smart move, both financially and in terms of lifestyle. Low-interest mortgage rates and earned equity in your primary home can help you realize your dream of a family getaway at the lake, by the seashore, or in the mountains.

For empty nesters, for whom a second house may become a retirement home, the location may be near a city, where there's access to cultural events, restaurants, and first-class healthcare. According to the National Association of

Realtors (NAR), about 50 percent of all second homes are used for fun. The rest are investments. "In many cases, vacation homeowners get the same mortgage-tax interest write-off they get for their first home," says the NAR. In addition, vacation homes, like all real estate, tend to appreciate in value, especially when they are in desirable locations. If you're looking for a way to diversify your financial portfolio, also consider this: all you have to do is live in the house two years out of the last five to be eligible to take the first $500,000 you make on re-sale, tax-free. Just remember to consult your tax advisor to find out where you stand.

A vacation home with the option of multiple dwellings, above right, can provide extra income.

Location is an important factor. Beachfront property, right, is highly sought-after and valuable.

A breakfast nook, below, is situated within a bay of windows that overlooks the ocean.

Plan #281002

Dimensions: 54' W x 33' D
Levels: 2
Square Footage: 1,859
Main Level Sq. Ft.: 959
Second Level Sq. Ft.: 900
Bedrooms: 3
Bathrooms: 1 full, 2 half
Foundation: Basement
Materials List Available: Yes
Price Category: C

Images provided by designer/architect.

This lovely three-bedroom home has the layout and amenities you need for comfortable living.

Features:

- Ceiling Height: 8 ft. unless otherwise noted.
- Foyer: Guests will walk through the lovely and practical front porch into this attractive foyer, with its vaulted ceiling.

- Living/Dining Room: Family and friends will be drawn to the warmth of the cozy, convenient gas fireplace in this combination living/dining room.
- Master Suite: You'll enjoy retiring at the end of the day to this luxurious master suite. It has a private sitting area with built-in storage for your books and television. Relax in the bath under its skylight.
- Kitchen: At the center of the main floor you will find this kitchen, with its eating nook that takes full advantage of the view and is just the right size for family meals.
- Deck: This large deck is accessible from the master suite, eating nook, and living/dining room.

Upper Level Floor Plan

Main Level Floor Plan

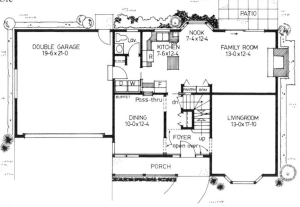

Copyright by designer/architect.

Plan #101015

Dimensions: 28' W x 46' D

Levels: 2

Square Footage: 1,647

Main Level Sq. Ft.: 1,288

Upper Level Sq. Ft.: 359

Bedrooms: 2

Bathrooms: 1

Foundation: Slab

Materials List Available: No

Price Category: C

Illustration provided by designer/architect.

• Bath: Also located downstairs is a compartmented bath with a 2-ft.-8-in. door that allows wheelchair access.

• Loft: Upstairs is an enormous loft with an 11-ft. ceiling. Use it to augment the two downstairs bedrooms or for recreation space.

This comfortable vacation retreat has handsome board-and-batten siding with stone accents.

Features:

• Ceiling Height: 20 ft. unless otherwise noted.

• Front Porch: This delightful front porch is perfect for spending relaxing vacation time in an old-fashioned rocker or porch swing.

• Great Room: From the porch you'll enter this enormous great room, where the whole family will enjoy spending time together under its 20-ft. vaulted ceiling.

• Kitchen: Within the great room is this open kitchen. An island provides plenty of food-preparation space, and there's a breakfast bar for casual vacation meals. The large pantry area provides space for a stacked washer and dryer.

Main Level Floor Plan

Upper Level Floor Plan

Copyright by designer/architect.

Illustration provided by designer/architect.

Plan #291005

Dimensions: 16' W x 36'10" D
Levels: 2
Square Footage: 896
Main Level Sq. Ft.: 448
Upper Level Sq. Ft.: 448
Bedrooms: 2
Bathrooms: 1½
Foundation: Crawl space
Materials List Available: No
Price Category: A

You'll be as charmed by the interior of this small home as you are by the wood-shingled roof, scroll-saw rake detailing, and board-and-batten siding on the exterior.

Features:

• **Porch:** Relax on this porch, which is the ideal spot for a couple of rockers or a swing.

• **Entryway:** Double doors reveal an open floor plan that makes everyone feel welcome.

• **Living Room:** Create a cozy nook by the windows here.

• **Kitchen:** Designed for convenience, this kitchen has ample counter space as well as enough storage to suit your needs. The stairway to the upper floor and the half-bath divide the kitchen from the living and dining areas.

• **Upper Level:** 9-ft. ceilings give a spacious feeling to the two bedrooms and full bathroom that you'll find on this floor.

Main Level Floor Plan

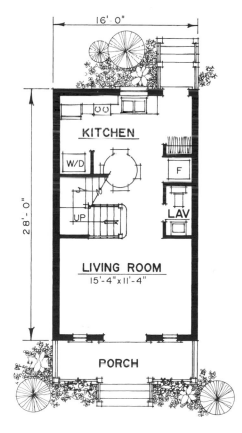

Upper Level Floor Plan

Copyright by designer/architect.

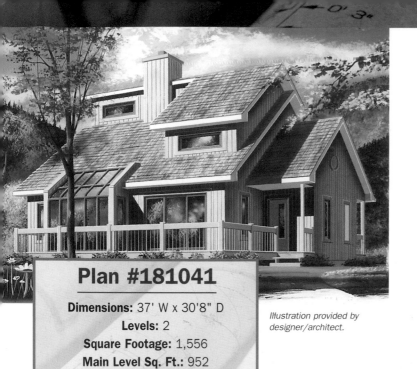

Plan #181041

Dimensions: 37' W x 30'8" D
Levels: 2
Square Footage: 1,556
Main Level Sq. Ft.: 952
Upper Level Sq. Ft.: 604
Bedrooms: 3
Bathrooms: 2
Foundation: Full basement
Materials List Available: Yes
Price Category: C

Illustration provided by designer/architect.

Upper Level Floor Plan

Copyright by designer/architect.

Main Level Floor Plan

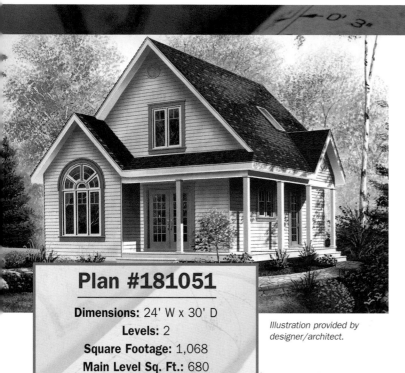

Plan #181051

Dimensions: 24' W x 30' D
Levels: 2
Square Footage: 1,068
Main Level Sq. Ft.: 680
Upper Level Sq. Ft.: 388
Bedrooms: 3
Bathrooms: 2
Foundation: Full basement
Materials List Available: Yes
Price Category: B

Illustration provided by designer/architect.

Upper Level Floor Plan

Copyright by designer/architect.

Main Level Floor Plan

Main Level Floor Plan

24'-0"

25'-4"

1'-4"

UTILITY (HW)
D
W
F
PR
UP
FP
PANTRY
KITCHEN
10'-0" x 8'-3"
LIVING ROOM
12'-0" x 13'-8"
OPEN TO ABOVE
DINING ROOM
10'-2" x 9'-0"
ENTRY
PORCH

Plan #291006

Dimensions: 24' W x 25'4" D

Levels: 2

Square Footage: 965

Main Level Sq. Ft.: 547

Upper Level Sq. Ft.: 418

Bedrooms: 1

Bathrooms: 1½

Foundation: Crawl space

Materials List Available: No

Price Category: A

Illustrations provided by designer/architect.

Upper Level Floor Plan

LOFT
12'-0" x 8'-0"
(8'-0" CLG)
DN
OPEN TO ABOVE
RIDGE BEAM
OPEN TO BELOW
TUB/SHWR
BATH
MASTER BEDROOM
12'-0" x 11'-0"
(12'-0" CEILING)
PLANT SHELF
W.I.C.

Copyright by designer/architect.

Plan #291007

Dimensions: 24' W x 31' D

Levels: 2

Square Footage: 1,065

Main Level Sq. Ft.: 576

Upper Level Sq. Ft.: 489

Bedrooms: 1

Bathrooms: 1½

Foundation: Crawl space

Materials List Available: No

Price Category: B

Illustrations provided by designer/architect.

Upper Level Floor Plan

5'-0" KNEEWALL
CEILING CLIP
LOFT
12'-4" x 8'-0"
DN
WOOD RAIL
BATH
EXPOSED BEAM
VAULTED CEILING
MASTER BED
13'-2" x 11'-0"
CEILING CLIP
W.I.C.
5'-0" KNEEWALL

Main Level Floor Plan

24'-0"

31'-0"

D UTIL. (WH)
W
F
PR
UP
FP
KITCHEN
11'-0" x 8'-4"
LIVING ROOM
13'-0" x 13'-8"
OPEN TO ABOVE
DINING
15'-0" x 9'-0"
ENTRY
PORCH
24'-0" x 7'-0"

Copyright by designer/architect.

Outdoor Living

Many homeowners treat their decks and patios as another room of the house. To gain the fullest use of these areas, homeowners often add cooking areas, outdoor lighting centers, and other features to their outdoor living areas.

Cooking Centers

As the trend toward outdoor entertaining gains popularity, many people are setting up complete, permanent outdoor cooking centers, which often become the focus of their decks. Others content themselves with a simple grill. In either case, practical planning makes outdoor cooking efficient and more enjoyable, whether it is for everyday family meals or for a host of guests.

Decide exactly what features you want in the outdoor kitchen area. If you prefer to keep it simple with just a grill, you'll still have some decisions to make. Do you want a charcoal, gas, or electric unit? A charcoal grill is the least expensive option; a natural gas grill will cost you the most because it must be professionally installed. (Check with your local building department beforehand. Some localities will require a permit or may not allow this installation.) Extra features and accessories, such as rotisseries, woks, burners, smoke ovens, and warming racks increase the cost, too. Just remember: if you intend to locate the grill in a wooden enclosure, choose a model designed for this application.

In addition to a grill, do you want an elaborate setup with a sink, countertop, or a refrigerator? If so, these amenities will need protection from the elements. However, some refrigerators designed specifically for outdoor use can withstand harsh weather conditions. These high-end units are vented from the front and can be built-in or freestanding on casters.

Typically, outdoor refrigerators are countertop height (often the same size as standard wine chilling units that mount underneath a kitchen countertop) and have shelving for food trays or drinks and indoor storage for condiments. Outdoor refrigerators intended strictly for cold beer storage come with a tap and can accommodate a half-keg.

More Entertainment Options

Do you entertain frequently? Think about including a custom-designed wet bar and countertop in your plans. Besides a sink, the unit can offer enclosed storage for beverages, ice, and glasses, and the countertop will be handy for serving or buffets. But if you can't handle the expense, consider a prefabricated open-air wet bar. It can be portable or built-in. Some portable wet-bars feature: a sink that you can hook up to the house plumbing or a garden hose (with a filter), ice bins with sliding lids, sectioned compartments for garnishes, a speed rail for bottles, and a beverage-chilling well. Deluxe models may come with extra shelves and side-mounted food warmers.

Practical Advantages

Integrating a cooking center with your deck provides easy access to the kitchen indoors. Remember, elaborate outdoor kitchens require gas, electricity, and plumbing; it is easier and less expensive to run those lines when the cooking area isn't at the other end of the yard. However, you'll have to carefully plan the cooktop so that it isn't too close to the house and so that the heat and smoke are directed away from seating areas.

In general, when arranging any outdoor cooking area, be sure that all accouterments—including serving platters, insulated mitts, basting brushes, spatulas, forks and knives, and long-handled tongs—are

readily at hand for the cook. And don't forget to plan enough surface room for setting down a tray of spices, condiments, sauces, and marinade or swiftly unloading a plate of hot grilled meats or vegetables. Because you'll have to juggle both uncooked and cooked foods, a roll-around cart may suffice. For safety's sake, always keep the pathway from the kitchen to the outdoor cooking area clear, and as a precaution, keep a fire extinguisher nearby.

Countertop Options

Any outdoor countertop should be able to withstand varying weather conditions. Rain, snow, and bright sunlight will pit and rot some materials, so choose carefully. Tile, concrete, or natural stone (such as slate) are the best options. Concrete can be tinted and inlaid for decorative effect but, like stone, it is porous and must be sealed. Avoid a surface laminate unless it's for use in a well-protected area because exposure to the weather causes the layers to separate. Solid-surfacing material is more durable, but it's better left to a sheltered location.

Think twice about using teak or other decay-resistant woods for a countertop. Although these woods weather handsomely, they are not sealed against bacteria, so you can't expose them directly to food. If you do select a wooden countertop, insert a tray or plate under any uncooked meats and vegetables. Decay-resistant woods such as redwood, cedar, teak, or mahogany are, however, good choices for outdoor cabinetry. Other types of wood will have to be sealed and stained or painted. Another option is oriented-strand board (OSB) that is weatherproof.

Side burners, opposite, help you prepare an entire meal at the grill.

Small, outdoor refrigerators, far right, save steps when entertaining outdoors.

What to Look for in a Grill

A grill cover should fit snugly. Some covers have adjustable lids, which allow airflow so that food cooks slowly and evenly.

Adjustable controls allow you to control the heat level of burners.

Side burners let you sauté toppings, simmer sauces, or fry side dishes. A side burner can come with a protective cover that also doubles as an extra landing surface for utensils.

A towel hook is a useful detail on a grill. Check for other extras, such as utility hooks for utensils, condiment compartments on side shelves, or warming racks.

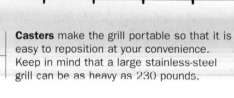

Casters make the grill portable so that it is easy to reposition at your convenience. Keep in mind that a large stainless-steel grill can be as heavy as 230 pounds.

Grill Checklist

Look for these important features:

■ **An electronic push-button ignition.** It starts better because it emits a continuous spark; knob igniters emit two to three sparks per turn.

■ **Insulated handles.** These are convenient because they don't get hot. Otherwise you'll need a grilling mitt to protect yourself from burns when using the controls.

■ **Easy access to the propane tank.** Some gas grills feature tilt-out bins, which make connecting and changing the tank a snap.

Safety Check

Hoses on gas grills can develop leaks. To check the hose on your gas grill, brush soapy water over it. If you see any bubbles, turn off the gas valve and disconnect the tank, then replace the hose.

Large grills, left, offer multiple, individually controlled burners, warming trays, and storage.

Selecting a Grill

It's not the size of the grill that counts; it's whether you have the space on the deck to accommodate it. Measure the intended cooking area before shopping, and take those measurements with you to the store or home center. Depending upon your budget, you may also want to consider one of the high-end units that luxury kitchen appliance manufacturers have introduced into the marketplace. They have lots of features and are built to last, but they are expensive and must be professionally installed. Serious cooks like them.

Think about the grill's location in relationship to the traffic, dining, and lounging zones. How far away will the grill be from the house? If your space is limited or if you expect a lot of activity—large crowds or kids underfoot—you may have to relegate the cooking area to someplace close, but not on the deck itself. Also consider how many people you typically cook for. Check out the grill's number of separate heating zones (there should be at least two) before buying it. If you have a large family or entertain frequently, you'll need a grill that can accommodate large quantities or different types of food at the same time.

Grill Features

Because you'll probably be using your new grill more often and with a greater variety of foods, buy one that has some important basic options. Are there any special features that you'd like with your grill? Extra burners, a rotisserie, a warming rack, or a smoker? What do you like to cook? Today, you can prepare more than hamburgers and barbecued chicken on your grill. In fact, tasty, healthy grilled food is popular year-round, and so you may be cooking outdoors from spring through late fall.

Many models now come with two burners, but larger ones have more. The burners should have adjustable temperature controls that will allow you to set the heat at high, medium, or low. Ideally, a unit should sustain an even cooking temperature and provide at least 33,000 Btu (British thermal units, the measurement for heat output) when burners are set on high. Generally, the larger the grill the higher the Btu output. A slow-roasting setting is optional on some models. Another good option is gauge that records the temperature when the lid is closed. If you enjoy sauces, make sure your grill comes with adjustable side burners, which can accommodate pots.

Outdoor Lighting

In terms of lighting and electricity, a deck can be as fully functional as any room inside your house. And if you add outdoor lighting, you will find that you get much more use out of your deck, patio, or outdoor living area. In addition to natural light, a pleasing combination of even, diffused general (also called "ambient") light, as well as accent and task lighting from artificial sources, can illuminate your deck for use after the sun goes down.

Developing an outdoor lighting plans differs from developing an interior lighting scheme. The basics are the same, but exterior lighting relies heavily on low-voltage systems. These operate on 12 volts as opposed to the 120 volts of a standard line system. A good outdoor plan will combine both types of lighting.

Developing a Lighting Planning

First decide how much light you need and where it should go. Besides general overall illumination, locate fixtures near activity zones: the food preparation and cooking area, the wet bar, or wherever you plan to set up drinks, snacks, or a buffet when you entertain. Be sure that there is adequate light near the dining table, conversation areas, and recreational spots, such as the hot tub, if you plan to use them in the evening. You may want separate switches for each one, and you might consider dimmers; you don't need or want the same intensity of light required for barbecuing as you do for relaxing in the hot tub.

What type of fixtures should you choose? That partly depends on the location. Near a wall or under a permanent roof, sconces and ceiling fixtures will provide light while staying out of the way. For uncovered areas, try post or railing lamps.

Lighting the Way

Walkways and staircases need lighting for safety. There are a number of practical options: path lights (if the walkway is ground level), brick lights that can be inserted into your walls near the steps, and railing fixtures that can be tucked under

deck railings or steps. Less-functional but more-decorative lighting such as post lamps can provide illumination for high traffic areas; sconces can be effective on stair landings or near doors. Walk lights also provide a needed measure of safety.

Don't forget about areas that may call for motion-sensitive floodlights, such as entrances into the house and garage, underneath a raised deck, and deep yards are all excellent locations for floodlights. Keep these fixtures on separate switches so that they don't interfere with the atmosphere you want to create while you are using the deck.

Railing- and bench-mounted lights, above, provide a subtle lighting option. They illuminate small areas without casting glare into the eyes of those on the deck.

Step lights, right, are a must for stairs leading down into the yard. Use these lights sparingly as shown. A little outdoor light goes a long way.

Provide a lighted backdrop to your outdoor living area by installing yard and garden lighting, above. Use lights to line walks, accent flower beds, or highlight a fountain or pond.

Adding Accent Light

Are there any noteworthy plantings or objects in your garden that you can highlight? By using in-ground accent lighting or spotlights, you can create dramatic nighttime effects or a focal point. Artful lighting can enhance the ambience of your deck by drawing attention to the shape of a handsome tree, a garden statue, a fountain or pond, or an outdoor pool.

Choosing the Right Fixture

If your home is formal, traditional fixtures in brass or an antique finish will complement the overall scheme nicely. For a modern setting, choose streamlined fixtures with matte or brushed-metal finishes. Landscape lighting is often utilitarian, but it is intended to blend unobtrusively into the landscape; the light, not the fixture, is noticeable. Path and post lighting, however, can be decorative and comes in a variety of styles and finishes, from highly polished metals to antique and matte looks.

Depending on the lighting system you buy, you may be able to install the fixtures yourself. But working with electricity does pose technical, code, and safety concerns. It's probably best to hire a qualified professional for the installation. For complex projects, you may also want to consult a landscape lighting professional. Home centers sometimes provide this type of expertise. If you decide to plot a design yourself, remember not to overlight the deck.

Other Considerations

As you plan to install deck lighting, think about the space's other electrical or wiring needs. If there is an outdoor kitchen, a grill area, or a bar, you may want outlets for a refrigerator or small appliances. You might include additional outlets for a stereo or speakers, or even a TV. Don't overlook a phone jack for the modem on your laptop computer. Some decking systems come prewired and are ready to be hooked up. So with forethought, you can incorporate everything you need into your outdoor living plans.

Water Features

There is nothing like the sight and sound of water to add a refreshing quality to your deck or patio. In fact, water can be a dynamic element in both the deck's design and its function. It can be in the form of one of the ultimate outdoor luxuries—a pool, spa, or hot tub—or in a water feature such as a fountain, waterfall, or pond. In any case, because of the relaxing qualities of water, you should consider integrating some form of it into your plans.

Planning a deck or patio near a pool requires taking the size and shape of the pool into consideration. In most cases, the pool will be a focal point in a landscape, so the design of the surrounding deck, including the flooring patterns, materials, and other details, can either enhance or detract

from its appeal. Aside from looks, think about how a pool deck will function.

Adding a Spa. Another way to enjoy water with your deck is with a soothing spa. Requiring less space than a pool, a spa uses hydrojets to move heated water. One type, a hot tub, is a barrel-like enclosure filled with water. It may or may not have jets and usually features an adjustable but simple bench. It offers a deeper soak—as much as 4 feet—than other types of spas, and many homeowners like the look of an aboveground hot tub's wood exterior. The tub comes with a vinyl or plastic liner.

A built-in spa is set into a deck or the ground (in-ground). It can be acrylic, or it can be constructed of poured concrete, gunite, or shotcrete. A spa can stand alone or be integrated with a large pool.

A portable spa is a completely self-contained unit that features an acrylic shell, a wooden surround, and all of the equipment needed to heat and move the water. A small portable spa costs less than an in-ground unit, and it runs on a standard 120-volt circuit. You can locate a portable spa on a concrete slab. But you can also install one on the deck. Just make sure there is proper structural support underneath the deck to sustain the additional weight of the unit, the water, and bathers.

Small, portable spas, opposite, are self-contained units that run on standard line-voltage electricity. Check weight restrictions if installing a spa on a deck.

Spas complete an outdoor living area, above. This sunken spa is a natural complement to the nearby pool and to the large multilevel deck.

Plan #181062

Dimensions: 58' W x 55' D
Levels: 2
Square Footage: 1,953
Main Level Sq. Ft.: 1,301
Second Level Sq. Ft.: 652
Bedrooms: 2
Bathrooms: 2½
Foundation: Half basement,
half crawl space
Materials List Available: Yes
Price Category: D

Images provided by designer/architect.

Features:

- Ceiling Height: 8 ft.

- Wall of Doors: The entire back of the house is filled by five sets of multi-pane glass doors.

- Formal Dining Room: This dining room is located adjacent to the kitchen for convenient entertaining.

- Kitchen: This efficient kitchen is a pleasure in which to work, thanks to plenty of counter

space, a pantry, double sinks, and access to the laundry room.

- Great Room: This great room is open to the atrium. As a result it is filled with warmth and natural light. You'll love gathering around the handsome fireplace.

- Master Suite: This private first-floor retreat features a walk-in closet and a luxurious full bath with dual vanities.

A magnificent glass enclosed vertical atrium is the focal point of this beautiful country home.

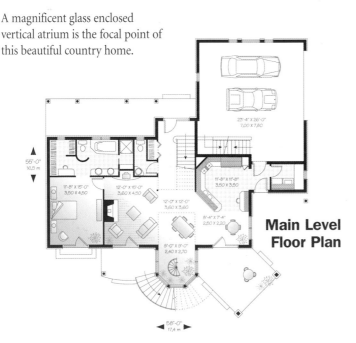

Main Level Floor Plan

Copyright by designer/architect.

Upper Level Floor Plan

Plan #181128

Dimensions: 36' W x 36' D
Levels: 2
Square Footage: 1,634
Main Level Sq. Ft.: 1,087
Second Level Sq. Ft.: 547
Bedrooms: 3
Bathrooms: 2
Foundation: Basement
Materials List Available: Yes
Price Category: C

Illustration provided by designer/architect.

This stone-accented rustic vacation home offers the perfect antidote to busy daily life.

Features:

- Ceiling Height: 8 ft. unless otherwise noted.
- Family Room: Family and friends will be unable to resist relaxing in this airy two-story family room, with its own handsome fireplace. French doors lead to the front deck.
- Kitchen: This eat-in kitchen features double sinks, ample counter space, and a pantry. It offers plenty of space for the family to gather for informal vacation meals.

- Master Suite: This first-floor master retreat occupies almost the entire length of the home. It includes a walk-in closet and a lavish bath.
- Secondary Bedrooms: On the second floor, two family bedrooms share a full bath.
- Mezzanine: This lovely balcony overlooks the family room.
- Basement: This full unfinished basement offers plenty of space for expansion.

Main Level Floor Plan

Upper Level Floor Plan

Copyright by designer/architect.

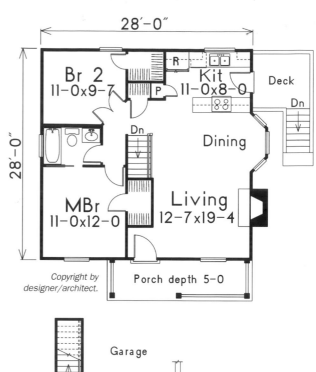

28'-0"

Br 2
11-0x9-7

Kit
11-0x8-0

Deck

Dn

P

R

Dn

Dining

28'-0"

MBr
11-0x12-0

Living
12-7x19-4

*Copyright by
designer/architect.*

Porch depth 5-0

*Illustration provided by
designer/architect.*

Plan #321025

Dimensions: 28' W x 28' D

Levels: 1

Square Footage: 914

Bedrooms: 2

Bathrooms: 1

Foundation: Daylight basement

Materials List Available: Yes

Price Category: A

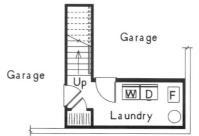

Garage

Garage

Up

W D F

Laundry

**Optional
Basement Level
Floor Plan**

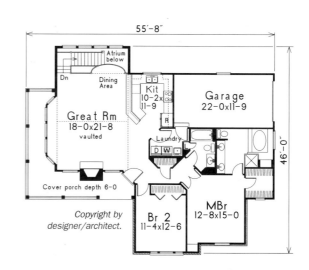

55'-8"

Atrium
below

Dn

Dining
Area

Kit
10-2x
11-9

Garage
22-0x11-9

Great Rm
18-0x21-8
vaulted

R

Laundry

D W

46'-0"

Cover porch depth 6-0

Br 2
11-4x12-6

MBr
12-8x15-0

*Copyright by
designer/architect.*

Plan #321035

Dimensions: 55'8" W x 46' D

Levels: 1

Square Footage: 1,384

Bedrooms: 2

Bathrooms: 2

Foundation: Basement

Materials List Available: Yes

Price Category: B

*Illustration provided by
designer/architect.*

Rear View

Up

Patio

**Optional
Basement
Level
Floor Plan**

Family Rm
25-0x21-4

Unexcavated

Unfinished
Basement

Main Level Floor Plan

Upper Level Floor Plan

Illustration provided by designer/architect.

Plan #181126

Dimensions: 35' W x 30' D

Levels: 2

Square Footage: 1,468

Main Level Sq. Ft.: 958

Upper Level Sq. Ft.: 510

Bedrooms: 3

Bathrooms: 2

Foundation: Full basement

Materials List Available: Yes

Price Category: B

Copyright by designer/architect.

Main Level Floor Plan

Upper Level Floor Plan

Illustration provided by designer/architect.

Plan #181053

Dimensions: 56' W x 53'2" D

Levels: 2

Square Footage: 2,353

Main Level Sq. Ft.: 1,606

Upper Level Sq. Ft.: 747

Bedrooms: 3

Bathrooms: 2½

Foundation: Basement, crawl space

Materials List Available: Yes

Price Category: E

Copyright by designer/architect.

Plan #181131

Dimensions: 26'4" W x 37' D

Levels: 2

Square Footage: 1,442

Main Level Sq. Ft.: 922

Upper Level Sq. Ft.: 520

Bedrooms: 3

Bathrooms: 2

Foundation: Full basement

Materials List Available: Yes

Price Category: B

Illustration provided by designer/architect.

Main Level Floor Plan

Upper Level Floor Plan

Copyright by designer/architect.

Plan #181132

Dimensions: 44' W x 26' D

Levels: 2

Square Footage: 1,437

Main Level Sq. Ft.: 856

Upper Level Sq. Ft.: 581

Bedrooms: 3

Bathrooms: 1½

Foundation: Walk-out basement

Materials List Available: Yes

Price Category: B

Illustration provided by designer/architect.

Main Level Floor Plan

Upper Level Floor Plan

Copyright by designer/architect.

Plan #181108

Dimensions: 26' W x 48' D

Levels: 2

Square Footage: 1,484

Main Level Sq. Ft.: 908

Second Level Sq. Ft.: 576

Bedrooms: 3

Bathrooms: 2

Foundation: Basement

Materials List Available: Yes

Price Category: B

This delightful home is well suited to a waterfront property with great views.

Features:

- Ceiling Height: 8 ft.

- Sunroom: This elevated front sunroom fills the house with warmth and is the perfect place in which to watch the sun set over a lake. A lovely deck adjoins the sunroom.

- Family Room: From the sunroom, walk through sliding doors into this inviting room with angled wood-burning fireplace.

- Dining Room: Also accessible from the sunroom, this dining room shares the family room fireplace. The dining room and the family room both get plenty of light from full-length multi-pane windows.

Illustration provided by designer/architect.

- Kitchen: This kitchen has a breakfast bar at the large center island, double sinks, and a pantry.

- Master Suite: Upstairs you'll find this master getaway with walk-in closet, luxurious full bathroom, and whirlpool tub.

Main Level Floor Plan

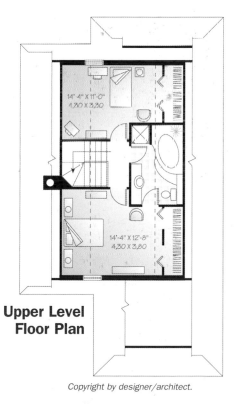

Upper Level Floor Plan

Copyright by designer/architect.

Plan #281010

Dimensions: 34' W x 31' D

Levels: 1

Square Footage: 884

Bedrooms: 2

Bathrooms: 1

Foundation: Crawl space

Materials List Available: Yes

Price Category: A

This cute vacation or retirement home is modest in size yet contains all the necessary amenities.

Features:

- Ceiling Height: 8 ft.

- Open Plan: The living room, dining room, and kitchen are all contained in one open space. This makes the space versatile and allows plenty of room for entertaining despite the home's small size.

- Covered Deck: Step outdoors and enjoy warm breezes on this covered deck, which is accessible from the open main living area.

- Master Bedroom: This master bedroom is separated from the other bedroom to allow maximum privacy.

- Second Bedroom: This bedroom is perfect for when friends and family come to spend the night.

- Cedar Siding: This vertical cedar siding weathers to a beautiful silver gray when left unstained.

Illustration provided by designer/architect.

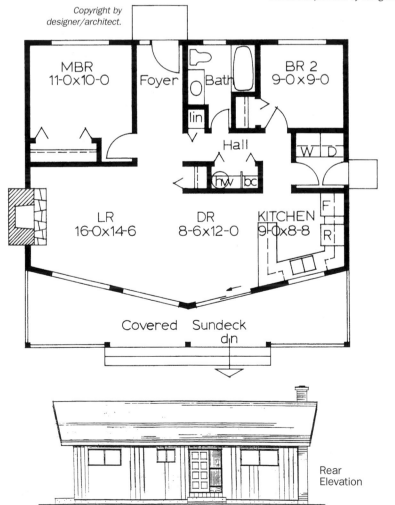

Plan #181109

Dimensions: 22'8" W x 26'8" D
Levels: 2
Square Footage: 991
Main Level Sq. Ft.: 596
Second Level Sq. Ft.: 395
Bedrooms: 2
Bathrooms: 2
Foundation: Crawl space
Materials List Available: Yes
Price Category: A

This charming home with beautiful windows is the perfect starter or retirement home.

Illustration provided by designer/architect.

Features:

- Ceiling Height: 8 ft. unless otherwise noted.

- Living Room: This front living room is the centerpiece of a well-designed floor plan that makes excellent use of space. The living room itself has plenty of room for family and friends to gather and relax.

- Kitchen: This bright and efficient kitchen includes an eat-in area that is perfect for informal dining. The eating area flows easily into the living room.

- Guest Bedroom: Guests will stay in comfort thanks to this pleasant downstairs guest room with its own closet and full bath.

- Master Suite: Retire at the end of the day in comfort and privacy in this upstairs master suite, which features a nicely appointed full bathroom and a walk-in closet.

- Mezzanine: This lovely balcony is open to the family room below. It provides space for a reading area or a home office.

Main Level Floor Plan

9'-4" X 10'-4"
2,80 X 3,10

8'-0" X 14'-4"
2,40 X 4,30

13'-0" X 12'-0"
3,90 X 3,60

10'-0" X 24'-0"
3,00 X 7,20

26'-8"
8,0 m

22'-8"
6,8 m

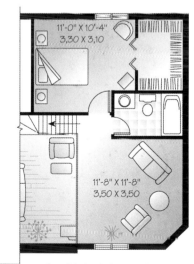

11'-0" X 10'-4"
3,30 X 3,10

11'-8" X 11'-8"
3,50 X 3,50

Copyright by designer/architect.

Upper Level Floor Plan

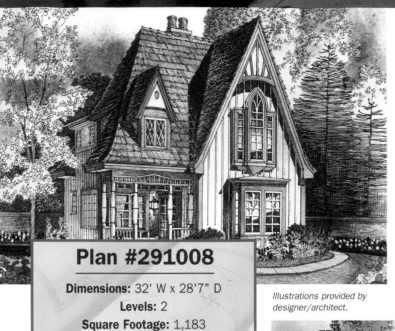

Main Level Floor Plan

32'-0"

KIT.
8'-0" x
9'-8"

STOR.

LIVING ROOM
15'-7" x 14'-0"

WALL ABOVE

UP

PORCH

28'-7"

DINE
11'-0" x 8'-3"

ENTRY

B 2

BEDROOM #2
10'-0" x 9'-0"
(+BAY)

PORCH

SEATS

Plan #291008

Dimensions: 32' W x 28'7" D

Levels: 2

Square Footage: 1,183

Main Level Sq. Ft.: 772

Upper Level Sq. Ft.: 411

Bedrooms: 2

Bathrooms: 2

Foundation: Crawl space

Materials List Available: No

Price Category: B

Illustrations provided by designer/architect.

Upper Level Floor Plan

DOWN

D

OPEN TO LIVING ROOM

W

WOOD BEAMS

BATH #1

WIC

MASTER BEDROOM
10'-5" x 13'-8"
(11'-8" CEILING)

BUILT-IN CABINETS

Plan #281006

Dimensions: 34' W x 56' D

Levels: 2

Square Footage: 1,702

Main Level Sq. Ft.: 1,238

Upper Level Sq. Ft.: 464

Bedrooms: 3

Bathrooms: 2

Foundation: Walk-out basement

Materials List Available: Yes

Price Category: C

Illustration provided by designer/architect.

BR 3
11-4 x 11-0

BR 2
14-0 x 11-6

lin

up

up

R F

BATH

KITCHEN
11-4 x 9-0

FOYER

DINING
11-4 x 9-0

dn

up

loft over

railing

LIVINGROOM
25-0 x 15-4

SUNDECK

Main Level Floor Plan

DECK

MASTER SUITE
14-0 x 11-6

attic

attic

Dressing

Bath

Walk-in Closet

dn

LOFT

railing

Livingroom below

Upper Level Floor Plan

Copyright by designer/architect.

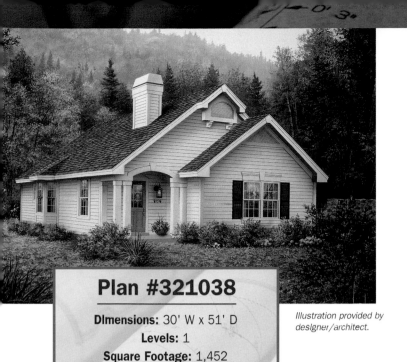

Plan #321038

Dimensions: 30' W x 51' D

Levels: 1

Square Footage: 1,452

Bedrooms: 4

Bathrooms: 2

Foundation: Basement

Materials List Available: Yes

Price Category: B

Illustration provided by designer/architect.

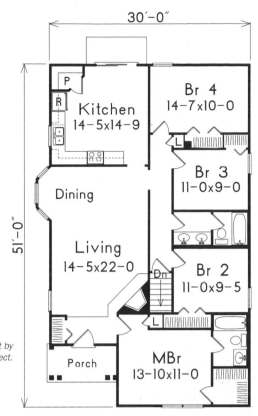

30'-0"

51'-0"

P
R
Kitchen
14-5x14-9

Br 4
14-7x10-0

Dining

L

Br 3
11-0x9-0

Living
14-5x22-0

Dn

Br 2
11-0x9-5

L

Porch

MBr
13-10x11-0

Copyright by designer/architect.

Plan #321040

Dimensions: 35' W x 40'8" D

Levels: 1

Square Footage: 1,084

Bedrooms: 2

Bathrooms: 2

Foundation: Basement

Materials List Available: Yes

Price Category: B

Illustration provided by designer/architect.

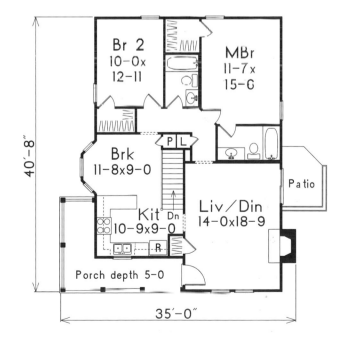

40'-8"

Br 2
10-0x
12-11

MBr
11-7x
15-6

Brk
11-8x9-0

P L

Patio

Kit
10-9x9-0

Dn

Liv/Din
14-0x18-9

R

Porch depth 5-0

35'-0"

Copyright by designer/architect.

Plan #321009

Dimensions: 55'8" W x 46'4" D
Levels: 1
Square Footage: 2,295
Bedrooms: 3
Bathrooms: 2
Foundation: Basement
Materials List Available: Yes
Price Category: E

Illustration provided by designer/architect.

If you've got a site with great views, you'll love this home, which is designed to make the most of them.

Features:

• **Porch:** This wraparound porch is an ideal spot to watch the sun come up or go down. Add potted plants to create a lush atmosphere or grow some culinary herbs.

• **Great Room:** You couldn't ask for more luxury than this room provides, with its vaulted ceiling, large bay window, fireplace, dining balcony, and atrium window wall.

• **Kitchen:** No matter whether you're an avid cook or not, you'll relish the thoughtful design of this room.

• **Master Suite:** This suite is truly a retreat you'll treasure. It has two large walk-in closets for good storage space, and sliding doors that open to an exterior balcony where you can sit out to enjoy the stars. The amenity-filled bath adds to your enjoyment of this suite.

Rear View

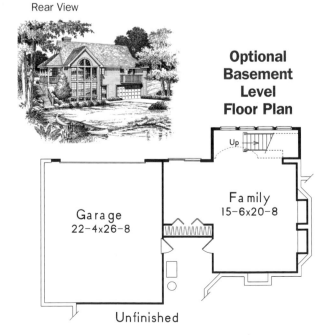

55'–8"

Balcony

MBr
18-4x13-0

Kit
10-2x
11-9

Dining   Dn

Great Rm
16-0x21-4
vaulted

Entry

Porch depth 6-0

46'–4"

W D

Br 2
12-8x14-0

Br 3
11-4x12-6

Copyright by designer/architect.

Optional Basement Level Floor Plan

Up

Garage
22-4x26-8

Family
15-6x20-8

Unfinished

Illustration provided by designer/architect.

Plan #181081

Dimensions: 58' W x 33' D
Levels: 2
Square Footage: 2,350
Main Level Sq. Ft.: 1,107
Second Level Sq. Ft.: 1,243
Bedrooms: 3
Bathrooms: 2½
Foundation: Basement
Materials List Available: Yes
Price Category: E

This traditional country home features a wrap-around porch and a second-floor balcony.

Features:

- Ceiling Height: 8 ft. unless otherwise noted.
- Family Room: Double French doors and a fireplace in this inviting front room enhance the beauty and warmth of the home's open floor plan.
- Kitchen: You'll love working in this bright and convenient kitchen. The breakfast bar is the perfect place to gather for informal meals.
- Master Suite: You'll look forward to retiring to this elegant upstairs suite at the end of a busy day. The suite features a private bath with separate shower and tub, as well as dual vanities.
- Secondary Bedrooms: Two family bedrooms share a full bath with a third room that opens onto the balcony.
- Basement: An unfinished full basement provides plenty of storage and the potential to add additional finished living space.

Main Level Floor Plan

Copyright by designer/architect.

Upper Level Floor Plan

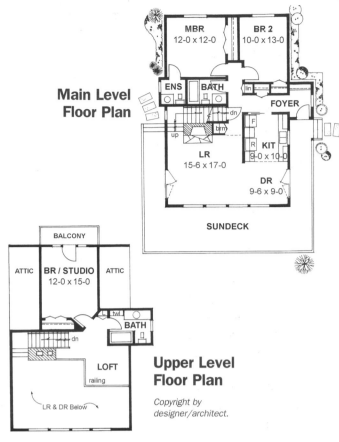

**Main Level
Floor Plan**

MBR
12-0 x 12-0

BR 2
10-0 x 13-0

ENS BATH lin

FOYER

up brm dn

F
R KIT
9-0 x 10-0

LR
15-6 x 17-0

DR
9-6 x 9-0

SUNDECK

BALCONY

ATTIC BR / STUDIO
12-0 x 15-0 ATTIC

twl

BATH

dn

LOFT

railing

LR & DR Below

**Upper Level
Floor Plan**

*Illustration provided by
designer/architect.*

*Copyright by
designer/architect.*

Plan #281004

Dimensions: 36' W x 50' D

Levels: 2

Square Footage: 1,426

Main Level Sq. Ft.: 1,086

Upper Level Sq. Ft.: 340

Bedrooms: 3

Bathrooms: 2½

Foundation: Walk-out basement

Materials List Available: Yes

Price Category: B

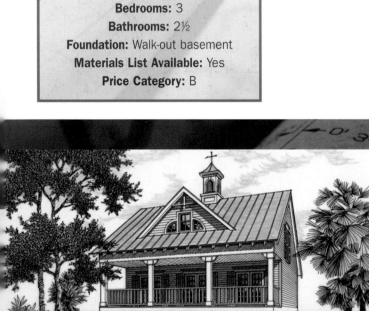

**Ground
Level
Floor
Plan**

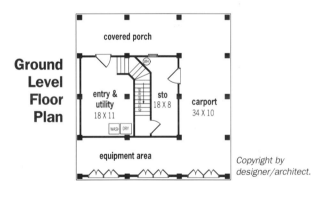

covered porch

entry &
utility
18 X 11

sto
18 X 8

carport
34 X 10

WASH DRY

equipment area

*Copyright by
designer/architect.*

Plan #211081

Dimensions: 32' W x 34' D

Levels: 2

Square Footage: 1,110

Main Level Sq. Ft.: 832

Upper Level Sq. Ft.: 278

Bedrooms: 2

Bathrooms: 2

Foundation: Crawl space

Materials List Available: No

Price Category: B

*Illustration provided by
designer/architect.*

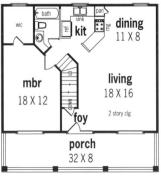

wic bath

ref sink pan

kit rng

dining
11 X 8

mbr
18 X 12

up

living
18 X 16

dwn

2 story clg

foy

porch
32 X 8

Main Level Floor Plan

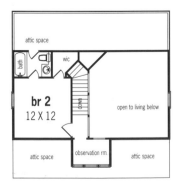

attic space

bath wic

br 2
12 X 12

dwn

open to living below

attic space observation rm attic space

Upper Level Floor Plan

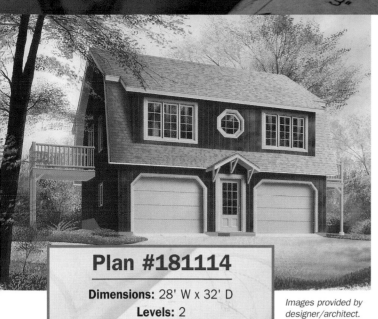

Plan #181114

Dimensions: 28' W x 32' D

Levels: 2

Square Footage: 992

Garage Level Sq. Ft.: 96

Second Level Sq. Ft.: 896

Bedrooms: 2

Bathrooms: 1½

Foundation: Slab

Materials List Available: Yes

Price Category: A

Images provided by designer/architect.

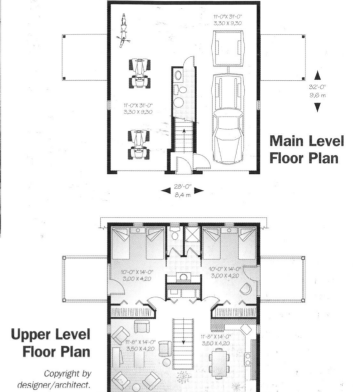

Main Level Floor Plan

Upper Level Floor Plan

Copyright by designer/architect.

Plan #181001

Dimensions: 38' W x 28' D

Levels: 1

Square Footage: 920

Bedrooms: 2

Bathrooms: 1

Foundation: Basement

Materials List Available: Yes

Price Category: A

Images provided by designer/architect.

Copyright by designer/architect.

Illustration provided by designer/architect.

Plan #181120

Dimensions: 32' W x 40' D
Levels: 2
Square Footage: 1,480
Main Level Sq. Ft.: 1,024
Second Level Sq. Ft.: 456
Bedrooms: 2
Bathrooms: 2
Foundation: Basement
Materials List Available: Yes
Price Category: B

Escape to this charming all-season vacation home with lots of view-capturing windows.

Features:

- Ceiling Height: 8 ft. unless otherwise noted.

- Living/Dining Area: The covered back porch opens into this large, inviting combined area. Its high ceiling adds to the sense of spaciousness.

- Family Room: After relaxing in front of the fireplace that warms this family room, family and guests can move outside onto the porch to watch the sun set.

- Kitchen: Light streams through a triple window in this well-designed kitchen. It's conveniently located next to the dining area and features a center island with a breakfast bar and double sinks.

- Master Suite: This first floor suite is located in the front of the house and is enhanced by its large walk-through closet and the adjoining private bath.

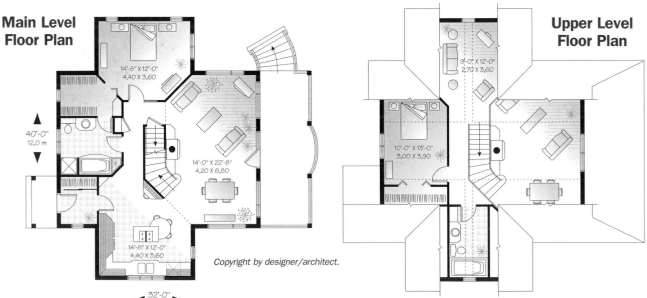

Main Level Floor Plan

14'-8" X 12'-0"
4,40 X 3,60

40'-0"
12,0 m

14'-0" X 22'-8"
4,20 X 6,80

14'-8" X 12'-0"
4,40 X 3,60

32'-0"
9,6 m

Copyright by designer/architect.

Upper Level Floor Plan

9'-0" X 12'-0"
2,70 X 3,60

10'-0" X 13'-0"
3,00 X 3,90

Plan #181133

Dimensions: 38' W x 40' D
Levels: 2
Square Footage: 1,832
Main Level Sq. Ft.: 1,212
Second Level Sq. Ft. 620
Bedrooms: 3
Bathrooms: 2
Foundation: Basement
Materials List Available: Yes
Price Category: D

You'll enjoy sunshine indoors and out with a wraparound deck and windows all around.

Illustration provided by designer/architect.

Features:

- Ceiling Height: 8 ft.
- Family Room: Family and friends will be drawn to this large sunny room. Curl up with a good book before the beautiful see-through fireplace.
- Screened Porch: This porch shares the see-through fireplace with the family room so you can enjoy an outside fire on cool summer nights.

- Master Suite: This romantic first-floor master suite offers a large walk-in closet and a luxurious private bathroom enhanced by dual vanities.
- Secondary Bedrooms: Upstairs you'll find two generous bedrooms with ample closet space. These bedrooms share a full bathroom.
- Basement: This large walkout basement with large glass door is perfectly suited for future expansion.

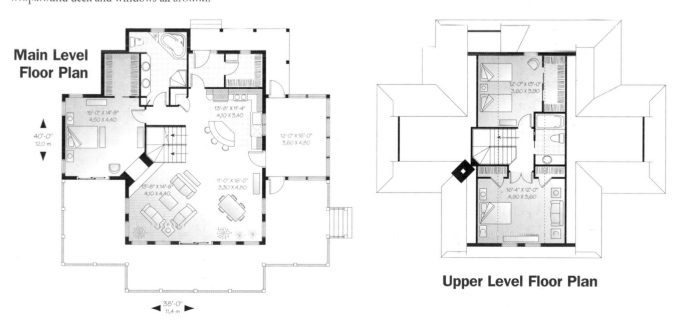

Main Level Floor Plan

Upper Level Floor Plan

Upper Level Floor Plan

Copyright by designer/architect.

Plan #181112

Dimensions: 28' W x 26' D

Levels: 2

Square Footage: 1,148

Main Level Sq. Ft.: 728

Upper Level Sq. Ft.: 420

Bedrooms: 1

Bathrooms: 1½

Foundation: Full basement

Materials List Available: Yes

Price Category: B

Images provided by designer/architect.

Main Level Floor Plan

Plan #181121

Dimensions: 27'8" W x 48' D

Levels: 2

Square Footage: 1,484

Main Level Sq. Ft.: 908

Upper Level Sq. Ft.: 576

Bedrooms: 3

Bathrooms: 2

Foundation: Walk-out basement

Materials List Available: Yes

Price Category: B

Images provided by designer/architect.

Main Level Floor Plan

Upper Level Floor Plan

Copyright by designer/architect.

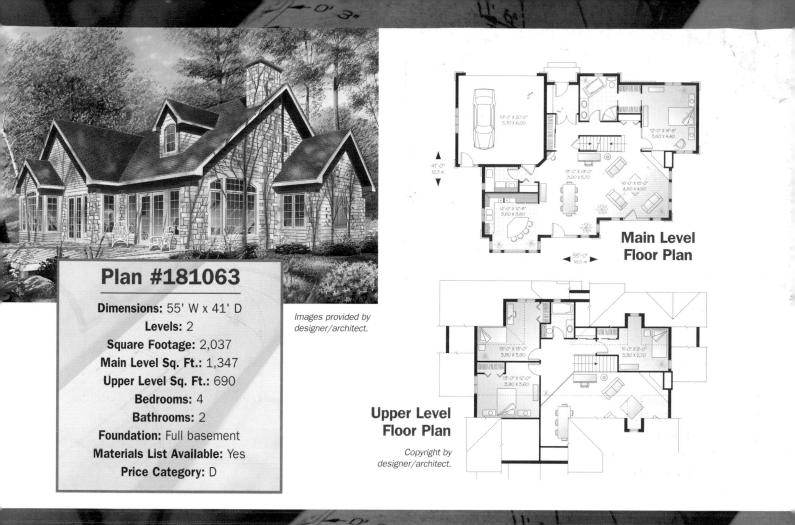

Plan #181063

Dimensions: 55' W x 41' D

Levels: 2

Square Footage: 2,037

Main Level Sq. Ft.: 1,347

Upper Level Sq. Ft.: 690

Bedrooms: 4

Bathrooms: 2

Foundation: Full basement

Materials List Available: Yes

Price Category: D

Images provided by designer/architect.

Main Level Floor Plan

Upper Level Floor Plan

Copyright by designer/architect.

Plan #281005

Dimensions: 35' W x 40' D

Levels: 2

Square Footage: 1,362

Main Level Sq. Ft.: 864

Upper Level Sq. Ft.: 498

Bedrooms: 2

Bathrooms: 2

Foundation: Crawl space

Materials List Available: Yes

Price Category: B

Images provided by designer/architect.

Upper Level Floor Plan

Main Level Floor Plan

Copyright by designer/architect.

Plan #271053

Dimensions: 70' W x 34' D
Levels: 2
Square Footage: 2,458
Main Level Sq. Ft.: 1,067
Upper Level Sq. Ft.: 346
Bedrooms: 3
Bathrooms: 2½
Foundation: Daylight basement or crawl space
Materials List Available: No
Price Category: E

Photo provided by designer/architect.

The octagonal shape and window-filled walls of this home create a powerful interior packed with panoramic views.

Features:

• Great Room: Straight back from the angled entry, this room is brightened by sunlight through windows and sliding glass doors. Beyond the doors, a huge wraparound deck offers plenty of space for tanning or relaxing. A spiral staircase adds visual interest.

• Kitchen: This efficient space includes a convenient pantry.

• Master Suite: On the upper level, this romantic master suite overlooks the great room below. Several windows provide scenic outdoor views. A walk-in closet and a private bath round out this secluded haven.

• Basement: The optional basement includes a recreation room, as well as an extra bedroom and bath.

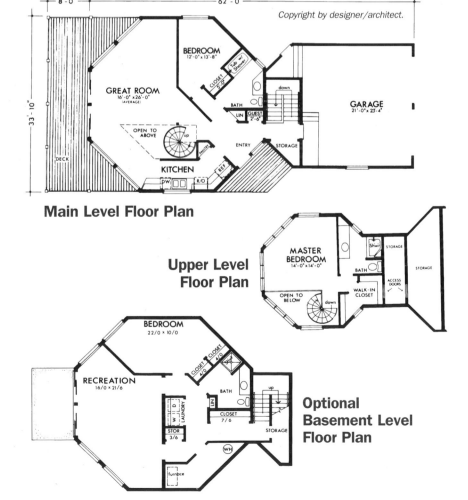

Copyright by designer/architect.

Main Level Floor Plan

Upper Level Floor Plan

Optional Basement Level Floor Plan

Let Us Help You
Plan Your
Dream Home

Whether you've always dreamed of building your own home or you can't find the right house from among the dozens you've toured, our collection of family–living home plans can help you achieve the home of your dreams. You could have an architect create a one-of-a-kind home for you, but the design services alone could end up costing up to 15 percent of the cost of construction—a hefty premium for any building project. Isn't it a better idea to select from among the hundreds of unique designs shown in our collection for a fraction of the cost?

What does Creative Homeowner Offer?

In this book, Creative Homeowner provides hundreds of home plans from the country's best architects and designers. Our designs are among the most popular available. Whether your taste runs from traditional to contemporary, Victorian to early American, you are sure to find the best house design for you and your family. Our plans packages include detailed drawings to help you or your builder construct your dream house. **(See page 344.)**

Can I Make Changes to the Plans?

Creative Homeowner offers three ways to help you achieve a truly unique home design. Our customizing service allows for extensive changes to our designs. **(See page 345.)** We also provide reverse images of our plans, or we can give you and your builder the tools for making minor changes on your own. **(See page 346.)**

Can You Help Me Stay on Budget?

Building a house is a large financial investment. To help you stay within your budget, Creative Homeowner can provide you with general construction costs based on your zip code. **(See page 346.)** Also, many of our plans come with the option of buying detailed materials lists to help you price out construction costs.

Is There Anything I Missed?

A typical construction crew consists of a number of skilled professionals. If you plan on doing all or part of the work yourself, or you want to keep tabs on your builder, we offer best-selling building and design books at attractive prices. Our book packages cover all phases of home construction, including framing and drywalling, interior decorating, kitchen and bath design, landscaping, and outdoor living. **(See pages 351–352.)**

Our Plans Packages Offer:

All of our home plans are the result of many hours of work by leading architects and professional designers. When you place an order for one of our home plans, you will receive the following.

Frontal Sheet
This artist's rendering of the front of the house gives you an idea of how the house will look once it is completed and the property landscaped.

Detailed Floor Plans
These plans show the size and layout of the rooms. They also provide the locations of doors, windows, fireplaces, closets, stairs, and electrical outlets and switches.

Foundation Plan
A foundation plan gives the dimensions of basements, walk-out basements, crawl spaces, pier foundations, and slab construction. Each house design lists the type of foundation included. If the plan you choose does not have the foundation type you require, our customer service department can help you customize the plan to meet your needs.

Roof Plan
In addition to providing the pitch of the roof, these plans also show the locations of dormers, skylights, and other elements.

Exterior Elevations
These drawings show the front, rear, and sides of the house as if you were looking at it head on. Elevations also provide information about architectural features and finish materials.

Interior Elevations and Details
Interior elevations show specific details of such elements as fireplaces, kitchen and bathroom cabinets, built-ins, and other unique features of the design.

Cross Sections
These show the structure as if it were sliced to reveal construction requirements, such as insulation, flooring, and roofing details.

Frontal Sheet

Floor Plan

Foundation Plan

Roof Plan

Cross Sections

Stair Details

Elevation

Illustrations provided by designer/architect

Customize Your Plans in 4 Easy Steps

1 **Select the home plan** that most closely meets your needs. Purchase of a reproducible master is necessary in order to make changes to a plan.

2 **Call 1-800-523-6789 to place your order.** Tell our sales representative you are interested in customizing your plan. To receive your customization cost estimate, we will send you a checklist (via fax or email) for you to complete indicating the changes you would like to make to your plan. There is a $50 nonrefundable consultation fee for this service. If you decide to continue with the custom changes, the $50 fee is credited to the total amount charged.

3 **Fax the completed checklist** to 1-201-760-2431 or email it to us at customize@creativehomeowner.com. Within three business days of receipt of your checklist, a detailed cost estimate will be provided to you.

4 **Once you approve the estimate,** a 75% retainer fee is collected and customization work begins. Preliminary drawings typically take 10 to 15 business days. After approval, we will collect the balance of your customization order cost before shipping the completed plans. You will receive five sets of blueprints or a reproducible master, plus a customized materials list if desired.

Modification Pricing Guide

Categories	Average Cost From...	To
Add or remove living space	Quote required	
Bathroom layout redesign	$120	$280
Kitchen layout redesign	$120	$280
Garage: add or remove	$400	$680
Garage: front entry to side load or vice versa	Starting at $300	
Foundation changes	Starting at $220	
Exterior building materials change	Starting at $200	
Exterior openings: add, move, or remove	$55 per opening	
Roof line changes	$360	$630
Ceiling height adjustments	$280	$500
Fireplace: add or remove	$90	$200
Screened porch: add	$280	$600
Wall framing change from 2x4 to 2x6	Starting at $200	
Bearing and/or exterior walls changes	Quote required	
Non-bearing wall or room changes	$55 per room	
Metric conversion of home plan	$400	
Adjust plan for handicapped accessibility	Quote required	
Adapt plans for local building code requirements	Quote required	
Engineering stamping only	Quote required	
Any other engineering services	Quote required	
Interactive illustrations (choices of exterior materials)	Quote required	

Note: *Any home plan can be customized to accommodate your desired changes. The average prices above are provided only as examples of the most commonly requested changes, and are subject to change without notice. Prices for changes will vary according to the number of modifications requested, plan size, style, and method of design used by the original designer. To obtain a detailed cost estimate, please contact us.*

Terms & Copyright

These home plans are protected under the terms of United States Copyright Law and may not be copied or reproduced in any way, by any means, unless you have purchased reproducible masters, which clearly indicate your right to copy or reproduce. We authorize the use of your chosen home plan as an aid in the construction of one single-family home only. You may not use this home plan to build a second or multiple dwellings without purchasing another blueprint or blueprints, or paying additional home plan fees.

Architectural Seals

Because of differences in building codes, some cities and states now require an architect or engineer licensed in that state to review and "seal" a blueprint, or officially approve it, prior to construction. Delaware, Nevada, New Jersey, and New York require that all plans for houses built in those states be redrawn by an architect licensed in the state in which the home will be built.

Before Customization

After

Decide What Type of Plan Package You Need

How many Plans Should You Order?

Standard 8-Set Package. We've found that our 8-set package is the best value for someone who is ready to start building. Once the process begins, a number of people will require their own set of blueprints. The 8-set package provides plans for you, your builder, the subcontractors, mortgage lender, and the building department.
Minimum 4-Set Package. If you are in the bidding process, you may want to order only four sets for the bidding round and reorder additional sets as needed.
1-Set Study Package. The 1-set package allows you to review your home plan in detail. The plan will be marked as a study print, and it is illegal to build a house from a study print alone. It is a violation of copyright law to reproduce a blueprint without permission.

Buying Additional Sets

If you require additional copies of blueprints for your home construction, you can order additional sets within 60 days of the original order date at a reduced price. The cost is $45.00 for each additional set. For more information, contact customer service.

Reproducible Masters

If you plan to make minor changes to one of our home plans, you can purchase reproducible masters. Drawn on vellum paper, an erasable paper that you can reproduce in a copying machine, reproducible masters allow an architect, designer, or builder to alter our plans to give you a customized home design. This package also allows you to print as many copies of the modified plans as you need for construction.

Mirror-Reverse Sets

Plans can be printed in mirror-reverse—we can "flip" plans to create a mirror image of the design. This is useful when the house would fit your site or personal preferences if all the rooms were on the opposite side than shown. As the image is reversed, the lettering and dimensions will also be reversed, meaning they will read backwards. Therefore, when ordering mirror-reverse drawings, you must order at least one set of right-reading plans. A $50.00 fee per order will be charged for mirror-reverse (regardless of the number of mirror-reverse sets ordered).

Determine Your Construction Costs

EZ Quote: Home Cost Estimator

EZ Quote is our response to one of the most frequently asked questions we hear from customers: "How much will the house cost me to build?" EZ Quote: Home Cost Estimator will enable you to obtain a calculated building cost to construct your new home, based on labor rates and building material costs within your zip code area. This summary building cost report is particularly useful for first-time buyers who might be concerned with the total construction costs before purchasing sets of home plans. It will also provide a certain level of comfort when you begin soliciting bids from builders. The cost is $29.95 for the first EZ Quote and $14.95 for each additional EZ Quote.

Materials List

Available for most of our plans, the Materials List provides you an invaluable resource in planning and estimating the cost of your home. Each Materials List outlines the quantity, dimensions, and type of materials needed to build your home (with the exception of mechanical systems). You will get faster, more-accurate bids from your contractors and building suppliers—and avoid paying for unused materials. Included are framing lumber, windows and doors, kitchen and bath cabinetry, rough and finish hardware, and much more. A Materials List may only be ordered with the purchase of a set of home plans.

Order Toll Free by Phone
1-800-523-6789
By Fax: 201-760-2431

Regular office hours are
8:30AM–9:00PM ET, Mon–Fri

Orders received 3PM ET, will be processed
and shipped within two business days.

Order Online
www.ultimateplans.com

Mail Your Order
Creative Homeowner
Attn: Home Plans
24 Park Way
Upper Saddle River, NJ 07458

Canadian Customers
Order Toll Free 1-800-393-1883

Before You Order

Our Exchange Policy

Blueprints are nonrefundable. However, should you find that the plan you have purchased does not fit your needs, you may exchange that plan for another plan in our collection within 60 days from the date of your original order. The entire content of your original order must be returned before an exchange will be processed. You will be charged a processing fee of 20% of the amount of the original plan set, the cost difference between the new plan set and the original plan set (if applicable), and shipping costs for the new plans. Contact our customer service department for more information. Please note: reproducible masters may only be exchanged if the package is unopened.

Building Codes and Requirements

At the time of creation, our plans meet the building code requirements published by the Building Officials and Code Administrators International, the Southern Building Code Congress International, the International Conference of Building Officials, or the Council of American Building Officials. Because building codes vary from area to area, some drawing modifications and/or the assistance of a professional designer or architect may be necessary to comply with your local codes or to accommodate specific building site conditions. We strongly advise you to consult with your local building official for information regarding codes governing your area.

Blueprint Price Schedule

Price Code	1 Set	4 Sets	8 Sets	Reproducible Masters	Materials List
A	$275	$315	$365	$490	$60
B	$350	$390	$440	$555	$60
C	$400	$440	$490	$590	$60
D	$450	$490	$540	$630	$70
E	$500	$540	$590	$675	$70
F	$550	$590	$640	$725	$70
G	$600	$640	$690	$820	$70
H	$675	$715	$765	$865	$70
I	$780	$820	$870	$905	$80

Shipping & Handling

	1-4 Sets	5-7 Sets	8+ Sets or Reproducibles
US Regular (7–10 business days)	$15	$20	$25
US Priority (3–5 business days)	$25	$30	$35
US Express (1–2 business days)	$35	$40	$45
Canada Reg. (8–12 business days)	$25	$30	$35
Canada Exp. (3–5 business days)	$40	$40	$45

Overseas Shipping: Contact customer service for shipping costs.

Note: *All delivery times are from date the blueprint and package is shipped.*

Order Form

Please send me the following:

Plan Number: _____

Price Code: _____ (see Plan Index)
Indicate Foundation Type: (see plan page for availability)
❏ Slab   ❏ Crawl space   ❏ Basement   ❏ Walk out basement

Basic Blueprint Package	Cost
❏ Reproducible Masters	$_____
❏ 8-Set Plan Package	$_____
❏ 4-Set Plan Package	$_____
❏ 1-Set Study Package	$_____
❏ Additional plan sets: __ sets at $45.00 per set	$_____
❏ Print in mirror-reverse. $50.00 per order __ sets printed in mirror-reverse	$_____

Important Extras

❏ Materials List	$_____
❏ EZ Quote for Plan #_____ at $29.95	$_____
❏ Additional EZ Quotes for Plan #s_____ at $14.95 each	$_____

Shipping (see chart above)	$_____
SUBTOTAL	$_____
Sales Tax (NJ residents add 6%)	$_____
TOTAL	$_____

Order Toll Free: 1-800-523-6789   By Fax: 201-760-2431
Creative Homeowner
24 Park Way
Upper Saddle River, NJ 07458

Name _____
(Please print or type)

Street _____
(Please do not use a P.O. Box)

City _____ State _____

Country _____ Zip _____

Daytime telephone ( ) _____

Fax ( ) _____
(Required for reproducible orders)

E-Mail _____

Payment ❏ Check/money order *Make checks payable to Creative Homeowner*

❏ VISA   ❏ MasterCard   ❏ American Express   ❏ DISCOVER

Credit card number _____

Expiration date (mm/yy) _____

Signature _____

Please check the appropriate box:
❏ Licensed builder/contractor   ❏ Homeowner   ❏ Renter

SOURCE CODE **CA400**

Index

Plan #	Price Code	Page	Total Finished Area Square Feet	Materials List Available
101004	C	74	1787	No
101005	D	183	1992	Yes
101014	C	61	1598	No
101015	C	314	1647	No
101016	D	86	1985	No
101019	F	259	2954	No
111005	H	256	3590	No
111012	G	271	3366	No
121001	D	198	1911	Yes
121008	C	104	1651	Yes
121020	E	148	2480	Yes
121050	D	174	1996	Yes
121051	D	141	1808	Yes
121052	D	161	2093	Yes
121053	E	293	2456	Yes
121055	C	22	1622	Yes
121056	B	77	1479	Yes
121057	E	169	2311	Yes
121058	C	29	1554	Yes
121059	C	29	1782	Yes
121061	G	237	3025	Yes
121062	G	245	3448	Yes
121063	G	272	3473	Yes
121064	D	48	1846	Yes
121065	G	268	3407	Yes
121066	D	49	2078	Yes
121067	F	167	2708	Yes
121068	E	310	2391	Yes
121069	F	263	2914	Yes
121070	D	297	2139	Yes
121071	F	262	2957	Yes
121072	G	277	3031	Yes
121073	E	302	2579	Yes
121074	E	303	2486	Yes
121075	E	160	2345	Yes
121076	G	276	3067	Yes
121081	G	286	3623	Yes
121082	F	244	2932	Yes
121083	F	154	2695	Yes
121084	C	9	1728	Yes
121085	D	109	1948	Yes
121086	D	23	1998	Yes
121087	D	23	2103	Yes
121088	E	292	2340	Yes
121092	D	193	1887	Yes
121097	E	155	2417	Yes
131001	D	59	1615	Yes
131002	D	20	1709	Yes
131003	C	95	1466	Yes
131004	C	81	1097	Yes
131005	D	96	1595	Yes
131007	D	12	1595	Yes
131014	C	224	1380	Yes
131027	F	206	2567	Yes
131030	F	114	2470	Yes
131032	F	144	2455	Yes
131034	C	210	1040	Yes
131035	E	220	1892	Yes
131036	F	219	2585	Yes
131041	D	45	1679	Yes
131043	E	54	1945	Yes
131044	E	220	1994	Yes
131046	F	118	2245	Yes
131050	G	213	2874	Yes
141004	C	85	1514	No
141007	D	169	1854	No
141009	C	87	1683	No
141010	C	90	1765	No

Plan #	Price Code	Page	Total Finished Area Square Feet	Materials List Available
141012	D	92	1870	yes
141013	D	99	1936	no
141014	D	211	2091	Yes
141015	E	171	2364	Yes
141016	E	192	2416	Yes
141017	E	182	2480	No
141019	F	278	2826	yes
141020	F	282	3140	No
141021	F	225	2614	Yes
141023	C	101	1715	Yes
141025	C	232	1749	Yes
141026	D	22	1993	Yes
141027	D	93	2088	Yes
141028	E	142	2215	Yes
141029	E	142	2289	Yes
141030	E	162	2323	Yes
141031	E	143	2367	No
141032	E	143	2476	Yes
141034	H	202	3656	Yes
141037	C	100	1735	no
151002	E	292	2444	Yes
151004	D	140	2107	Yes
151005	D	196	1940	Yes
151010	B	94	1379	Yes
151014	F	197	2698	Yes
151015	F	188	2789	yes
151018	F	124	2755	yes
151054	C	57	1746	Yes
151057	F	265	2951	Yes
151059	B	57	1382	Yes
151068	D	151	1880	Yes
151089	D	119	1921	Yes
151094	E	172	2372	Yes
151100	E	179	2247	Yes
151105	D	165	2039	Yes
151108	F	305	2742	Yes
151113	D	152	2186	Yes
151117	D	177	1957	Yes
151121	G	242	3108	Yes
151125	F	304	2606	Yes
151144	F	301	2624	Yes
161001	C	30	1782	Yes
161003	C	65	1508	Yes
161006	C	55	1755	Yes
161007	C	44	1611	Yes
161015	c	80	1768	No
161016	D	311	2101	No
161017	F	125	2653	No
161018	F	283	2816	No
161020	D	296	2082	yes
161021	D	91	1897	No
161025	F	117	2738	No
161026	D	128	2041	No
161027	E	111	2388	No
161028	H	273	3570	Yes
161029	I	248	4589	Yes
161030	I	269	4562	Yes
161032	I	238	4517	Yes
161038	E	204	2209	No
161040	E	306	2403	Yes
161042	D	309	2198	Yes
161045	I	285	4652	Yes
171001	B	75	1277	Yes
171002	B	53	1458	Yes
171003	D	146	2098	Yes
171004	E	195	2256	Yes
171005	E	164	2276	Yes
171006	E	176	2296	Yes

Index

Plan #	Price Code	Page	Total Finished Area Square Feet	Materials List Available
171007	C	63	1650	Yes
171008	C	89	1652	Yes
171009	C	88	1771	Yes
171010	D	146	1972	Yes
171011	D	139	2069	Yes
171013	G	233	3084	Yes
171014	D	224	1815	Yes
171015	D	215	2089	Yes
171016	E	216	2482	Yes
171017	E	123	2558	Yes
171018	E	203	2599	Yes
181001	A	337	920	Yes
181034	F	203	2687	Yes
181041	C	316	1556	Yes
181051	B	316	1068	Yes
181053	E	327	2353	Yes
181061	D	228	2111	Yes
181062	D	324	1953	Yes
181063	D	341	2037	Yes
181074	C	229	1760	Yes
181077	D	185	2119	Yes
181079	G	246	3016	Yes
181081	E	335	2350	Yes
181085	D	218	2183	Yes
181094	D	101	2099	Yes
181101	D	205	1936	YES
181102	E	229	2265	Yes
181107	D	84	1879	Yes
181108	B	329	1484	Yes
181109	A	331	991	Yes
181112	B	340	1148	Yes
181114	A	337	992	YES
181120	B	338	1480	Yes
181121	B	340	1484	Yes
181123	B	84	1482	Yes
181126	B	327	1468	Yes
181128	C	325	1634	Yes
181131	B	328	1442	Yes
181132	B	328	1437	Yes
181133	D	339	1832	Yes
181136	E	162	2426	Yes
181140	D	184	2172	Yes
181143	B	66	1056	Yes
181151	E	134	2283	Yes
101001	D	166	2156	No
191002	C	52	1716	No
191003	C	103	1785	No
191008	D	173	2188	No
191009	D	138	2172	No
191010	D	173	2189	No
191015	E	178	2340	No
191017	F	308	2605	No
201040	C	104	1754	YES
201043	D	126	1887	Yes
201044	D	126	1869	Yes
201053	D	147	1959	Yes
201054	D	147	1987	Yes
201061	E	189	2387	Yes
201062	E	298	2551	Yes
201067	F	309	2735	Yes
201084	D	234	2056	Yes
201089	D	225	1873	Yes
201103	E	184	2490	Yes
201126	H	246	3813	Yes
211002	C	21	1792	Yes
211004	D	116	1828	Yes
211005	D	149	2000	Yes
211006	D	136	2177	Yes

Plan #	Price Code	Page	Total Finished Area Square Feet	Materials List Available
211007	E	189	2252	Yes
211009	E	137	2396	Yes
211011	F	293	2791	Yes
211016	B	46	1191	Yes
211017	B	34	1212	No
211018	B	34	1266	Yes
211019	B	46	1395	Yes
211020	B	35	1346	Yes
211021	B	35	1375	Yes
211024	B	42	1418	Yes
211026	B	38	1415	Yes
211029	C	38	1672	Yes
211030	C	42	1600	Yes
211032	C	39	1751	Yes
211036	D	43	1800	Yes
211037	D	39	1800	Yes
211039	D	168	1868	Yes
211042	D	56	1800	Yes
211046	D	152	1936	Yes
211047	D	150	2009	Yes
211048	D	193	2002	Yes
211049	D	168	2023	Yes
211050	D	196	2000	Yes
211051	D	150	2123	Yes
211057	E	153	2366	No
211064	F	265	2936	No
211065	G	264	3158	Yes
211067	I	264	4038	Yes
211069	C	58	1600	Yes
211070	I	200	4242	Yes
211077	I	287	5560	No
211081	B	336	1110	No
211086	C	77	1704	Yes
211103	F	113	2605	Yes
211111	G	258	3035	Yes
211125	I	271	4440	Yes
221001	F	289	2600	No
221004	C	18	1763	No
221015	D	194	1926	No
221022	G	280	3382	No
221023	H	226	3511	No
221024	C	32	1732	No
221025	G	275	3009	No
231001	D	215	2177	No
231003	A	178	2254	No
231004	A	62	1463	No
231006	A	188	1961	No
231008	A	216	1941	No
231009	A	221	2765	No
231011	F	290	2716	No
231013	F	122	2780	No
231015	E	122	2360	No
231020	D	192	2166	No
231023	G	247	3215	No
231025	E	163	2501	No
231026	H	247	3784	No
231030	I	278	4726	No
231035	D	93	1954	No
241001	E	156	2350	No
241003	D	112	2080	No
241005	C	223	1670	No
241007	D	230	2036	No
241008	E	212	2526	No
241009	D	208	1974	No
241010	D	299	2044	No
241012	E	214	2743	No
241013	F	208	2779	No
241014	G	214	3046	No

Index

Plan #	Price Code	Page	Total Finished Area Square Feet	Materials List Available
251001	B	102	1253	Yes
251002	B	106	1333	Yes
251003	B	43	1393	Yes
251004	C	107	1550	Yes
251005	C	15	1631	Yes
251006	D	151	1849	Yes
251007	C	63	1597	Yes
251008	D	98	1808	Yes
251009	D	217	1829	No
251010	D	202	1854	Yes
251012	D	217	2009	Yes
251013	D	294	2073	Yes
251014	E	232	2210	Yes
261001	H	274	3746	No
261002	F	228	2976	No
261003	F	261	2974	No
261004	F	186	2707	No
261005	E	191	2419	No
261006	I	261	4583	No
261007	F	187	2635	No
261008	E	190	2226	No
261009	I	260	4048	No
261010	F	170	2724	No
271012	B	108	1359	Yes
271025	E	180	2223	Yes
271027	E	181	2463	Yes
271030	D	33	1926	Yes
271053	E	342	2458	No
271057	D	222	2195	No
271095	G	279	3220	No
281001	E	175	2423	Yes
281002	D	313	1859	Yes
281003	E	123	2370	Yes
281004	B	336	1426	Yes
281005	B	341	1362	Yes
281006	C	332	1702	Yes
281007	B	16	1206	Yes
281009	B	89	1423	Yes
281010	A	330	884	Yes
281011	B	41	1314	Yes
281012	B	17	1368	Yes
281013	B	17	1407	Yes
291001	C	40	1550	No
291002	C	37	1550	No
291003	D	159	1890	No
291004	E	301	2529	No
291005	A	315	896	No
291006	A	317	965	No
291007	B	317	1065	No
291008	B	332	1183	No
291009	C	10	1655	No
291010	C	92	1776	No
291011	D	16	1898	No
291012	E	163	2415	No
291013	H	209	3553	No
291014	I	209	4372	No
301001	F	305	2720	Yes
301002	D	121	1845	Yes
301003	E	294	2485	Yes
301005	D	120	1930	Yes
301006	D	179	2162	Yes
301007	E	231	2398	Yes
311002	E	221	2402	Yes
311003	E	201	2428	Yes
311005	E	235	2497	Yes
321001	C	19	1721	Yes
321002	B	60	1400	Yes
321003	C	26	1791	Yes
321004	F	241	2808	Yes

Plan #	Price Code	Page	Total Finished Area Square Feet	Materials List Available
321005	E	307	2483	Yes
321006	D	157	1977	Yes
321007	F	291	2695	Yes
321008	C	36	1761	Yes
321009	E	334	2295	Yes
321010	C	25	1787	Yes
321011	F	279	2874	Yes
321012	D	153	1882	Yes
321013	B	25	1360	Yes
321014	C	24	1676	Yes
321015	C	24	1501	Yes
321016	H	270	3814	Yes
321017	E	295	2531	Yes
321018	E	295	2523	Yes
321019	E	304	2452	Yes
321020	D	159	1882	Yes
321021	C	56	1708	Yes
321022	B	28	1140	Yes
321023	B	28	1092	Yes
321024	B	53	1403	Yes
321025	A	326	914	Yes
321026	C	62	1712	Yes
321027	F	300	2758	Yes
321028	F	300	2723	Yes
321029	E	158	2334	Yes
321030	D	158	2029	Yes
321031	G	243	3200	Yes
321032	I	243	4826	Yes
321033	B	52	1268	Yes
321034	H	270	3508	Yes
321035	B	326	1384	Yes
321036	F	240	2900	No
321037	E	172	2397	Yes
321038	B	333	1452	Yes
321039	B	88	1231	Yes
321040	B	333	1084	Yes
321041	E	127	2286	yes
321050	E	185	2336	yes
321051	F	199	2624	yes
321052	D	164	2182	yes
321054	F	242	2828	yes
321055	E	127	2505	yes
321057	C	76	1524	yes
321060	C	76	1575	yes
321063	G	284	3222	yes
321064	C	64	1769	yes
341003	B	14	1200	Yes
341004	B	11	1101	Yes
341005	B	47	1334	Yes
341009	B	27	1280	Yes
341010	B	47	1261	Yes
341012	B	50	1316	Yes
341013	B	105	1363	Yes
341018	B	50	1191	Yes
341019	B	51	1258	Yes
341021	B	51	1208	Yes
341022	B	85	1281	Yes
341023	B	100	1469	Yes
341024	B	66	1310	Yes
341025	B	67	1392	Yes
341026	B	78	1009	Yes
341027	C	83	1657	Yes
341028	B	79	1248	Yes
341029	C	79	1737	Yes
341030	C	82	1660	Yes
341031	B	82	1400	Yes
341032	C	83	1528	Yes
341033	B	78	1297	Yes
341034	B	67	1445	Yes

Books To Help You Build

Creative Homeowner offers an extensive selection of leading how-to books.
Choose any of the book packages below to get started.

Home Building Package

Build and repair your home—inside and out—with these essential titles.

Retail Price: $74.80
Your Price: $65.95
Order #: 267095

Wiring: Complete Projects for the Home
Provides comprehensive information about the home electrical system. Over 750 color photos and 75 illustrations. 288 pages.

Plumbing: Basic, Intermediate & Advanced Projects
An overview of the plumbing system with code-compliant, step-by-step projects. Over 750 full-color photos, illustrations. 272 pages.

House Framing
Walks you through the framing basics, from assembling simple partitions to cutting compound angles for dormers. 500 full-color illustrations and photos. 208 pages.

Drywall: Pro Tips for Hanging and Finishing
Covers tools and materials, estimating, cutting, hanging, and finishing gypsum wallboard. 250 color photos and illustrations. 144 pages.

Kitchen & Bath Package

Learn to design and build kitchens and bathrooms like a pro.

Retail Price: $79.80
Your Price: $69.95
Order #267080

The *New* Smart Approach to Kitchen Design
Includes all the answers to help plan a project, hire a contractor, shop for appliances, and decorate like a design pro. More than 260 color photos. 208 pages.

Kitchens: Plan, Remodel, Build
A complete design and installation package, including design trends and step-by-step projects. More than 550 full-color photos and illustrations. 256 pages.

The *New* Smart Approach to Bath Design
The latest and best materials and products on the market for master baths, family baths, and powder rooms. More than 260 color photos. 208 pages.

Bathrooms: Plan, Remodel, Build
Includes step-by-step projects, storage options, products, materials, and lighting possibilities. Over 100 illustrations and 550 color photographs. 256 pages.

Landscaping Package

Create a yard you'll love with these comprehensive landscape guides.

Retail Price: $73.80
Your Price: $64.95
Order # 267075

Complete Home Landscaping
Covers everything from design principles to construction projects, from plant selection to plant care. More than 800 full-color photos and illustrations. 320 pages.

Trees, Shrubs & Hedges
Create a landscape, match plants to growing conditions, and learn to plant, transplant, and prune. Over 500 color photos and paintings. 208 pages.

Smart Guide: Ponds & Fountains
Plan, build, and maintain with projects and easy-to-understand text. Covers plant and fish selection. 175 -color illustrations, 40 color photos. 80 pages.

Annuals, Perennials & Bulbs
Lavishly illustrated with portraits of over 100 flowering plants; filled with instructional techniques and tips. More than 500 color photos and illustrations. 208 pages.

Decks & Patios Package

Design and build decks and patios for your new home.

Retail Price$66.80
Your Price $55.95
Order # 267090

Decks: Planning, Designing, Building
Takes you through every step involved in designing and building a beautiful deck. 600 color photos and illustrations. 192 pages.

Deck Designs Plus Railings, Planters, Benches
The best plans from top deck designers. Includes planters, railings, benches, and trellises. 300 color photos and drawings. 192 pages.

Walks, Walls & Patios: Design, Plan & Build
Includes the ideas and how to you'll need to integrate popular hardscape designs into a home landscape. Over 500 color photos and illustrations. 240 pages.

Design Ideas for Decks
Everything you'll need to create a beautiful deck for your home. Learn about the newest deck styles, designs, and patterns. More than 250 photos. 128 pages.

Decorating Package

Save money and design like a professional with these must-have decorating books.

Retail Price $66.85
Your Price $59.95
Order # 267085

The New Smart Approach to Home Decorating
Introduces the classic design theories, showcases interior design trends, and teaches how to make the most of any space. Over 440 color photos. 288 pages.

Lyn Peterson's Real Life Decorating
Noted interior designer gives easy-to-live-with solutions to the most daunting decorating dilemmas. More than 300 color photos and illustrations. 304 pages.

Color in the American Home
Shows how the power of color can transform even the plainest room into a beauty. Over 200 color photos. 176 pages.

Outdoor Projects Package

Use these project guides to accessorize the largest room in your home—your yard.

Retail Price $51.85
Your Price $45.95
Order # 267060

Trellises & Arbors
Features inspiring photos, planning advice, design ideas, plant information, and 10 step by step trellis projects. Over 160 photos and illustrations. 160 pages.

Yard & Garden Furniture
Contains 20 step-by-step projects, from the comfortable lines of an Adirondack chair to the sturdy serviceability- of a family picnic table. Over 600 color photos and illustrations. 208 pages.

Gazebos & Other Outdoor Structures
Design fundamentals, step-by-step building techniques, and custom options for the perfect gazebo, arbor, or pavilion. 480 color illustrations and photos. 160 pages.

Home Reference Package

*Find it, fix it, design it, create it—
if it's in your home, it's in here.*

Retail Price: $59.90
Your Cost: $49.95
Order # 267070

The Home Book
The largest, most complete home improvement book on the market—608 pages packed with over 2,300 photos, 800 drawings, and an understandable, practical text that covers your home top to bottom, inside and out. 608 pages.

The *New* Smart Approach to Home Decorating
Decorate every room in your home with the same confidence and flair as a professional designer. More than 440 color photos. 288 pages.

Family-Living Package

*Start your home off right with these family-oriented ideas
for the home and garden.*

Retail Price: $69.80
Your Cost: $59.95
Order # 267065

Lyn Peterson's Real Life Decorating
Noted interior designer gives easy-to-live-with solutions to the most daunting decorating dilemmas. More than 300 color photos and illustrations. 304 pages.

Smart Approach to Kids' Rooms
Ideas for decorating, furnishing, designing, and organizing space for children with practical design advice and safety tips. Over 200 color photos. 176 pages.

Build a Kids' Play Yard
How to build a swing set, monkey bars, balance beam, playhouse, and more. Over 200 color photos and drawings. 144 pages.

National Wildlife Federation®
Attracting Birds, Butterflies and Other Backyard Wildlife
Wildlife-friendly gardening, landscape designs, and family projects from the National Wildlife Federation. Over 200 color photos and illustrations. 128 pages.

Order Form for Books to Help Complete Your Home

Qty.	Description	Order #	Price	Cost
Book Packages:				
___	Home Building Package	267095	$65.95	___
___	Kitchen & Bath Package	267080	69.95	___
___	Landscaping Package	267075	64.95	___
___	Decks & Patios Package	267090	55.95	___
___	Decorating Package	267085	59.95	___
___	Outdoor Projects Package	267060	45.95	___
___	Home Reference Package	267070	49.95	___
___	Family-Living Package	267065	59.95	___
Individual Titles from Creative Homeowner:				
___	Wiring: Basic and Advanced Projects	278237	$19.95	___
___	Plumbing: Basic, Intermediate & Advanced Projects	278210	19.95	___
___	House Framing	277655	19.95	___
___	Drywall: Pro Tips for Hanging and Finishing	278315	14.95	___
___	The New Smart Approach to Kitchen Design	279946	19.95	___
___	Kitchens: Plan, Remodel, Build	277061	19.95	___
___	The New Smart Approach to Bath Design	279234	19.95	___
___	Bathrooms: Plan, Remodel, Build	278627	19.95	___
___	Complete Home Landscaping	274615	24.95	___
___	Trees, Shrubs & Hedges	274238	19.95	___
___	Smart Guide: Ponds & Fountains	274643	8.95	___
___	Annuals, Perennials & Bulbs	274032	19.95	___
___	The New Smart Approach to Home Decorating	279672	24.95	___
___	Lyn Peterson's Real Life Decorating	279382	21.95	___
___	Color in the American Home	287264	19.95	___
___	Decks: Planning, Designing, Building	277162	16.95	___
___	Deck Designs	277369	16.95	___
___	Walks, Walls & Patios	277997	19.95	___
___	Design Ideas for Decks	277155	12.95	___
___	Trellises & Arbors	274804	16.95	___

Qty.	Description	Order #	Price	Cost
Individual Titles from Creative Homeowner:				
___	Yard & Garden Furniture	277462	$19.95	___
___	Gazebos & Other Outdoor Structures	277138	14.95	___
___	The Home Book	267855	34.95	___
___	The Smart Approach to Kids' Rooms	279473	19.95	___
___	Build a Kids' Play Yard	277662	14.95	___
___	Attracting Birds, Butterflies & and Other Backyard Wildlife	274955	12.95	___

Shipping* _____

SUBTOTAL _____

Sales Tax (NJ residents add 6%) _____

TOTAL _____

*Shipping Costs:
For book packages: $5.95 per package
For individual titles: $4.75 for first book
$1.75 for each additional book

Make check payable to Creative Homeowner
To order, send form to:
Creative Homeowner
P.O. Box 38
24 Park Way
Upper Saddle River, NJ 07458

Or call
1-800-523-6789

CREATIVE
HOMEOWNER®

SHIP TO:

Name _____
(Please print)

Address _____

City _____ State:____ Zip:_____ Phone #_____